P. VERGILI MARONIS

AENEIDOS

LIBER QVINTVS

P. VERGILI MARONIS

AENEIDOS

LIBER QVINTVS

EDITED WITH A COMMENTARY

BY

R. D. WILLIAMS

SENIOR LECTURER IN CLASSICS
IN THE
UNIVERSITY OF READING

OXFORD
AT THE CLARENDON PRESS
1960

Oxford University Press, Amen House, London E.C.

GLASGOW NEW YORK TORONTO MELBOURNE WELLINGTON
BOMBAY CALCUTTA MADRAS KARACHI KUALA LUMPUR
CAPE TOWN IBADAN NAIROBI ACCRA

PRINTED IN GREAT BRITAIN

Je sent
for

PREFACE

THE fifth book of the *Aeneid* is outshone in brilliance by the
books before and after it, but it is indispensable to both. In
the structure of the poem it makes possible the progression
from the tragic events of Book IV to the mystery and
majesty of Book VI; it interposes a different kind of scenery
between the conquest of two mountain summits. Here we
see the skill with which Virgil handles his transitions of tone
and intensity, for in the course of Book V the tension is
gradually released and gradually built up again. We see too
the skill with which the intensity is changed without any
change in the major themes of the poem as it moves; the
scenery is different but entirely harmonious. A careful reading of Books IV, V, and VI will do much to illuminate how
a great epic poet builds up his structure in such a way that
his poem will not fall apart, a fate which often overtakes the
lesser epics.

   In preparing this edition of *Aeneid* V I have endeavoured
to meet the needs of students in the upper forms of schools
and in universities, and at the same time to make some con-
tribution to more advanced Virgilian scholarship. I have
paid particular attention throughout the commentary to
stylistic and metrical features, both in order to explain
Virgilian usage, and to try to show how rhythmic effects
(whether of metre or sound) are employed to support and
emphasize the meaning and tone of a passage; in brief, to
comment on what Dryden tried to imitate in his translation,
the way in which Virgil chooses and places his words 'for the
sweetness of the sound'. I am indeed aware that there must
be a subjective element in aesthetic appreciation of this
kind, and that it is easy to go too far, but I have thought
it better to venture suggestions rather than to keep silent,
and each reader may judge for himself how far he is prepared
to go. I have commented often on sense pauses, because it
is here that Virgil differs most from his predecessors, and on
the division of words within the line, which I have discussed
mainly by use of the terms ictus and accent (though other
terms which may be preferred, such as diaeresis and caesura,

would give much the same result). The student of Milton will easily appreciate the importance of these two elements of verse movement.

The debt which I owe to the great Virgilian commentators and critics of the past cannot be acknowledged at each point, because it is their formative influence, not their specific comments at one place or another, which has left the main impact. Those who have helped me most are included in the list on pp. 29–31. But Servius is in a category of his own, and I have cited him very frequently in the commentary in order to give a picture both of his merits and of his limitations.

The text of this edition is reproduced from Hirtzel's Oxford Classical Text, by kind permission of the Delegates of the Clarendon Press. I have indicated in the notes that I would prefer a different reading or punctuation from the Oxford Text in the following places: 112, 238, 279, 317, 326, 349, 486, 512, 768, 776.

My grateful thanks are due to Mr. F. Robertson for the profit which this book has derived from many long discussions on every aspect of it; to Professor J. M. R. Cormack and Mr. A. E. Wardman for ready help of all kinds; to Mr. H. H. Huxley and Mr. A. G. Lee for valuable criticisms and suggestions on many points; and to Professor R. G. Austin for the constant assistance which I have had from his edition of Book IV, and for personal help in many places in Book V. For the errors and omissions which remain I am myself responsible.

I wish to acknowledge my thanks to the authors and publishers for permission to make citations from the translations of the *Aeneid* by Mr. W. F. Jackson Knight (Penguin Books, 1956) and Mr. C. Day Lewis (Hogarth Press, 1952).

Reading, 1959   R. D. W.

CONTENTS

INTRODUCTION

I. *The Purpose of Book V*

THE major part of Book V is concerned with the anniversary games held in honour of Anchises. The description which Virgil gives recalls again and again Homer's account in *Iliad* XXIII of the funeral games for Patroclus, and it is plain that among the main reasons which led Virgil to include an account of athletic contests in the *Aeneid* was his desire to recall this element of Homer's poetry to his Roman readers, and to transfer into a Roman context and the idiom of a later day the heritage which as an epic poet he had received from Homer. The poems of Homer had cast their spell upon him; the magic of their artistry and the love of life in so many of its varied aspects which they breathe had captured the poet in him, just as the grandeur of his vision of Rome had captured the patriot in him. The roots of the *Aeneid* took their nourishment not only—as is so very evident —from Roman ways and Roman ideals, from the national model of Ennius' epic and the great new prospects of Roman destiny, but equally (and in some ways perhaps primarily) from Virgil's love of Homer's poems. This truism is not best stated in phrases like 'imitation of Homer', as if Homer was Virgil's model and therefore to Homer he had to go. Rather we should think of how Homer had fired Virgil's poetic imagination, shaped and sharpened his appreciation of countless aspects of human activity seen through a poet's eyes, impelled him to wish to re-create—in his own language and from a very different standpoint—the situations and events in which the Homeric heroes had played their parts. We should not expect Virgil to have recaptured the *élan* of Homer's games (indeed no Roman was likely to see athletics as the Greeks saw them); but what he has done is to recall and reshape the narrative of Homer, substituting the grave cadences of his own hexameter for the dancing movement of the Greek, and reorganizing in a closely woven artistic unity the rapid and direct poetic style of *Iliad* XXIII.

The desire to recall Homer then was certainly one of the main reasons why Virgil included athletic games in his epic;[1] but there was another major reason. A revival of interest in athletics was being shown in the Roman world, and this was encouraged and stimulated by Augustus.[2] The great Pan-Hellenic festivals at Olympia, Delphi, Corinth, and Nemea were winning fresh popularity, and upon them Augustus modelled his Actian games,[3] a festival of great magnificence to commemorate the victory at Actium. They were celebrated at Nicopolis, the site of Augustus' camp during the battle of Actium, for the first time in 28 B.C. and subsequently every four years; they included athletic and

---

[1] It is not known that Ennius included any account of athletic contests in his epic; the Berne scholiast on *Geo.* 2. 384 says that Ennius mentioned the games which Romulus held at the dedication of the temple to Jupiter Feretrius (Vahlen³, p. 15), but there is no suggestion that they were described at any length. See also note on p. 114 f.

[2] See Suet. *Aug.* 43, *Mon. Ancyr.* 22 (with Gagé's notes), E. N. Gardiner, *Athletics of the Ancient World*, pp. 46 f. A fondness for games and shows was always characteristic of the Romans, but athletic contests (with the exception of chariot-racing) generally played a relatively small part compared with the exhibition of wild animals, gladiatorial combats, and pageantry of various kinds. Two famous examples of games of this latter sort were given by Augustus: one in 44 B.C., the occasion of the comet (see note on 523–4), and one in 29 B.C., at the dedication of the temple to Caesar (Dio 51. 22, Ov. *Fast.* 3. 704). But the Actian games with their revival of the Greek type of athletic contest were quite different, and there was an increasing emphasis on athletics in the many festivals held at Rome after their inauguration.

[3] For the Actian games see W. H. Willis, *T.A.Ph.A.*, 1941, pp. 404 f., J. Gagé, *Mél. d'arch. et d'hist.*, vol. 53 (1936), pp. 92 f., D. L. Drew, *The Allegory of the Aeneid*, Blackwell, 1927, pp. 51 f., and Reisch in *R.E.*, s.v. *Aktia*.

equestrian events and a regatta. In the *Aeneid*, when the Trojans on their voyage towards Italy put in at Actium, Virgil mentions the celebration of games (*Aen.* 3. 278 f.). Finally the equestrian display known as the *lusus Troiae*,[1] with which Virgil concludes his account of the games, played a prominent part in Augustus' encouragement of organizations for the training of the young in Rome and Italy. Thus we see that Virgil's description of the games was associated with contemporary social events as well as with the Homeric precedent, and in the course of it Virgil could link the past with the present (as he very often does in the *Aeneid*) by showing the time-honoured origin of contemporary customs in which the Trojan ancestors of Roman families played a leading part (116 f., 568 f.).

These then were two of the main motives which led Virgil to include a description of athletic games in the *Aeneid*. We may next ask what he has achieved by placing them at this particular point in the poem, or in other words what function the episode plays in the pattern of the whole *Aeneid*.

Above all the games serve to diminish the tension after the powerful and moving tragedy of the fourth book, and to give relief and variation before the majestic unfolding of Book VI. In this respect we may compare the function of Book III, where the tension is less marked than in the books before and after it, and (in a different way) that of Book VIII,[2] with its serenity and peace set in contrast with the war scenes of VII and IX. The principle of variation in emotional tension, of contrast between light and darkness, between storm and peace, is one of the most marked features of the structure of the *Aeneid*,[3] and nowhere is it more

---

[1] For a full discussion of this see note on 545 f.

[2] See J. R. Bacon, *C.R.*, 1939, pp. 97 f.

[3] On this see V. Pöschl, *Die Dichtkunst Virgils*, 1950, *passim*, R. S. Conway, *Harvard Lectures on the Vergilian Age*, 1928, pp. 129 f., G. E. Duckworth, *A.J.Ph.*, 1954, pp. 1 f., and *T.A.Ph.A.*, 1957, pp. 1 f.

Book V

marked than in this instance. The tone of the description of the games is lighter than perhaps any other part of the *Aeneid*. But while Virgil's aim here was to alter the colour and tension of his narrative, to slow its movement, to lessen its power, it was vital that the interest should not flag. The games could not be a wholly detached episode. The relevance to the larger theme had to be maintained, and no sense of bathos or purposeless digression (such as is often found in lesser epics, as for example in Statius' *Thebaid*) could be allowed. This problem Virgil solved partly by the extreme skill with which he led into the games and led away from them again within the book (see Section III), and partly by the religious association of the games with Anchises.

Great stress is laid, both before the games begin (42–103) and after their conclusion (603, 759–61), on the religious significance of the ceremony in honour of Anchises of which the games themselves form a part.[1] The filial piety of Aeneas is one of the dominant themes of the poem, corresponding with the closeness of family relationships in contemporary Roman life. While Anchises lives he plays a large part in guiding and advising Aeneas; after his death his shade appears to Aeneas in his hour of trial (722 f.), and he it is who makes the final revelation to Aeneas in the underworld (6. 724 f.). Aeneas pays honour to him not only from the obligation of duty but also in proper recognition of all that he does in reality owe to him. Book V thus lays much emphasis on the religious aspects of Roman family life and on the religious side of Aeneas' character, so that in combining his athletic games with the religious ceremonies paid by a son to a father Virgil has succeeded in interweaving his 'episode' with the whole texture of his poem.

Finally, now that we have considered the main poetic

---

[1] See note on 42 f. for a discussion of the significance of the honours paid to Anchises, and the points of similarity with the Roman *parentatio* and with *ludi funebres*.

functions which Book V fulfils, we should not overlook the
fact that Virgil had to make modifications in the existing
legend of Aeneas' wanderings in order to achieve his purposes. Anchises had died in Drepanum (*Aen.* 3. 707 f.)
before Aeneas was driven by the storm to Carthage, and as
far as we know there was nothing in the legend either about
funeral games then or about a second visit by the Trojans
to Sicily. By introducing the second visit to Sicily a year
later,[1] and making the games anniversary celebrations (not
funeral games as in Homer), Virgil has at one stroke
achieved several important aims. He has placed the games
in that part of the poem where for structural reasons he
wanted them; he has associated them closely with the religious aspects of Roman family life; and he has laid special
stress on Sicily[2] of all the places which Aeneas visited in his
voyage, so that its particularly close relationship with Italy
from earliest times is given appropriate prominence.[3]

II. *The Description of the Games*

In the selection and arrangement of the contests Virgil
adopts the attitude towards his Homeric source-material
which we see so often elsewhere in the *Aeneid*: he recalls
Homeric episodes, incidents, and diction frequently and
closely, but he does so in a way which is appropriate to his
own purposes and requirements. In *Iliad* XXIII there are
eight contests in the following order: chariot-race (the
account of which occupies well over half the total description of the games), boxing, wrestling, foot-race, spear-
fight, discus, archery, javelin. Virgil has four contests (ship-
race, foot-race, boxing, archery) followed by the pageant

[1] For the chronological difficulties caused by this alteration in the
legend see Section V.

[2] For Sicily and the Trojans see on 718.

[3] See Heinze, *Virgils Epische Technik*, pp. 145 f., for a discussion
of why the games could not be placed elsewhere in the poem, or
given in honour of anyone other than Anchises. I have laid stress on
the positive rather than the negative reasons for Virgil's choice.

of the *lusus Troiae*. The ship-race[1] corresponds quite closely to Homer's chariot-race (e.g. in the events at the turning-point), and all the other contests[2] have marked points of similarity with their Homeric counterparts (e.g. the fall in the foot-race, the plight of the loser in the boxing, the cutting of the cord in the archery). But it was obviously not possible for Virgil to reproduce the vigour and swing and directness of Homer's account, and he has aimed instead at the more elaborate formal composition which literary epic requires. By describing fewer contests than Homer he has made a tighter unity possible. The arrangement of the contests is carefully balanced; the long accounts of the ship-race and the boxing alternate with the shorter descriptions of the foot-race and the archery. In a number of ways Virgil has sought to give the variety appropriate to literary epic: the announcement and presentation of the prizes is made differently in each instance (see on 249 f.); those taking part range in age from young Euryalus in the foot-race to Entellus in the boxing and Acestes in the archery; the number of competitors varies from event to event and (except of course in the boxing) as many as four or five of them play some decisive part in each contest.

A major difference, worth considering at some length, between Virgil's games and Homer's is that in the *Iliad* the contestants are the chief figures of the poem, Ajax, Odysseus and the rest, well known to us already and immediately capturing our interest and attention. In Virgil this is not so, because in the *Aeneid* there are no great and well-known Trojan leaders standing by Aeneas' side. Consequently Virgil has the problem of interesting us in his competitors, and he solves it in a very typical way, by concentrating attention on their characters as revealed in the incidents of the contest. Thus in the ship-race the characters of those

---

[1] For the reasons which led Virgil to include a ship-race, and for fuller details about it and Homeric parallels, see note on 114 f.

[2] For details of the other contests see notes on 286 f., 362 f., 485 f.

taking part are clearly depicted and directly influence the action: Sergestus is rash and impetuous, and runs aground; Gyas is hot-tempered and foolish, and loses his chance of success through a fit of anger; Mnestheus is gallant and determined, and comes very near to victory; Cloanthus has kept going steadily, and at the end holds off Mnestheus' challenge by a timely prayer to the deities of the sea.

In the foot-race the action turns on the friendship of Nisus and Euryalus, and the character sketch of these two which emerges from the events is very clear and compelling: Euryalus young and keen and popular, Nisus unscrupulous and coolly brazen about his conduct, over which Salius for his part is splendidly and very rightly indignant. The picture of the two friends is vivid enough to live in the memory until their partnership later in the poem under grimmer circumstances, when they pay with their lives for their daring in trying to relieve the blockade of the Trojan camp (*Aen.* 9. 176 f.).

Virgil handles the description of the boxing match on a much more mythological level. It was a brutal sport in Roman days (see on 364), and Roman nobles did not engage in it. Virgil himself most clearly had little liking for it, and he therefore transfers his account of it to a plane rather removed from ordinary human activity in which anyone might join, and makes it instead a contest between two specialists of distant days and superhuman strength and prowess, Dares who had defeated the giant Butes of the Bebrycian race, and Entellus who possessed the gauntlets in which his teacher Eryx had fought against Hercules. Unlike the competitors in the other events these two do not figure again in the *Aeneid*; their place is entirely in the remote past of heroes and demi-gods, in a quasi-symbolic world of mythology (see on 362 f.). Within these limits Virgil draws very powerful pictures of them—Dares the braggart who meets his match, Entellus the older man who still has enough left of his fabulous skill and strength to win this last contest.

In the archery contest we return from the mythological world to witness the skill of Aeneas' Trojan companions, and the presence of Acestes himself as a competitor prepares us for important events. The dove has already been brought down before Acestes' turn comes, but he nevertheless shoots an arrow into the sky, and it bursts into flames as it goes. This supernatural omen portends great events (see on 519 f., 523–4), and the level of poetic significance is thus raised at the conclusion of the games, and the way is prepared for the stately and impressive account of the *lusus Troiae* with its patriotic associations, and thus for the return to the high level of tension necessary in the narrative of the burning of the ships.

Thus for the linear development of the vivid narrative in Homer's games Virgil has substituted a curve of falling and then rising tension in order to link up with the events of the poem both before and after the games. While the similarities of episode between Homer and Virgil are many, the total effect of the two accounts is very different indeed. It would be as wrong to expect to find in Virgil the immediacy and vividness of Homer as to look in Homer for elaborate symmetry or variation of composition and intricate arrangement of tension.[1]

III. *The Setting of the Games and Their Sequel*

We may now turn to a fuller consideration of how Virgil leads up to his description of the games, and how he makes his transition from them. Book V begins on a note of sorrow, recalling the tragedy of Dido, and Virgil breaks away abruptly (see note on 8) with the account of the storm which motivates the second visit of the Trojans to Sicily. This visit is associated with the divine purpose, and is not to be thought accidental; Aeneas says (line 56) that it is evidently by the will of the gods that they have arrived in Sicily again

[1] For some additional remarks (with bibliographical references) on athletic games in epic poetry see note on 104 f.

at the site of Anchises' tomb. The religious ceremonies are described with a wealth of detail, focusing the attention on the high honour in which Anchises is held and on the filial devotion of his son, and showing the Roman reader that this was the first occurrence of rituals and rites which he still held sacred. After the due and proper fulfilment of the religious obligations a feeling of relaxation comes into the poem, and the mood of the games is light-hearted and carefree, not without humour and some quarrelling and a good deal of tact on the part of Aeneas. Just for a short while the weight is off his shoulders, and this lonely figure, whose lot is throughout the poem cast in troubled situations, is seen in a happier setting. As the games draw to their conclusion the note of happiness still prevails, and the level of poetic significance is raised (as we have seen) to prepare for the transition back to the narrative; the final event in the games ends with the omen of Acestes' arrow, and the concluding ceremony is the joyous pageant of the *lusus Troiae*, symbolizing the hopes placed in the younger generation whether in the times of Aeneas or in those of Virgil.

At this moment, when the colours are at their brightest and the mood is peaceful and serene, there comes a sharp change to impending disaster: *hinc primum Fortuna fidem mutata novavit* (604) . . . *Saturnia Iuno* (606) . . . *multa movens necdum antiquum saturata dolorem* (608). So Virgil introduces his account of the burning of the ships,[1] the frenzied action of the women who could not endure to wander any more. The return to the main narrative after the description of the games is made with great skill; there is a factual connexion because the absence of the men at the games made the action of the women possible, and there is a tensional connexion because of the dignity and impressiveness to which the account of the games had been raised by the omen of the arrow and by the *lusus Troiae*. The point is perhaps best appreciated by imagining the abruptness of

[1] See note on 604 f.

a transition to the narrative from the foot-race or the boxing contest.

In the description of the burning of the ships we meet one of the great themes of the poem: the conflict between the ordered world which it is the will of the gods that Aeneas should found, and the *furor*, the *violentia*, which are aroused against him in human agents by the machinations of Juno (see on 604 f.). And when this disaster comes upon Aeneas so soon after the peace and serenity of the games he is shaken in his purpose to such an extent that he comes near to abandoning his whole mission (700–3). It is only after the intervention by Nautes and the vision of Anchises that he decides to go on. It is at this stage in the poem that we see Aeneas' determination at its lowest point, so soon after the joy of the games, so shortly before the triumphant revelation in Book VI of Rome's destined greatness.

After the vision of Anchises has appeared to Aeneas, the Trojan city in Sicily is founded and the voyage to Italy begins. Now Venus intervenes on behalf of the Trojans to ask Neptune for a safe passage to Italy. Neptune grants her request, but it must involve the sacrifice of one life. Here again is a theme of the whole poem: achievements are counterbalanced by suffering, sometimes involving Aeneas and his companions, sometimes those who find themselves in opposition to the divine will, like Dido and Turnus.

> Unus erit tantum amissum quem gurgite quaeres;
> unum pro multis dabitur caput. (814–15.)

So the book ends with the deeply moving description of the faithful and loyal Palinurus,[1] holding fast to his duty until the god Sleep comes to overwhelm him—*te, Palinure, petens, tibi somnia tristia portans / insonti* (840–1). Still Palinurus will not desert his post, but the god is too strong, and the lament of Aeneas for his lost helmsman ends the book on the note of sorrow and sympathy which is so

---

[1] The story of Palinurus is discussed in the note on 827 f.

characteristic of Virgil's poetry. As the Trojans reach their promised land there is grief in the moment of triumph.

IV. *The Character of Aeneas and the Nature of His Mission*

As we have seen in the previous section, the events in Book V play a considerable part in Virgil's portrayal of the character of Aeneas. The great theme of the *Aeneid* is the fulfilment of Rome's destiny by the achievement of her first founder, who must symbolize the qualities through which his descendants made his little town become the heart of a mighty empire. It has often been said that Virgil's portrayal of Aeneas is unconvincing for this reason, and that he is an abstraction, a shadow of a man, too much a puppet of the gods.[1] But a proper consideration of the events throughout the poem shows that Virgil has taken great care to make sure that whatever Aeneas may symbolize he is above all a real person.

Virgil leaves us in no doubt about the nature of Aeneas' mission. It is laid upon him by fate (*fato profugus, Aen.* 1. 2); Jupiter himself early in the poem (1. 257 f.) promises a glorious future for Rome, and it is for this that Venus has rescued and protected Aeneas (4. 227 f.). Throughout the poem the human action takes place against a background of divinities and fate (see notes on 604 f., 722, 779 f.). Phrases indicating that Aeneas' voyage is a mission of destiny are used again and again in the poem (in this book cf. lines 82, 656, 703, 709, 784). The object of the mission is firstly to establish Rome's sway and secondly to bring religion and laws to the world (*Aen.* 1. 6, 4. 229 f., 6. 851 f., 12. 826 f.). The virtues which it requires in Aeneas are those which made Rome great, of which we constantly read in the pages of Livy, virtues of *pietas, temperantia, iustitia, fides, constantia.*

---

[1] For example, Page's *Aeneid I–VI*, Intro., pp. xvii f., J. Wight Duff, *A Literary History of Rome to the Close of the Golden Age*, pp. 463 f.

Inevitably then to some extent Virgil's Aeneas symbolizes these virtues.[1] He is above all *pius*—that is to say devoted to the duty of following out his divine mission (see note on 26); he shows *iustitia* and *fides* in contrast with Turnus, the victim of *violentia* and *furor*. He is deeply religious, an aspect of his character which (as we have seen) receives special prominence in Book V. In some ways (but by no means all)[2] he reminds us of the Stoic *sapiens* undergoing his testing-time; Stoic phrases are sometimes used in connexion with him (e.g. 5. 725). But these elements are certainly not the whole of his character. Above all else he is a complex human personality, subject to human frailties and doubts and weaknesses, following out as well as he is able a mission whose fulfilment is almost too difficult for him, isolated by the magnitude of his responsibilities, in a real sense (in T. R. Glover's phrase) 'the most solitary figure in literature'. *Tantae molis erat Romanam condere gentem.*

The feature of Aeneas' character then which gives it life is the inner conflict in him between his devotion to duty and his human frailties and warmer human emotions. It is not only that it sometimes seems as if he has not the strength to go on; sometimes too he is baffled and perplexed by the suffering which his mission apparently involves, as with Dido, with Turnus, with the countless young warriors who fall in battle.

A few illustrations of the human weaknesses and doubts of Aeneas must here suffice to dispel the suggestion that he is a marionette of the fates, an abstract personification of *pietas*. Whatever else he is or is not, he is a man of flesh and

---

[1] To the extent that Augustus had these virtues too Aeneas may be said to remind us of Augustus; it is as incorrect to dissociate Aeneas entirely from Augustus as it is to regard him as an allegorical representation of the Emperor.

[2] Some of the ways in which Aeneas fell short of the Stoic ideal of perfection are illustrated in the rest of this section; see also C. M. Bowra in *Greece and Rome*, 1933–4, pp. 8 f., and M. L. Clarke, *The Roman Mind*, pp. 32–41, 71.

blood. At the beginning of the poem (1. 92 f.) we see him in despair, a man who has suffered much and has more yet to suffer; still he goes on and heartens his companions after the storm, though his words of hope are feigned (1. 198 f.). When he meets his disguised mother he protests against the adversity which has come upon those carrying out a fated mission (1. 372 f.). In the temple at Carthage (1. 453 f.) the pictures of the Trojan War remind him once again of the suffering all around him, of the *lacrimae rerum*. In these opening scenes we have seen him pondering, sorely tried, sometimes in despair. The second book is full of the turmoil of his feelings in the last hours of Troy; in the third we are made to feel the toil and pain (as well as the hope) of ever striving onwards to an uncertain goal. In the fourth book more than anywhere we see the anguish brought upon Aeneas by the conflict between his emotions and his devotion to duty. Here our sympathy goes out to him as it does to Dido.[1] Both have suffered much; both grasp at a fleeting chance of happiness. Aeneas is reminded roughly and imperiously by Mercury that his divine mission requires a complete sacrifice of self, and he realizes with a shock what he should have realized long before, and in the conflict of loyalties his judgement decides (as it must) for Rome. The Trojans are all delighted at the divine intervention and the decision to go (4. 294 f.); among his rejoicing companions the lonely Aeneas has now nothing but sorrow before him. In the last scenes with Dido he tries to control his feelings and reconcile her to the imperative demands of duty upon him; but neither can understand the other's point of view, and when all is said they are farther apart than they were before.

The fifth book begins with the Trojans sailing away from Carthage, unaware of Dido's fate, but filled with sorrowful thoughts of what may have happened. The arrival at Anchises' tomb and the religious celebrations there alter

[1] See Austin's *Aeneid IV*, Intro., pp. xiv f.

the mood of the poem; after the completion of the rites the
games are described, the tension is lessened, and a sense of
serenity and joy comes into the narrative. The sudden
disaster of the burning of the ships is therefore all the more
difficult for Aeneas to bear, and his despair here is more deep
and complete than at any other stage. He calls on the gods
to save him now or else for ever strike him down (685 f.), and
even when his prayer is answered he is so shaken in heart
that he actually wonders whether to forget his mission and
stay in Sicily.

> At pater Aeneas casu concussus acerbo
> nunc huc ingentis, nunc illuc pectore curas
> mutabat versans, Siculisne resideret arvis
> oblitus fatorum, Italasne capesseret oras.   (700–3.)

It is only the advice of Nautes and the vision of Anchises
which give him the strength to go on. He founds the city of
Segesta and sets sail; but his joy at the prospect of a safe
arrival at last in his destined home (827 f.) is cruelly changed
to grief as the book ends with the loss of Palinurus and
Aeneas' final words of sorrow.

It is clear then from the events of the poem that Virgil
cannot justly be accused of depicting his hero as an abstraction, an unconvincing paragon of righteousness automatically carrying out a mission laid upon him. There would
be more truth in the opposite criticism, that Aeneas is too
liable to human frailty: he does not rise magnificently above
disaster, but he struggles with it and comes very near to the
limit of his physical and mental endurance. But this objection would be based on an un-Virgilian conception of what
is meant by heroism.

In the early part of Book VI the note of sorrow with
which Book V ended is dominant again, and when Aeneas
meets Dido in the underworld he is still looking backwards
towards the tragedy and suffering of the past rather than
forwards to the triumph of Rome. The first words of
Anchises to his son are:

> Venisti tandem, tuaque exspectata parenti
> vicit iter durum pietas?   (6. 687–8.)

Aeneas' sense of devotion to his mission has triumphed, but
by a narrow margin, and at a great cost. There follows the
pageant of Roman heroes, and after the vision of Augustus
Anchises breaks off to ask his son:

> Et dubitamus adhuc virtutem extendere factis,
> aut metus Ausonia prohibet consistere terra?   (6. 806–7.)

Now at last, after this profound experience, all doubts and
hesitation must be cast aside. Aeneas is finally strengthened
to continue with his mission until it is achieved.

The inner conflict in Aeneas' character corresponds in
some degree with the conflict in Virgil's own mind. Along
with the theme of Rome's destined greatness Virgil was pre-
occupied with the theme of pain and suffering, and as he
wrote the *Aeneid* he sought to harmonize the two themes.
The inner unity of the whole poem derives from the balance
and the tension of these major motives. The note of tenderness and sorrow, set against the triumph of Roman achievement, is sometimes dominant, and in the end the suffering
of Dido and Turnus, of Pallas and Euryalus, of Palinurus
and Marcellus, of Aeneas himself, is not wholly explained
by the Golden Age which Virgil saw dawning for Rome.
The *Aeneid* is indeed a national and patriotic expression of
the glory of Rome, but it extends beyond that—it is also
a universal poem of human experience.

V. *The Composition of Book V*

There are a number of reasons for believing that Book V
was not written, or at all events not completed, until after
the rest of the first half of the poem. There is nothing sur-
prising about this; we are told a good deal by Servius,
Donatus, and others about Virgil's method of composition,
and we know that after sketching out the poem in twelve
books and writing a prose draft he worked on different

sections at different times: *particulatim componere instituit, prout liberet quidque, et nihil in ordinem arripiens (Vit. Don. 23).*[1] In a discussion about the early or late composition of any part of the *Aeneid* it is necessary to guard firmly against any implication that Virgil constantly changed the whole plan of his work, or made haphazard later additions; nothing could be farther from the truth, though unfortunately this impression is often given by the listing and analysis of various contradictions and inconsistencies in the poem.[2] The structure of the *Aeneid*, both in factual content and in emotional and tensional arrangement, is of the most intricate and closely woven kind. The poem must have received many modifications and improvements in order to make the cohesion closer before it reached its present form; there are still some places where the cohesion is not perfect, but it must be emphasized that these are of relatively little significance compared with the total effect of structural unity.

Of the books in the first half of the poem the third and the fifth are those which show most indication of not having received their final touches. Book III was probably written early, and it is extremely likely that Virgil's projected visit to Greece in 19 B.C. was undertaken to give him the local colour and first-hand knowledge which he felt he needed for revision and (perhaps) partial recasting.[3] Book V seems to have been written comparatively late, perhaps when Virgil was working on the second half. It presents certain similarities of style with the later books; the directness and vigour of narrative and the relative rareness of Alexandrian motifs and descriptive phraseology link it with Virgil's later style. There are indications that in a number of passages Virgil had not yet given his final revision; the proportion of lines

[1] For the ancient evidence see M. M. Crump, *The Growth of the Aeneid*, Blackwell, 1920, pp. 2 f., Conington's edition, vol. ii, Intro., pp. lxvi f.

[2] For a well-put warning in this connexion see the study of Book III by R. B. Lloyd, *A.J.Ph.*, 1957, pp. 133 f.

[3] For inconsistencies connected with prophecies see note on 731 f.

which are repeated elsewhere in the *Aeneid* is high in Book V
compared with the rest of the poem,[1] and there are some
undoubted awkwardnesses of diction and construction.[2]
Finally there are two noticeable inconsistencies with other
parts of the poem, one concerned with Palinurus and the
other with the chronology of Aeneas' voyage.

(i) *Palinurus*

In the *Aeneid* as we now possess it there are undeniable
factual discrepancies between the story of Palinurus' death
in Book V and the account given by his shade in the underworld (6. 337 f.).[3] They are much too marked to be explained
away, and they show conclusively that the end of Book V
was not composed immediately before the beginning of
Book VI. They are as follows: (i) In Book V the god Sleep
throws Palinurus overboard, but in Book VI there is no
mention by Palinurus of divine intervention; in fact he
explicitly says *nec me deus aequore mersit.* (ii) Conversely,
in Book V Aeneas thinks Palinurus' death was an accident,
but in Book VI asks what god was responsible. (iii) In
Book V the sea is calm, in Book VI stormy. (iv) In Book V
Palinurus was on the journey from Sicily to Italy, but in
Book VI we read *qui Libyco nuper cursu . . .*[4] (v) In Book VI
Palinurus says that he was on the sea for three days and
nights, but in fact only one day has yet passed since the
events at the end of Book V.

To these five points of factual discrepancy, which suggest
irresistibly that the two accounts were composed separately
and have not been harmonized, we may add two further

---

[1] See Index, s.v. 'Repetition', and J. Sparrow, *Half-lines and
Repetitions in Virgil*, pp. 98 f., 104 f.

[2] See Index, s.v. 'Unrevised passages'.

[3] These have often been discussed; see especially P. Jacob, *Les
Études Classiques*, 1952, pp. 163 f., Norden on *Aen.* 6. 337–83, Heinze,
Virgils Epische Technik, p. 146, n. 1.

[4] This can only mean 'on the voyage to Libya'; and even if it
could be forced into the meaning 'on the voyage from Libya' the
stop in Sicily is far too important to be ignored.

points: (i) Servius (on *Aen.* 5. 871) says that the first two lines of Book VI were at the end of Book V until Varius and Tucca transferred them to the beginning of Book VI. (ii) There is a marked similarity between the fates of Misenus (6. 149 f.) and of Palinurus. When the Sibyl tells Aeneas that before he can get the golden bough he must first find and bury the dead body of one of his comrades, the reader immediately assumes that this refers to Palinurus (5. 871), and is surprised to discover that Misenus is meant.

There is no difficulty in determining which of the two versions is the earlier. We know that Book VI was relatively early in composition (it was read to Augustus in 23 B.C.); and the account of Palinurus in it is so clearly intended to resemble the appearance of Elpenor[1] to Odysseus in *Odyssey* XI that it must have been part of Virgil's Νέκυια from the start. Further, there is the evidence of Servius for alteration at the end of Book V. It seems highly likely that 5. 779–871 was composed a good deal later than Book VI, and probable that it was later than the rest of Book V, perhaps replacing a short passage describing the voyage to Italy. This would also explain one awkwardness in the present version of Book V, namely that the weather seems to be calm when Aeneas sets out (774 f.), yet Neptune, at Venus' instigation, drives away the storm-clouds and stills the waters (820 f.). Feeling that his transition in tone between Books V and VI was not yet exactly as he wanted it Virgil added or elaborated the Palinurus passage[2] and led into it with the conversation of Venus and Neptune. If we discern a modification of this kind in the original plan, it should suggest not the inadequacy of the previous plan but the great mastery which Virgil increasingly gained in the handling of mood and tone within the structure of the poem. The correction of consequent factual discrepancies (if not too

---

[1] See note on 827 f.

[2] It also gives a symmetry between the beginning and the end of the book; see Heinze, op. cit., pp. 451 f.

large) could be left until the final revision; the colour and
the movement and the development of the emotional motifs
were of primary importance.

The original account of the death of Palinurus to which
Book VI refers may then have been suppressed, it may have
been a passage which still had to be written, or it may have
been implied in the storm in Book I. There (*Aen.* 1. 113 f.) the
pilot of Orontes' ship, who is not named, is lost in the storm;
in *Aen.* 6. 333 f. the mention of Palinurus comes just after
a reference to Orontes and the storm. In many ways (but
not all) Palinurus' story in Book VI is consistent with this
storm, and it is possible that when composing Book VI
Virgil may have thought of the loss of Palinurus as having
occurred then. However that may be, there is no reasonable
doubt that the version of Palinurus' death in Book V was
written some considerable time after the version in Book
VI, and in factual detail the two passages had not been
harmonized.

A few words remain to be said about the Misenus–
Palinurus 'doublet'. Aeneas finds Misenus lying unburied
on the shore, burial rites are performed, and the name
Misenus is given to the place of his tomb. A little later the
shade of the unburied Palinurus is consoled by the promise
that a tomb will be erected for him and the place will be
called Palinurus. There are obvious points of similarity in
the stories, and it is sometimes thought that here we may
detect different strands in the composition of the poem.
First of all it should be observed that there is no reference
of any kind to Misenus in Book V. Servius and many since
have tried to find some, the favourite place being 5. 814–15;
but the death of Misenus, which occurs after the Trojans
have landed, has nothing whatever to do with Neptune's
prophecy about the voyage.[1] Secondly, there is no reason
to think that Book VI was ever without either Misenus or
Palinurus. It seems likely that they both figured in the

[1] On this see Heinze's excellent remarks, op. cit., p. 452, n. 1,

current version of the legend (Dion. Hal. 1. 53. 2 f. recounts them one after the other), and Virgil evidently decided to use both by basing each on a different aspect of the Homeric story of Elpenor.[1] The similarity of the two aetiological stories quite close to one another can be explained by Virgil's fondness for this way of linking the legendary past with the present, particularly now that the Trojans have reached the shores of Italy with their well-loved and familiar place-names.

(ii) *Chronology*

A second indication that Book V had not yet received its final revision may be found in the chronology of Aeneas' wanderings. Now it is true that we should not look in an epic poem for an historian's precision about dating, and it is also true that poetic considerations may override factual details of place and time; but the general organization of the *Aeneid* is such that we should expect Virgil's time background to be unobtrusively correct and consistent when the poem was finally finished. The chronology of Book III also presents difficulties, and it is probable that this background aspect of the poem was one of the features which Virgil would have reconsidered during final revision.[2]

In 5. 626 Iris disguised as Beroe says *septima post Troiae excidium iam vertitur aestas*; in *Aen.* 1. 755 f. Dido had said *nam te iam septima portat/ omnibus errantem terris et fluctibus aestas*. Clearly these two statements are irreconcilable, and Servius is right in his comment on 5. 626 'ergo constat quaestionem hanc unam esse de insolubilibus, quas non dubium est emendaturum fuisse Vergilium'. As we shall

---

[1] See Norden's *Aeneid VI*, p. 181.

[2] On the whole subject see L. A. Constans, *L'Énéide de Virgile*, Paris, 1938, Appendix I, and his review of R. Mandra, *The Time Element in the Aeneid* in *R.E.L.*, 1935, pp. 397 f.; see also Heinze, op. cit., pp. 348 f., Crump, *The Growth of the Aeneid*, pp. 25 f., E. de Saint-Denis, *R.E.L.*, 1942, pp. 79 f.

see, it is the line in Book V which is most strongly in contradiction with the rest of the poem.

The tradition of Aeneas' wanderings, as far as the evidence
shows us, gave a shorter period than seven years. The
narrative of Book III can hardly be extended to cover more
than three years. The number seven may well have been
suggested to Virgil's mind because of its host of ritual
associations, but these do not entitle us to divest it entirely
of its arithmetical significance in order to get over the
difficulty.

Many attempts have been made to reconcile Dido's
septima aestas with Beroe's words in Book V, but however
freely one interprets *aestas* as equivalent to *annus* the passages remain contradictory. It seems certain that Aeneas
arrived at Carthage late in the year, stayed for two or
three months, and left towards the end of winter (*Aen.* 4.
193 *nunc hiemem inter se luxu quam longa fovere*; *Aen.* 4. 309
quin etiam hiberno moliris sidere classem?); it is likely that
Virgil would conceive the celebration of the *parentatio* for
Anchises as happening at the appropriate time of the year
for the Roman festival, namely 13–21 February. It is
possible to account for the passage of a year from the death
of Anchises at Drepanum (*Aen.* 3. 707 f.) and the celebration
of the anniversary games by assuming that Aeneas stayed
for a considerable time at Drepanum before leaving for
Carthage.

What conclusions then can be drawn? No other conclusions than that in his plan of the poem Virgil had not yet
fully worked out the chronology. Other factors were more
important for him; he had decided to include a second visit
to Sicily in order to set the religious ceremonies and the
anniversary games in the region where he wanted them
and in the part of his poem where they were appropriate.
In this, as in his seven-year chronology, he was departing
from the normal tradition, and he had not yet set about
resolving the difficulties of the time factor. His mental

picture was of a seven-years' wandering; he had used the phrase *septima aestas* for Dido, and now for the moment he allowed it again for Beroe. It would have been easy to work through the poem later and to make changes; arithmetic could easily be altered. What could not be changed was the arrangement of episodes in the emotional and tensional order which Virgil had found to be the right one. We ought not, because of inconsistencies in the time scale which could very easily be removed, to be tempted to think that they imply major dislocations in the original plan. Book V plays the part in the poem which Virgil had intended for it; the alterations which his death prevented him from making were matters of detail.

SIGLA

F = Schedae Vaticanae   saec. iii init. vel iv
M = Codex Mediceus   saec. v
P = Codex Palatinus   saec. iv–v
R = Codex Romanus   saec. vi?
V = Schedae Veronenses rescriptae   saec. iv ?
γ = Codex Gudianus   saec. ix
a = Codex Bernensis 172 et Pari-   saec. ix
     sinus 7929
b = Codex Bernensis 165   saec. ix
c = Codex Bernensis 184   saec. ix
m = Codex Minoraugiensis   saec. xii?
π = Codex Pragensis   saec. ix
Serv. = Servii commentarii
D. Serv. = Servius Danielis (vel Deuteroservius quem
     vocat Georgii)

P. VERGILI MARONIS

AENEIDOS

LIBER V

Interea medium Aeneas iam classe tenebat
certus iter fluctusque atros Aquilone secabat
moenia respiciens, quae iam infelicis Elissae
conlucent flammis. quae tantum accenderit ignem
causa latet; duri magno sed amore dolores   5
polluto, notumque furens quid femina possit,
triste per augurium Teucrorum pectora ducunt.
ut pelagus tenuere rates nec iam amplius ulla
occurrit tellus, maria undique et undique caelum,
olli caeruleus supra caput astitit imber   10
noctem hiememque ferens et inhorruit unda tenebris.
ipse gubernator puppi Palinurus ab alta:
'heu quianam tanti cinxerunt aethera nimbi?
quidve, pater Neptune, paras?' sic deinde locutus
colligere arma iubet validisque incumbere remis,   15
obliquatque sinus in ventum ac talia fatur:
'magnanime Aenea, non, si mihi Iuppiter auctor
spondeat, hoc sperem Italiam contingere caelo.
mutati transversa fremunt et vespere ab atro
consurgunt venti, atque in nubem cogitur aër.   20
nec nos obniti contra nec tendere tantum
sufficimus. superat quoniam Fortuna, sequamur,
quoque vocat vertamus iter. nec litora longe
fida reor fraterna Erycis portusque Sicanos,
si modo rite memor)servata remetior astra.'   25
tum pius Aeneas: 'equidem sic poscere ventos

iamdudum et frustra cerno te tendere contra.
flecte viam velis. an sit mihi gratior ulla,
quove magis fessas optem demittere navis,
quam quae Dardanium tellus mihi servat Acesten   30
et patris Anchisae gremio complectitur ossa ? '
haec ubi dicta, petunt portus et vela secundi
intendunt Zephyri ; fertur cita gurgite classis,
et tandem laeti notae advertuntur harenae.

At procul ex celso miratus vertice montis   35
adventum sociasque rates occurrit Acestes,
horridus in iaculis et pelle Libystidis ursae,
Troia Criniso conceptum flumine mater
quem genuit. veterum non immemor ille parentum
gratatur reduces et gaza laetus agresti   40
excipit, ac fessos opibus solatur amicis.

Postera cum primo stellas Oriente fugarat
clara dies, socios in coetum litore ab omni
advocat Aeneas tumulique ex aggere fatur :
'Dardanidae magni, genus alto a sanguine divum,   45
annuus exactis completur mensibus orbis,
ex quo reliquias divinique ossa parentis
condidimus terra maestasque sacravimus aras.
iamque dies, nisi fallor, adest, quem semper acerbum,
semper honoratum (sic di voluistis) habebo.   50
hunc ego Gaetulis agerem si Syrtibus exsul,
Argolicove mari deprensus et urbe Mycenae,
annua vota tamen sollemnisque ordine pompas
exsequerer strueremque suis altaria donis.
nunc ultro ad cineres ipsius et ossa parentis   55
haud equidem sine mente, reor, sine numine divum
adsumus et portus delati intramus amicos.
ergo agite et laetum cuncti celebremus honorem :

27–36 *MP*; 37–58 *MPR*   29 demittere *cπ deteriores quidam*:
dimittere *ceteri Serv.*   38 Criniso *codd. Serv. ad* i. 550; *sed flumini
nomen erat Crimisso, unde* Crimiso *Güthling*   52 urbe] arce *P*[1]
Mycenis *R*

poscamus ventos, atque haec me sacra quotannis
urbe velit posita templis sibi ferre dicatis.   60
bina boum vobis Troia generatus Acestes
dat numero capita in navis; adhibete penatis
et patrios epulis et quos colit hospes Acestes.
praeterea, si nona diem mortalibus almum
Aurora extulerit radiisque retexerit orbem,   65
prima citae Teucris ponam certamina classis;
quique pedum cursu valet, et qui viribus audax
aut iaculo incedit melior levibusque sagittis,
seu crudo fidit pugnam committere caestu,
cuncti adsint meritaeque exspectent praemia palmae.   70
ore favete omnes et cingite tempora ramis.'
    Sic fatus velat materna tempora myrto.
hoc Helymus facit, hoc aevi maturus Acestes,
hoc puer Ascanius, sequitur quos cetera pubes.
ille e concilio multis cum milibus ibat   75
ad tumulum magna medius comitante caterva.
hic duo rite mero libans carchesia Baccho
fundit humi, duo lacte novo, duo sanguine sacro,
purpureosque iacit flores ac talia fatur:
'salve, sancte parens, iterum salvete, recepti   80
nequiquam cineres animaeque umbraeque paternae.
non licuit finis Italos fataliaque arva
nec tecum Ausonium, quicumque est, quaerere Thybrim.'
dixerat haec, adytis cum lubricus anguis ab imis
septem ingens gyros, septena volumina traxit   85
amplexus placide tumulum lapsusque per aras,
caeruleae cui terga notae maculosus et auro
squamam incendebat fulgor, ceu nubibus arcus
mille iacit varios adverso sole colores.
obstipuit visu Aeneas. ille agmine longo   90

59–72 *MPR*; 73–90 *MPRV*   59, 60 *primae redactionis esse suspicatur Deuticke*   68 levibusve *Rb*   77 '*ut libaret de mero baccho i.e. puro' Serv., et sic Güthling*   80 *post* iterum *distinguunt alii*   87 auri *Klouček*   89 iacit] trahit *Rγ²abcπ*

tandem inter pateras et levia pocula serpens
libavitque dapes rursusque innoxius imo
successit tumulo et depasta altaria liquit.
hoc magis inceptos genitori instaurat honores,
incertus geniumne loci famulumne parentis   95
esse putet; caedit binas de more bidentis
totque sues, totidem nigrantis terga iuvencos,
vinaque fundebat pateris animamque vocabat
Anchisae magni manisque Acheronte remissos.
nec non et socii, quae cuique est copia, laeti   100
dona ferunt, onerant aras mactantque iuvencos;
ordine aëna locant alii fusique per herbam
subiciunt veribus prunas et viscera torrent.
  Exspectata dies aderat nonamque serena
Auroram Phaethontis equi iam luce vehebant,   105
famaque finitimos et clari nomen Acestae
excierat: laeto complerant litora coetu
visuri Aeneadas, pars et certare parati.
munera principio ante oculos circoque locantur
in medio, sacri tripodes viridesque coronae   110
et palmae pretium victoribus, armaque et ostro
perfusae vestes, argenti aurique talentum;
et tuba commissos medio canit aggere ludos.
  Prima pares ineunt gravibus certamina remis
quattuor ex omni delectae classe carinae.   115
velocem Mnestheus agit acri remige Pristim,
mox Italus Mnestheus, genus a quo nomine Memmi,
ingentemque Gyas ingenti mole Chimaeram,
urbis opus, triplici pubes quam Dardana versu
impellunt, terno consurgunt ordine remi;   120
Sergestusque, domus tenet a quo Sergia nomen,

  91–98 *MPRV*; 99–108 *MPR*; 109–21 *FMPR*   93 linquit *M¹m*
96 caedit binas *M*: caeditque binas *R*: mactat binas *D. Serv. ad* iv.
200: caedit quinas *PVγabcmπ Nonius Serv. ad v.* 78   97 totque]
atque *Klouček*   107 complebant *M*   112 talenta *FRbcm Serv.*
Ribbeck   120 terno . . . remi *uncis secludit Ribbeck*

Centauro invehitur magna, Scyllaque Cloanthus
caerulea, genus unde tibi, Romane Cluenti.

    Est procul in pelago saxum spumantia contra
litora, quod tumidis summersum tunditur olim   125
fluctibus hiberni condunt ubi sidera Cori;
tranquillo silet immotaque attollitur unda
campus et apricis statio gratissima mergis.
hic viridem Aeneas frondenti ex ilice metam
constituit signum nautis pater, unde reverti   130
scirent et longos ubi circumflectere cursus.
tum loca sorte legunt ipsique in puppibus auro
ductores longe effulgent ostroque decori;
cetera populea velatur fronde iuventus
nudatosque umeros oleo perfusa nitescit.   135
considunt transtris, intentaque bracchia remis;
intenti exspectant signum, exsultantiaque haurit
corda pavor pulsans laudumque arrecta cupido.
inde ubi clara dedit sonitum tuba, finibus omnes,
haud mora, prosiluere suis; ferit aethera clamor   140
nauticus, adductis spumant freta versa lacertis.
infindunt pariter sulcos, totumque dehiscit
convulsum remis rostrisque tridentibus aequor.
non tam praecipites biiugo certamine campum
corripuere ruuntque effusi carcere currus,   145
nec sic immissis aurigae undantia lora
concussere iugis pronique in verbera pendent.
tum plausu fremituque virum studiisque faventum
consonat omne nemus, vocemque inclusa volutant
litora, pulsati colles clamore resultant.   150

    Effugit ante alios primisque elabitur undis
turbam inter fremitumque Gyas; quem deinde Cloanthus
consequitur, melior remis, sed pondere pinus
tarda tenet. post hos aequo discrimine Pristis
Centaurusque locum tendunt superare priorem;   155

   122–55 *FMPR*   133 longe] auro *Priscianus*   154 aequo]
aliquo *F*[1]

et nunc Pristis habet, nunc victam praeterit ingens
Centaurus, nunc una ambae iunctisque feruntur
frontibus et longa sulcant vada salsa carina.
iamque propinquabant scopulo metamque tenebant
cum princeps medioque Gyas in gurgite victor   160
rectorem navis compellat voce Menoeten:
'quo tantum mihi dexter abis? huc derige gressum;
litus ama et laeva stringat sine palmula cautes;
altum alii teneant.' dixit; sed caeca Menoetes
saxa timens proram pelagi detorquet ad undas.   165
'quo diversus abis?' iterum 'pete saxa, Menoete!'
cum clamore Gyas revocabat, et ecce Cloanthum
respicit instantem tergo et propiora tenentem.
ille inter navemque Gyae scopulosque sonantis
radit iter laevum interior subitoque priorem   170
praeterit et metis tenet aequora tuta relictis.
tum vero exarsit iuveni dolor ossibus ingens
nec lacrimis caruere genae, segnemque Menoeten
oblitus decorisque sui sociumque salutis
in mare praecipitem puppi deturbat ab alta;   175
ipse gubernaclo rector subit, ipse magister
hortaturque viros clavumque ad litora torquet.
at gravis ut fundo vix tandem redditus imo est
iam senior madidaque fluens in veste Menoetes
summa petit scopuli siccaque in rupe resedit.   180
illum et labentem Teucri et risere natantem
et salsos rident revomentem pectore fluctus.
    Hic laeta extremis spes est accensa duobus,
Sergesto Mnestheique, Gyan superare morantem.
Sergestus capit ante locum scopuloque propinquat,   185
nec tota tamen ille prior praeeunte carina;
parte prior, partim rostro premit aemula Pristis.

    156–8 FMPR; 159–87 MPR   158 longe deteriores   carinae
F¹π: longae … carinae Serv. ad iii. 495   162 dirige Mbcπ   gressum]
cursum M²bcπ Seneca   163 laevas Rγ²b²c   187 partim] partem
M probat Deuticke

at media socios incedens nave per ipsos
hortatur Mnestheus: 'nunc, nunc insurgite remis,
Hectorei socii, Troiae quos sorte suprema   190
delegi comites; nunc illas promite viris,
nunc animos, quibus in Gaetulis Syrtibus usi
Ionioque mari Maleaeque sequacibus undis.
non iam prima peto Mnestheus neque vincere certo
(quamquam o!—sed superent quibus hoc, Neptune, dedisti),
extremos pudeat rediisse: hoc vincite, cives,   196
et prohibete nefas.' olli certamine summo
procumbunt: vastis tremit ictibus aerea puppis
subtrahiturque solum, tum creber anhelitus artus
aridaque ora quatit, sudor fluit undique rivis.   200
attulit ipse viris optatum casus honorem.
namque furens animi dum proram ad saxa suburget
interior spatioque subit Sergestus iniquo,
infelix saxis in procurrentibus haesit.
concussae cautes et acuto in murice remi   205
obnixi crepuere inlisaque prora pependit.
consurgunt nautae et magno clamore morantur
ferratasque trudes et acuta cuspide contos
expediunt fractosque legunt in gurgite remos.
at laetus Mnestheus successuque acrior ipso   210
agmine remorum celeri ventisque vocatis
prona petit maria et pelago decurrit aperto.
qualis spelunca subito commota columba,
cui domus et dulces latebroso in pumice nidi,
fertur in arva volans plausumque exterrita pennis   215
dat tecto ingentem, mox aëre lapsa quieto
radit iter liquidum celeris neque commovet alas:
sic Mnestheus, sic ipsa fuga secat ultima Pristis
aequora, sic illam fert impetus ipse volantem.
et primum in scopulo luctantem deserit alto   220
Sergestum brevibusque vadis frustraque vocantem

 188–221 *MPR* 198 aurea *M¹P¹* 202 animo *Pγ¹* prora *M*
208 sudes *M* 212 pelago] caelo *Quintilianus*

auxilia et fractis discentem currere remis.
inde Gyan ipsamque ingenti mole Chimaeram
consequitur; cedit, quoniam spoliata magistro est.

   Solus iamque ipso superest in fine Cloanthus: 225
quem petit et summis adnixus viribus urget.
tum vero ingeminat clamor cunctique sequentem
instigant studiis, resonatque fragoribus aether.
hi proprium decus et partum indignantur honorem
ni teneant, vitamque volunt pro laude pacisci;   230
hos successus alit: possunt, quia posse videntur.
et fors aequatis cepissent praemia rostris,
ni palmas ponto tendens utrasque Cloanthus
fudissetque preces divosque in vota vocasset:
'di, quibus imperium est pelagi, quorum aequora curro, 235
vobis laetus ego hoc candentem in litore taurum
constituam ante aras voti reus, extaque salsos
proiciam in fluctus et vina liquentia fundam.'
dixit, eumque imis sub fluctibus audiit omnis
Nereidum Phorcique chorus Panopeaque virgo,   240
et pater ipse manu magna Portunus euntem
impulit: illa noto citius volucrique sagitta
ad terram fugit et portu se condidit alto.

   Tum satus Anchisa cunctis ex more vocatis
victorem magna praeconis voce Cloanthum   245
declarat viridique advelat tempora lauro,
muneraque in navis ternos optare iuvencos
vinaque et argenti magnum dat ferre talentum.
ipsis praecipuos ductoribus addit honores:
victori chlamydem auratam, quam plurima circum   250
purpura Maeandro duplici Meliboea cucurrit,
intextusque puer frondosa regius Ida
velocis iaculo cervos cursuque fatigat

   222–40 MPR; 241–53 $MPRV$ 226 enixus $P\gamma$ 228 resonat
clamoribus $P\gamma\pi$ 235 pelagi est $M^2Rc\pi$ aequore $R\gamma$ 238 poriciam
M^2: porriciam $Macrobius$, $agnoscit$ $Serv$.   et] ac $P\gamma b$ 241 Neptunus γ^1 247 aptare $\gamma^2bcm\pi$ 249 praecipue M $Nonius$

acer, anhelanti similis, quem praepes ab Ida
sublimem pedibus rapuit Iovis armiger uncis: 255
longaevi palmas nequiquam ad sidera tendunt
custodes, saevitque canum latratus in auras.
at qui deinde locum tenuit virtute secundum,
levibus huic hamis consertam auroque trilicem
loricam, quam Demoleo detraxerat ipse 260
victor apud rapidum Simoenta sub Ilio alto,
donat habere, viro decus et tutamen in armis.
vix illam famuli Phegeus Sagarisque ferebant
multiplicem conixi umeris; indutus at olim
Demoleos cursu palantis Troas agebat. 265
tertia dona facit geminos ex aere lebetas
cymbiaque argento perfecta atque aspera signis.
iamque adeo donati omnes opibusque superbi
puniceis ibant evincti tempora taenis,
cum saevo e scopulo multa vix arte revulsus 270
amissis remis atque ordine debilis uno
inrisam sine honore ratem Sergestus agebat.
qualis saepe viae deprensus in aggere serpens,
aerea quem obliquum rota transiit aut gravis ictu
seminecem liquit saxo lacerumque viator; 275
nequiquam longos fugiens dat corpore tortus
parte ferox ardensque oculis et sibila colla
arduus attollens; pars vulnere clauda retentat
nexantem nodis seque in sua membra plicantem:
tali remigio navis se tarda movebat; 280
vela facit tamen et velis subit ostia plenis.
Sergestum Aeneas promisso munere donat
servatam ob navem laetus sociosque reductos.

254–83 *MPRV* 254 ab Ida] ab alto *Burman*: ab aethra
Schrader; *sed vide Henry ad hunc locum* 257 in] ad *P* 260 ipsi
M¹ (?) 262 *interpunxit Schröter, vulgo* donat habere viro *iungunt*
270 revolsam *R* 278 vulnera *Pγ¹* cauda *M¹P²V* 279 nexantem *RV* (*teste Henry*) *γ²bπ Priscianus*: netentem *M ab ipsa prima
manu correctus*: nixantem *M¹Pγ¹c* 280 ferebat *Pγ* 281 plenis
subit ostia velis *M*

olli serva datur operum haud ignara Minervae,
Cressa genus, Pholoe, geminique sub ubere nati.   285
   Hoc pius Aeneas misso certamine tendit
gramineum in campum, quem collibus undique curvis
cingebant silvae, mediaque in valle theatri
circus erat ; quo se multis cum milibus heros
consessu medium tulit exstructoque resedit.   290
hic, qui forte velint rapido contendere cursu,
invitat pretiis animos, et praemia ponit.
undique conveniunt Teucri mixtique Sicani,
Nisus et Euryalus primi,
Euryalus forma insignis viridique iuventa,   295
Nisus amore pio pueri ; quos deinde secutus
regius egregia Priami de stirpe Diores ;
hunc Salius simul et Patron, quorum alter Acarnan,
alter ab Arcadio Tegeaeae sanguine gentis :
tum duo Trinacrii iuvenes, Helymus Panopesque,   300
adsueti silvis, comites senioris Acestae ;
multi praeterea, quos fama obscura recondit.
Aeneas quibus in mediis sic deinde locutus :
'accipite haec animis laetasque advertite mentes.
nemo ex hoc numero mihi non donatus abibit.   305
Gnosia bina dabo levato lucida ferro
spicula caelatamque argento ferre bipennem ;
omnibus hic erit unus honos. tres praemia primi
accipient flavaque caput nectentur oliva.
primus equum phaleris insignem victor habeto ;   310
alter Amazoniam pharetram plenamque sagittis
Threiciis, lato quam circum amplectitur auro
balteus et tereti subnectit fibula gemma ;
tertius Argolica hac galea contentus abito.'

   284–92 *MPRV* ; 293–314 *MPR*   285 ubera *M P¹Rγ*   290 con-
sensu *M¹* : consessum *Gossrau* : consessum in *Klouček*   295 insigni
Pγ¹   296 quem *Pγ¹*   299 Arcadia *Pγbc*   Tegeaeae sanguine *P¹*
Mentelianus alter : Tegeae de *M²P²γcπ*, *utrumque testatur Serv.*, *illud
praefert* : Tegere de *M¹* : Tegaea de *R*   309 flava] fulva *invenisse
videtur Serv.*   310 equam *M¹*   312 circumplectitur *M*

Haec ubi dicta, locum capiunt signoque repente   315
corripiunt spatia audito limenque relinquunt,
effusi nimbo similes: simul ultima signant.
primus abit longeque ante omnia corpora Nisus
emicat et ventis et fulminis ocior alis;
proximus huic, longo sed proximus intervallo,   320
insequitur Salius; spatio post deinde relicto
tertius Euryalus;
Euryalumque Helymus sequitur; quo deinde sub ipso
ecce volat calcemque terit iam calce Diores
incumbens umero, spatia et si plura supersint   325
transeat elapsus prior ambiguumque relinquat.
iamque fere spatio extremo fessique sub ipsam
finem adventabant, levi cum sanguine Nisus
labitur infelix, caesis ut forte iuvencis
fusus humum viridisque super madefecerat herbas.   330
hic iuvenis iam victor ovans vestigia presso
haud tenuit titubata solo, sed pronus in ipso
concidit immundoque fimo sacroque cruore.
non tamen Euryali, non ille oblitus amorum:
nam sese opposuit Salio per lubrica surgens,   335
ille autem spissa iacuit revolutus harena:
emicat Euryalus et munere victor amici
prima tenet, plausuque volat fremituque secundo.
post Helymus subit et nunc tertia palma Diores.
hic totum caveae consessum ingentis et ora   340
prima patrum magnis Salius clamoribus implet,
ereptumque dolo reddi sibi poscit honorem.
tutatur favor Euryalum lacrimaeque decorae,
gratior et pulchro veniens in corpore virtus.
adiuvat et magna proclamat voce Diores,   345
qui subiit palmae frustraque ad praemia venit

315–46 *MPR*   323 quo] quod *MR*: quem *P*[1]   326 ambiguumque *codd.*: -ve '*codices nostri omnes*' *Nic. Heinsius, sed quales
non liquet*: -ve *Bentley Ribbeck alii*   327 ipsum *M*[2]   337 amico
M[1]   340 consensum *M*[1]*Ry*[1]*b*[1]

ultima, si primi Salio reddentur honores.
tum pater Aeneas 'vestra' inquit 'munera vobis
certa manent, pueri et palmam movet ordine nemo;
me liceat casus miserari insontis amici.'   350
sic fatus tergum Gaetuli immane leonis
dat Salio villis onerosum atque unguibus aureis.
hic Nisus 'si tanta' inquit 'sunt praemia victis,
et te lapsorum miseret, quae munera Niso
digna dabis, primam merui qui laude coronam   355
ni me, quae Salium, fortuna inimica tulisset?'
et simul his dictis faciem ostentabat et udo
turpia membra fimo. risit pater optimus olli
et clipeum efferri iussit, Didymaonis artis,
Neptuni sacro Danais de poste refixum.   360
hoc iuvenem egregium praestanti munere donat.
    Post, ubi confecti cursus et dona peregit:
'nunc, si cui virtus animusque in pectore praesens,
adsit et evinctis attollat bracchia palmis.'
sic ait, et geminum pugnae proponit honorem,   365
victori velatum auro vittisque iuvencum,
ensem atque insignem galeam solacia victo.
nec mora; continuo vastis cum viribus effert
ora Dares magnoque virum se murmure tollit,
solus qui Paridem solitus contendere contra,   370
idemque ad tumulum quo maximus occubat Hector
victorem Buten immani corpore, qui se
Bebrycia veniens Amyci de gente ferebat,
perculit et fulva moribundum extendit harena.
talis prima Dares caput altum in proelia tollit,   375
ostenditque umeros latos alternaque iactat
bracchia protendens et verberat ictibus auras.
quaeritur huic alius; nec quisquam ex agmine tanto

347–78 *MPR*   347 reddantur $M^1R\gamma^2\pi$: redduntur *M* (*ab ipsa prima manu correctus*) *bc*   349 *interpunxit Nauck, vulgo* pueri *vocative scribunt*   350 misereri P^1Rbc^1 354 munera] praemia *M*   359 artem *PRγ*   364 vinctis $P\gamma^1b^1$ 374 percutit Rb^1

audet adire virum manibusque inducere caestus.
ergo alacris cunctosque putans excedere palma   380
Aeneae stetit ante pedes, nec plura moratus
tum laeva taurum cornu tenet atque ita fatur:
'nate dea, si nemo audet se credere pugnae,
quae finis standi? quo me decet usque teneri?
ducere dona iube.' cuncti simul ore fremebant   385
Dardanidae reddique viro promissa iubebant.
   Hic gravis Entellum dictis castigat Acestes,
proximus ut viridante toro consederat herbae:
'Entelle, heroum quondam fortissime frustra,
tantane tam patiens nullo certamine tolli   390
dona sines? ubi nunc nobis deus ille (magister
nequiquam memoratus) Eryx? ubi fama per omnem
Trinacriam et spolia illa tuis pendentia tectis?'
ille sub haec: 'non laudis amor nec gloria cessit
pulsa metu; sed enim gelidus tardante senecta   395
sanguis hebet, frigentque effetae in corpore vires.
si mihi quae quondam fuerat quaque improbus iste
exsultat fidens, si nunc foret illa iuventas,
haud equidem pretio inductus pulchroque iuvenco
venissem, nec dona moror.' sic deinde locutus   400
in medium geminos immani pondere caestus
proiecit, quibus acer Eryx in proelia suetus
ferre manum duroque intendere bracchia tergo.
obstipuere animi: tantorum ingentia septem
terga boum plumbo insuto ferroque rigebant.   405
ante omnis stupet ipse Dares longeque recusat,
magnanimusque Anchisiades et pondus et ipsa
huc illuc vinclorum immensa volumina versat.
tum senior talis referebat pectore voces:
'quid, si quis caestus ipsius et Herculis arma   410
vidisset tristemque hoc ipso in litore pugnam?
haec germanus Eryx quondam tuus arma gerebat

379–412 *MPR*   382 laevo *Pγ¹*   384 quae] qui *M²*   387 his
Nonius   388 herba *Rc¹*   398 iuventus *Pγ¹mπ*

(sanguine cernis adhuc sparsoque infecta cerebro),
his magnum Alciden contra stetit, his ego suetus,
dum melior viris sanguis dabat, aemula necdum   415
temporibus geminis canebat sparsa senectus.
sed si nostra Dares haec Troius arma recusat
idque pio sedet Aeneae, probat auctor Acestes,
aequemus pugnas. Erycis tibi terga remitto
(solve metus), et tu Troianos exue caestus.'   420
haec fatus duplicem ex umeris reiecit amictum
et magnos membrorum artus, magna ossa lacertosque
exuit atque ingens media consistit harena.
tum satus Anchisa caestus pater extulit aequos
et paribus palmas amborum innexuit armis.   425
constitit in digitos extemplo arrectus uterque
bracchiaque ad superas interritus extulit auras.
abduxere retro longe capita ardua ab ictu
immiscentque manus manibus pugnamque lacessunt,
ille pedum melior motu fretusque iuventa,   430
hic membris et mole valens; sed tarda trementi
genua labant, vastos quatit aeger anhelitus artus.
multa viri nequiquam inter se vulnera iactant,
multa cavo lateri ingeminant et pectore vastos
dant sonitus, erratque auris et tempora circum   435
crebra manus, duro crepitant sub vulnere malae.
stat gravis Entellus nisuque immotus eodem
corpore tela modo atque oculis vigilantibus exit.
ille, velut celsam oppugnat qui molibus urbem
aut montana sedet circum castella sub armis,   440
nunc hos, nunc illos aditus, omnemque pererrat
arte locum et variis adsultibus inritus urget.
ostendit dextram insurgens Entellus et alte
extulit: ille ictum venientem a vertice velox

413–44 *MPR*   421 deiecit *P¹*   422 -que *om. P²m*
423 exuit] extulit *Macrobius*   425 intexuit *M¹*   428 redduxere
Marius Victorinus   434 pectora *Hamburgensis alter, probat Schaper*
435 sonitum *Pγ¹*

praevidit celerique elapsus corpore cessit;   445
Entellus viris in ventum effudit et ultro
ipse gravis graviterque ad terram pondere vasto
concidit, ut quondam cava concidit aut Erymantho
aut Ida in magna radicibus eruta pinus.
consurgunt studiis Teucri et Trinacria pubes;   450
it clamor caelo primusque accurrit Acestes
aequaevumque ab humo miserans attollit amicum.
at non tardatus casu neque territus heros
acrior ad pugnam redit ac vim suscitat ira;
tum pudor incendit viris et conscia virtus,   455
praecipitemque Daren ardens agit aequore toto
nunc dextra ingeminans ictus, nunc ille sinistra.
nec mora nec requies: quam multa grandine nimbi
culminibus crepitant, sic densis ictibus heros
creber utraque manu pulsat versatque Dareta.   460
    Tum pater Aeneas procedere longius iras
et saevire animis Entellum haud passus acerbis,
sed finem imposuit pugnae fessumque Dareta
eripuit mulcens dictis ac talia fatur:
'infelix, quae tanta animum dementia cepit?   465
non viris alias conversaque numina sentis?
cede deo.' dixitque et proelia voce diremit.
ast illum fidi aequales genua aegra trahentem
iactantemque utroque caput crassumque cruorem
ore eiectantem mixtosque in sanguine dentes   470
ducunt ad navis; galeamque ensemque vocati
accipiunt, palmam Entello taurumque relinquunt.
hic victor superans animis tauroque superbus
'nate dea, vosque haec' inquit 'cognoscite, Teucri,
et mihi quae fuerint iuvenali in corpore vires   475
et qua servetis revocatum a morte Dareta.'

445–7 *MPR*; 448–76 *MPRV*   446 effundit *P*[1]   449 radicitus *R*γ[2]*c*[1] *testatur Priscianus, probat Ribbeck*   457 ille] deinde *Mm*
470 ore eiectantem *P*γ[1]: ore iectantem *Mc*[1]: ore iactantem *R*: ore
reiectantem γ[2]   473 animo *V*

dixit, et adversi contra stetit ora iuvenci
qui donum astabat pugnae, durosque reducta
libravit dextra media inter cornua caestus
arduus, effractoque inlisit in ossa cerebro: 480
sternitur exanimisque tremens procumbit humi bos.
ille super talis effundit pectore voces:
'hanc tibi, Eryx, meliorem animam pro morte Daretis
persolvo; hic victor caestus artemque repono.'

    Protinus Aeneas celeri certare sagitta   485
invitat qui forte velint et praemia dicit,
ingentique manu malum de nave Seresti
erigit et volucrem traiecto in fune columbam,
quo tendant ferrum, malo suspendit ab alto.
convenere viri deiectamque aerea sortem   490
accepit galea; et primus clamore secundo
Hyrtacidae ante omnis exit locus Hippocoontis;
quem modo navali Mnestheus certamine victor
consequitur, viridi Mnestheus evinctus oliva.
tertius Eurytion, tuus, o clarissime, frater,   495
Pandare, qui quondam iussus confundere foedus
in medios telum torsisti primus Achivos.
extremus galeaque ima subsedit Acestes,
ausus et ipse manu iuvenum temptare laborem.
tum validis flexos incurvant viribus arcus   500
pro se quisque viri et depromunt tela pharetris,
primaque per caelum nervo stridente sagitta
Hyrtacidae iuvenis volucris diverberat auras,
et venit adversique infigitur arbore mali.
intremuit malus timuitque exterrita pennis   505
ales, et ingenti sonuerunt omnia plausu.
post acer Mnestheus adducto constitit arcu
alta petens, pariterque oculos telumque tetendit.

    477–99 *MPRV*; 500–8 *MPR*   477 aversi *Pγb*   480 in
om. R Güthling   484 reponit *Rc¹ Serv.*   486 dicit] ponit
MRVbcπ Nonius   491 primum *RV*   499 manum *V*   labore *V*
503 volucris iuvenis *Pγ¹b*

ast ipsam miserandus avem contingere ferro
non valuit; nodos et vincula linea rupit   510
quis innexa pedem malo pendebat ab alto;
illa Notos atque alta volans in nubila fugit.
tum rapidus, iamdudum arcu contenta parato
tela tenens, fratrem Eurytion in vota vocavit,
iam vacuo laetam caelo speculatus et alis   515
plaudentem nigra figit sub nube columbam.
decidit exanimis vitamque reliquit in astris
aetheriis fixamque refert delapsa sagittam.

  Amissa solus palma superabat Acestes,
qui tamen aërias telum contorsit in auras   520
ostentans artemque pater arcumque sonantem.
hic oculis subitum obicitur magnoque futurum
augurio monstrum; docuit post exitus ingens
seraque terrifici cecinerunt omina vates.
namque volans liquidis in nubibus arsit harundo   525
signavitque viam flammis tenuisque recessit
consumpta in ventos: caelo ceu saepe refixa
transcurrunt crinemque volantia sidera ducunt.
attonitis haesere animis superosque precati
Trinacrii Teucrique viri, nec maximus omen   530
abnuit Aeneas, sed laetum amplexus Acesten
muneribus cumulat magnis ac talia fatur:
'sume pater; nam te voluit rex magnus Olympi
talibus auspiciis exsortem ducere honores.
ipsius Anchisae longaevi hoc munus habebis,   535
cratera impressum signis, quem Thracius olim
Anchisae genitori in magno munere Cisseus
ferre sui dederat monimentum et pignus amoris.'
sic fatus cingit viridanti tempora lauro

   509–39 *MPR*   512 alta] atra *MRγ²bcπ*   516 figit nigram
P¹: figit nigra *γ*   518 aeriis *MRm*: aereis *γ²bc*   520 contendit *M¹R Nonius, probat Bentley*   522 subitum *deteriores
pauci*: subito *ceteri*   526 flammis] lamnis *M¹*   534 honorem
M²γ²bc

et primum ante omnis victorem appellat Acesten.   540
nec bonus Eurytion praelato invidit honori,
quamvis solus avem caelo deiecit ab alto.
proximus ingreditur donis qui vincula rupit,
extremus volucri qui fixit harundine malum.

    At pater Aeneas nondum certamine misso   545
custodem ad sese comitemque impubis Iuli
Epytiden vocat, et fidam sic fatur ad aurem:
'vade age et Ascanio, si iam puerile paratum
agmen habet secum cursusque instruxit equorum,
ducat avo turmas et sese ostendat in armis   550
dic' ait. ipse omnem longo discedere circo
infusum populum et campos iubet esse patentis.
incedunt pueri pariterque ante ora parentum
frenatis lucent in equis, quos omnis euntis
Trinacriae mirata fremit Troiaeque iuventus.   555
omnibus in morem tonsa coma pressa corona;
cornea bina ferunt praefixa hastilia ferro,
pars levis umero pharetras; it pectore summo
flexilis obtorti per collum circulus au.ri
tres equitum numero turmae ternique vagantur   560
ductores; pueri bis seni quemque secuti
agmine partito fulgent paribusque magistris.
una acies iuvenum, ducit quam parvus ovantem
nomen avi referens Priamus, tua clara, Polite,
progenies, auctura Italos; quem Thracius albis   565
portat equus bicolor maculis, vestigia primi
alba pedis frontemque ostentans arduus albam.
alter Atys, genus unde Atii duxere Latini,
parvus Atys pueroque puer dilectus Iulo.
extremus formaque ante omnis pulcher Iulus   570
Sidonio est invectus equo, quem candida Dido
esse sui dederat monimentum et pignus amoris.

    540–72 *MPR*   541 honore *P¹ Ribbeck*   548 paratus *P¹*
551 decedere *MRγ²bcπ*   558 it *M²c² Serv.*: et *M¹Rγ¹b¹*: iet *P*
(*erasa* i): id *γ²*   564 cara *P¹*   570 formam *M¹*

cetera Trinacriis pubes senioris Acestae
fertur equis.
excipiunt plausu pavidos gaudentque tuentes 575
Dardanidae, veterumque agnoscunt ora parentum.
postquam omnem laeti consessum oculosque suorum
lustravere in equis, signum clamore paratis
Epytides longe dedit insonuitque flagello.
olli discurrere pares atque agmina terni 580
diductis solvere choris, rursusque vocati
convertere vias infestaque tela tulere.
inde alios ineunt cursus aliosque recursus
adversi spatiis, alternosque orbibus orbis
impediunt pugnaeque cient simulacra sub armis; 585
et nunc terga fuga nudant, nunc spicula vertunt
infensi, facta pariter nunc pace feruntur.
ut quondam Creta fertur Labyrinthus in alta
parietibus textum caecis iter ancipitemque
mille viis habuisse dolum, qua signa sequendi 590
frangeret indeprensus et inremeabilis error:
haud alio Teucrum nati vestigia cursu
impediunt texuntque fugas et proelia ludo,
delphinum similes qui per maria umida nando
Carpathium Libycumque secant [luduntque per undas]. 595
hunc morem cursus atque haec certamina primus
Ascanius, Longam muris cum cingeret Albam,
rettulit et priscos docuit celebrare Latinos,
quo puer ipse modo, secum quo Troia pubes;
Albani docuere suos; hinc maxima porro 600
accepit Roma et patrium servavit honorem;

573–601 *MPR*   573 Trinacriis *deteriores quidam, editores plerique*:
Trinacrii *P¹Rb Serv. Ribbeck*: Trinacriae *MP²γa²cπ*   577 cossen-
sum *M¹*: concessum *Pγ¹*   580 ternis *γ¹b*   581 deductis *MR*
584 adversis *Pγbc*   alternisque *R*   591 frangeret *PRγbc²m Serv.*:
falleret *Mc¹*   592 alioter *R¹*: aliter *R²bmπ*   nati Teucrum *Pγ*
595 luduntque per undas *om. M¹Pγ¹m*

Troiaque nunc pueri, Troianum dicitur agmen.
hac celebrata tenus sancto certamina patri.
  Hinc primum Fortuna fidem mutata novavit.
dum variis tumulo referunt sollemnia ludis,   605
Irim de caelo misit Saturnia Iuno
Iliacam ad classem ventosque aspirat eunti,
multa movens necdum antiquum saturata dolorem.
illa viam celerans per mille coloribus arcum
nulli visa cito decurrit tramite virgo.   610
conspicit ingentem concursum et litora lustrat
desertosque videt portus classemque relictam.
at procul in sola secretae Troades acta
amissum Anchisen flebant, cunctaeque profundum
pontum aspectabant flentes. heu tot vada fessis   615
et tantum superesse maris, vox omnibus una.
urbem orant, taedet pelagi perferre laborem.
ergo inter medias sese haud ignara nocendi
conicit et faciemque deae vestemque reponit;
fit Beroe, Tmarii coniunx longaeva Dorycli,   620
cui genus et quondam nomen natique fuissent,
ac sic Dardanidum mediam se matribus infert.
'o miserae, quas non manus' inquit 'Achaica bello
traxerit ad letum patriae sub moenibus! o gens
infelix, cui te exitio Fortuna reservat?   625
septima post Troiae excidium iam vertitur aestas,
cum freta, cum terras omnis, tot inhospita saxa
sideraque emensae ferimur, dum per mare magnum
Italiam sequimur fugientem et volvimur undis.
hic Erycis fines fraterni atque hospes Acestes: 630
quis prohibet muros iacere et dare civibus urbem?
o patria et rapti nequiquam ex hoste penates,

    602-32 *MPR*   602 *ante* pueri *interpungunt editores plerique*
pueri] ludi *proponit Nettleship*   604 hic *Mc*   609 celebrans
*M*¹; *cf.* iv. 641   611 consessum *M*¹   620 Tmarii] Ismarii
deteriores quidam: Martii *Klouček*   628 sidera] litora *Klouček*
631 qui *M*¹: quid *Rc Henry*

nullane iam Troiae dicentur moenia? nusquam
Hectoreos amnis, Xanthum et Simoenta, videbo?
quin agite et mecum infaustas exurite puppis. 635
nam mihi Cassandrae per somnum vatis imago
ardentis dare visa faces: "hic quaerite Troiam;
hic domus est" inquit "vobis." iam tempus agi res,
nec tantis mora prodigiis. en quattuor arae
Neptuno; deus ipse faces animumque ministrat.' 640
haec memorans prima infensum vi corripit ignem
sublataque procul dextra conixa coruscat
et iacit. arrectae mentes stupefactaque corda
Iliadum. hic una e multis, quae maxima natu,
Pyrgo, tot Priami natorum regia nutrix: 645
'non Beroe vobis, non haec Rhoeteia, matres,
est Dorycli coniunx; divini signa decoris
ardentisque notate oculos; qui spiritus illi,
quis vultus vocisque sonus vel gressus eunti.
ipsa egomet dudum Beroen digressa reliqui 650
aegram, indignantem tali quod sola careret
munere nec meritos Anchisae inferret honores.'
haec effata.
at matres primo ancipites oculisque malignis
ambiguae spectare rates miserum inter amorem 655
praesentis terrae fatisque vocantia regna:
cum dea se paribus per caelum sustulit alis
ingentemque fuga secuit sub nubibus arcum.
tum vero attonitae monstris actaeque furore
conclamant, rapiuntque focis penetralibus ignem 660
(pars spoliant aras), frondem ac virgulta facesque
coniciunt. furit immissis Volcanus habenis
transtra per et remos et pictas abiete puppis.
    Nuntius Anchisae ad tumulum cuneosque theatri
incensas perfert navis Eumelus, et ipsi 665
respiciunt atram in nimbo volitare favillam.

633–66 *MPR*   640 animam *Rb¹ Ribbeck*   649 qui *Mγ²cπ* vel]
et *P*   660, 661 *interpunxit Henry*   666 atro *Klouček, recipit Schaper*

primus et Ascanius, cursus ut laetus equestris
ducebat, sic acer equo turbata petivit
castra, nec exanimes possunt retinere magistri.
'quis furor iste novus? quo nunc, quo tenditis' inquit, 670
'heu, miserae cives? non hostem inimicaque castra
Argivum, vestras spes uritis. en, ego vester
Ascanius!' — galeam ante pedes proiecit inanem,
qua ludo indutus belli simulacra ciebat.
accelerat simul Aeneas, simul agmina Teucrum. 675
ast illae diversa metu per litora passim
diffugiunt, silvasque et sicubi concava furtim
saxa petunt; piget incepti lucisque, suosque
mutatae agnoscunt excussaque pectore Iuno est.

Sed non idcirco flamma atque incendia viris 680
indomitas posuere; udo sub robore vivit
stuppa vomens tardum fumum, lentusque carinas
est vapor et toto descendit corpore pestis,
nec vires heroum infusaque flumina prosunt.
tum pius Aeneas umeris abscindere vestem 685
auxilioque vocare deos et tendere palmas:
'Iuppiter omnipotens, si nondum exosus ad unum
Troianos, si quid pietas antiqua labores
respicit humanos, da flammam evadere classi
nunc, pater, et tenuis Teucrum res eripe leto. 690
vel tu, quod superest, infesto fulmine morti,
si mereor, demitte tuaque hic obrue dextra.'
vix haec ediderat cum effusis imbribus atra
tempestas sine more furit tonitruque tremescunt
ardua terrarum et campi; ruit aethere toto 695
turbidus imber aqua densisque nigerrimus Austris,
implenturque super puppes, semusta madescunt
robora, restinctus donec vapor omnis et omnes
quattuor amissis servatae a peste carinae.

667–99 *MPR*   680 flamma P^1: flammam $M^1P^2\gamma^1$: flammae
$M^2R\gamma^2b\pi$ 685 excindere M 687 exosu's *Ribbeck*   695 campis
M^1P (*in rasura*) γ^1

At pater Aeneas casu concussus acerbo   700
nunc huc ingentis, nunc illuc pectore curas
mutabat versans, Siculisne resideret arvis
oblitus fatorum, Italasne capesseret oras.
tum senior Nautes, unum Tritonia Pallas
quem docuit multaque insignem reddidit arte   705
(haec responsa dabat, vel quae portenderet ira
magna deum vel quae fatorum posceret ordo)—
isque his Aenean solatus vocibus infit:
'nate dea, quo fata trahunt retrahuntque sequamur;
quidquid erit, superanda omnis fortuna ferendo est.   710
est tibi Dardanius divinae stirpis Acestes:
hunc cape consiliis socium et coniunge volentem;
huic trade amissis superant qui navibus et quos
pertaesum magni incepti rerumque tuarum est;
longaevosque senes ac fessas aequore matres   715
et quidquid tecum invalidum metuensque pericli est
delige, et his habeant terris sine moenia fessi;
urbem appellabunt permisso nomine Acestam.'
    Talibus incensus dictis senioris amici
tum vero in curas animo diducitur omnis.   720
et Nox atra polum bigis subvecta tenebat:
visa dehinc caelo facies delapsa parentis
Anchisae subito talis effundere voces:
'nate, mihi vita quondam, dum vita manebat,
care magis, nate, Iliacis exercite fatis,   725
imperio Iovis huc venio, qui classibus ignem
depulit, et caelo tandem miseratus ab alto est.
consiliis pare quae nunc pulcherrima Nautes
dat senior; lectos iuvenes, fortissima corda,
defer in Italiam. gens dura atque aspera cultu   730
debellanda tibi Latio est. Ditis tamen ante
infernas accede domos et Averna per alta

700–32 *MPR*   706 hac *c¹ Ribbeck alii*   719 accensus *R*
720 animum $\gamma^2b^2c^2\pi$ *Serv. Bentley*   722 facies caelo *Rγbcπ*
731 est Latio *P*

congressus pete, nate, meos. non me impia namque
Tartara habent, tristes umbrae, sed amoena piorum
concilia Elysiumque colo. huc casta Sibylla   735
nigrarum multo pecudum te sanguine ducet.
tum genus omne tuum et quae dentur moenia disces.
iamque vale; torquet medios Nox umida cursus
et me saevus equis Oriens adflavit anhelis.'
dixerat et tenuis fugit ceu fumus in auras.   740
Aeneas 'quo deinde ruis? quo proripis?' inquit,
'quem fugis? aut quis te nostris complexibus arcet?'
haec memorans cinerem et sopitos suscitat ignis,
Pergameumque Larem et canae penetralia Vestae
farre pio et plena supplex veneratur acerra.   745
    Extemplo socios primumque accersit Acesten
et Iovis imperium et cari praecepta parentis
edocet et quae nunc animo sententia constet.
haud mora consiliis, nec iussa recusat Acestes.
transcribunt urbi matres populumque volentem   750
deponunt, animos nil magnae laudis egentis.
ipsi transtra novant flammisque ambesa reponunt
robora navigiis, aptant remosque rudentisque,
exigui numero, sed bello vivida virtus.
interea Aeneas urbem designat aratro   755
sortiturque domos; hoc Ilium et haec loca Troiam
esse iubet. gaudet regno Troianus Acestes
indicitque forum et patribus dat iura vocatis.
tum vicina astris Erycino in vertice sedes
fundatur Veneri Idaliae, tumuloque sacerdos   760
ac lucus late sacer additur Anchiseo.
    Iamque dies epulata novem gens omnis, et aris
factus honos: placidi straverunt aequora venti
creber et aspirans rursus vocat Auster in altum.

733–64 *MPR*   734 tristesve *M²b²*   739 saevus] Foebus
Sacerdos   740 in] ad *P*: in ad *γ¹*   752 -que *om. π, probat
Kvičala commate post* ambesa *posito: idem proposuerat Peerlkamp*
761 additus *Pγ¹b*

exoritur procurva ingens per litora fletus;   765
complexi inter se noctemque diemque morantur.
ipsae iam matres, ipsi, quibus aspera quondam
visa maris facies et non tolerabile numen,
ire volunt omnemque fugae perferre laborem.
quos bonus Aeneas dictis solatur amicis   770
et consanguineo lacrimans commendat Acestae.
tris Eryci vitulos et Tempestatibus agnam
caedere deinde iubet solvique ex ordine funem.
ipse caput tonsae foliis evinctus olivae
stans procul in prora pateram tenet, extaque salsos   775
proicit in fluctus ac vina liquentia fundit.
prosequitur surgens a puppi ventus euntis;
certatim socii feriunt mare et aequora verrunt.

  At Venus interea Neptunum exercita curis
adloquitur talisque effundit pectore questus: 780
'Iunonis gravis ira neque exsaturabile pectus
cogunt me, Neptune, preces descendere in omnis;
quam nec longa dies pietas nec mitigat ulla,
nec Iovis imperio fatisque infracta quiescit.
non media de gente Phrygum exedisse nefandis   785
urbem odiis satis est nec poenam traxe per omnem
reliquias Troiae: cineres atque ossa peremptae
insequitur. causas tanti sciat illa furoris.
ipse mihi nuper Libycis tu testis in undis
quam molem subito excierit: maria omnia caelo   790
miscuit Aeoliis nequiquam freta procellis,
in regnis hoc ausa tuis.
per scelus ecce etiam Troianis matribus actis
exussit foede puppis et classe subegit

765–83 *MPR*; 784–94 *FMPR*   767 ipsi] ipsae *Nonius*
768 nomen M^1 *Nonius Ribbeck*: caelum *R*   772 agnos *M*
776 porricit *Heinsius*   777, 778 *inverso ordine* Pγ *Ribbeck*
782 in] ad *Serv. Güthling*   784 fatisve Fγbcmπ 785 ex-
cidisse *F*   786 traxere F^1P^1: traxisse $F^2M^1\gamma^1$ omnis P^1:
omnes γ 794 excussit $M^1P^1\gamma^1$

amissa socios ignotae linquere terrae. 795
quod superest, oro, liceat dare tuta per undas
vela tibi, liceat Laurentem attingere Thybrim,
si concessa peto, si dant ea moenia Parcae.'
tum Saturnius haec domitor maris edidit alti:
'fas omne est, Cytherea, meis te fidere regnis, 800
unde genus ducis. merui quoque; saepe furores
compressi et rabiem tantam caelique marisque.
nec minor in terris, Xanthum Simoentaque testor,
Aeneae mihi cura tui. cum Troia Achilles
exanimata sequens impingeret agmina muris, 805
milia multa daret leto, gemerentque repleti
amnes nec reperire viam atque evolvere posset
in mare se Xanthus, Pelidae tunc ego forti
congressum Aenean nec dis nec viribus aequis
nube cava rapui, cuperem cum vertere ab imo 810
structa meis manibus periurae moenia Troiae.
nunc quoque mens eadem perstat mihi; pelle timores.
tutus, quos optas, portus accedet Averni.
unus erit tantum amissum quem gurgite quaeres;
unum pro multis dabitur caput.' 815
his ubi laeta deae permulsit pectora dictis,
iungit equos auro genitor, spumantiaque addit
frena feris manibusque omnis effundit habenas.
caeruleo per summa levis volat aequora curru;
subsidunt undae tumidumque sub axe tonanti 820
sternitur aequor aquis, fugiunt vasto aethere nimbi.
tum variae comitum facies, immania cete,
et senior Glauci chorus Inousque Palaemon
Tritonesque citi Phorcique exercitus omnis;

795–814 FMPR; 815–24 MPR   795 ignota MPRγ¹   terra
MP²: terret γ   797 tibi] mihi Peerlkamp   805 inmitteret F¹
807 atque] neque P: qua Augustinus   810 eripui F²   811 peri-
turae FM¹   812 timorem Mc   814 quaeret deteriores quidam,
Ribbeck Deuticke: quaeris M²   821 equis M¹b¹   fugiuntque ex
aethere M²

laeva tenent Thetis et Melite Panopeaque virgo,   825
Nisaee Spioque Thaliaque Cymodoceque.
  Hic patris Aeneae suspensam blanda vicissim
gaudia pertemptant mentem; iubet ocius omnis
attolli malos, intendi bracchia velis.
una omnes fecere pedem pariterque sinistros,   830
nunc dextros solvere sinus; una ardua torquent
cornua detorquentque; ferunt sua flamina classem.
princeps ante omnis densum Palinurus agebat
agmen; ad hunc alii cursum contendere iussi.
iamque fere mediam caeli Nox umida metam   835
contigerat, placida laxabant membra quiete
sub remis fusi per dura sedilia nautae:
cum levis aetheriis delapsus Somnus ab astris
aëra dimovit tenebrosum et dispulit umbras,
te, Palinure, petens, tibi somnia tristia portans   840
insonti; puppique deus consedit in alta
Phorbanti similis funditque has ore loquelas:
'Iaside Palinure, ferunt ipsa aequora classem,
aequatae spirant aurae, datur hora quieti.
pone caput fessosque oculos furare labori.   845
ipse ego paulisper pro te tua munera inibo.'
cui vix attollens Palinurus lumina fatur:
'mene salis placidi vultum fluctusque quietos
ignorare iubes? mene huic confidere monstro?
Aenean credam (quid enim?) fallacibus auris   850
et caelo, totiens deceptus fraude sereni?'
talia dicta dabat, clavumque adfixus et haerens
nusquam amittebat oculosque sub astra tenebat.
ecce deus ramum Lethaeo rore madentem
vique soporatum Stygia super utraque quassat   855

825–55 *MPR*   825 tenet *Mγ²π Serv.*: tent *R*   829 velis]
remis *MR*   837 sedilia] silentia *P¹*   843 ipsa aequora] sua
flamina *M¹*   850 fallacius *Ti. Donatus*   austris *P²γc²π Ti.*
Donatus   851 caeli *MP²Rγ²b¹c²π* agnoscit *D. Serv.*   sereno *γ¹c¹*
852 dictabat *Pc*

tempora, cunctantique natantia lumina solvit.
vix primos inopina quies laxaverat artus,
et superincumbens cum puppis parte revulsa
cumque gubernaclo liquidas proiecit in undas
praecipitem ac socios nequiquam saepe vocantem;   860
ipse volans tenuis se sustulit ales ad auras.
currit iter tutum non setius aequore classis
promissisque patris Neptuni interrita fertur.
iamque adeo scopulos Sirenum advecta subibat,
difficilis quondam multorumque ossibus albos   865
(tum rauca adsiduo longe sale saxa sonabant),
cum pater amisso fluitantem errare magistro
sensit, et ipse ratem nocturnis rexit in undis
multa gemens casuque animum concussus amici:
'o nimium caelo et pelago confise sereno,   870
nudus in ignota, Palinure, iacebis harena.'

856–871 *MPR*   860 saepe] voce *M*   861 ad] in *Pγ*
Versus duo primos sexti libri ineuntis quinto adiunxisse Vergilium,
removisse Tuccam et Varium, narrat Servius, crediderunt Probus Ribbeck

LIST OF CHIEF WORKS CITED AND ABBREVIATIONS USED

Note. Abbreviated references to periodicals follow in general the system of *L'Année Philologique.* *C.A.H.* is used for the *Cambridge Ancient History*; *O.C.D.* for the *Oxford Classical Dictionary*; O.C.T. for Oxford Classical Text; *R.E.* for Pauly–Wissowa, *Real-Encyclopädie*; *Thes.L.L.* for the *Thesaurus Linguae Latinae.* Ennius is abbreviated according to Vahlen's third edition, thus: Enn. *Ann.* 205 V. Abbreviations used for a few of the works listed below are shown in square brackets.

AUSTIN, R. G. *Aeneid IV*, Oxford, 1955.

AXELSON, B. *Unpoetische Wörter*, Lund, 1945.

BAILEY, C. *Religion in Virgil*, Oxford, 1935.

BÜCHNER, K. Article s.v. *P. Vergilius Maro* in *R.E.*, 1955.

CONINGTON, J., and NETTLESHIP, H. *Vergili Opera*, ed. J. Conington: vol. ii, 4th ed. revised by H. Nettleship, London, 1884.

CONWAY, R. S. *Aeneid I*, Cambridge, 1935.

DAREMBERG, C., and SAGLIO, E. *Dictionnaire des antiquités grecques et romaines*, 9 vols., Paris, 1877–1919 [Daremberg–Saglio].

ERNOUT, A., and THOMAS, F. *Syntaxe Latine*, 2nd ed., Paris, 1953 [Ernout–Thomas].

FAIRCLOUGH, H. R. *Virgil*, Loeb Library, 2 vols., revised ed., 1934–5.

FLETCHER, F. *Aeneid VI*, Oxford, 1941.

FORBIGER, A. *Virgilii Opera*, 4th ed., Leipzig, 1872–5.

FOWLER, W. WARDE *The Death of Turnus*, Oxford, Blackwell, 1919.

GARDINER, E. N. *Athletics of the Ancient World*, Oxford, 1930.

—— *Greek Athletic Sports and Festivals*, London, 1910.

GLOVER, T. R. *Virgil*, 7th ed., London, 1942.

GOELZER, H., and BELLESSORT, A. *Virgile, Énéide I–VI*, Collection Budé; text by Goelzer, translation by Bellessort, Paris, 1925 [Bellessort].

HEINZE, R. *Virgils Epische Technik*, 3rd ed., Leipzig, 1928, reprinted 1957.

HENRY, JAMES *Aeneidea*, 5 vols., Leipzig–Dublin–Meissen, 1873–92.

HEYNE, C. G., and WAGNER, G. P. E. *Virgilii Opera*, 4th ed., 5 vols., Leipzig and London, 1830–41 (Heyne's 3rd ed. of 1801 reproduced with additional notes by Wagner).

JANELL, G. *Vergili Opera*, Teubner, Leipzig, 1930.

KNIGHT, W. F. JACKSON *Virgil, The Aeneid* (prose translation), Penguin Books, 1956.

KÜHNER, R., and STEGMANN, C. *Ausführliche Grammatik der lateinischen Sprache* by R. Kühner; vol. ii (Syntax) in two parts, 2nd ed. by C. Stegmann, Hanover, 1912–14 [Kühner–Stegmann].

LEUMANN, M., and HOFMANN, J. B. *Lateinische Grammatik*, the 5th ed. of Stolz–Schmalz, Munich, 1928 [Leumann–Hofmann].

LEWIS, C. DAY *The Aeneid of Virgil* (verse translation), London, 1952.

LÖFSTEDT, E. *Syntactica*, Lund; vol. i, 2nd ed., 1942, vol. ii, 1st ed., 1933.

MACKAIL, J. W. *The Aeneid of Virgil*, Oxford, 1930.

MAGUINNESS, W. S. *Aeneid XII*, London, 1953.

MAROUZEAU, J. *Traité de stylistique latine*, 2nd ed., Paris, 1946.

—— *L'Ordre des mots dans la phrase latine*, 3 vols., Paris, 1922–49.

MEHL, E. *Die Leichenspiele, Anhang* to Büchner's article in *R.E.*, s.v. *P. Vergilius Maro.*

—— Article s.v. *Troiaspiel* in *R.E.*, suppl. viii (1956), pp. 888 f.

NORDEN, E. *Aeneid VI*, 3rd ed., Leipzig, 1926, reprinted 1957.

PAGE, T. E. *Virgil*, 3 vols., London, 1894–1900.

PALMER, L. R. *The Latin Language*, London, 1954.

PEASE, A. S. *Aeneid IV*, Harvard, 1935.

PLATNAUER, M. *Latin Elegiac Verse*, Cambridge, 1951.

PLESSIS, F., and LEJAY, P. *Œuvres de Virgile* (*Aeneid* by Lejay), Paris, 1919 [Lejay].

PÖSCHL, V. *Die Dichtkunst Virgils, Bild und Symbol in der Äneis*, Innsbruck, 1950.

RICH, A. *Dictionary of Roman and Greek Antiquities* (with wood engravings), 5th ed., London, 1884 [Rich, *Dict. Antiq.*].

ROSCHER, W. H. *Ausführliche Lexicon der griechischen und römischen Mythologie*, Leipzig, 1884–1937.

SABBADINI, R. *Vergili Opera*, 2 vols., Rome, 1930.

SERVIUS and SERVIUS *AUCT.*, ed. by G. Thilo and H. Hagen, Leipzig, 1878–1902. (Servius *auct.* refers to the 'enlarged' version of Servius sometimes called Servius Danielis.)

SPARROW, J. *Half-lines and Repetitions in Virgil*, Oxford, 1931.

WAGNER, G. P. E. *Quaestiones Virgilianae*; in vol. iv of Heyne–Wagner, q.v. [Wagner, *Quaest. Virg.*].

WINBOLT, S. E. *Latin Hexameter Verse*, London, 1903.

COMMENTARY

1–7. *As they sail away from Carthage the Trojans look back and see a blaze in the city; although they do not know that it comes from Dido's pyre, they feel presentiments of disaster.*

1–7. This brief and reticent passage forms Virgil's transition from the tragic events of Book IV to the resumption of the narrative of Aeneas' journey towards Italy. The last mention of the Trojans was when they set sail from Carthage, and Dido at dawn watched their ships leaving her shore (4. 582 f.). The rest of Book IV describes Dido's death on the pyre, closing on the quiet note of Juno's intervention to prevent further suffering. Now Virgil returns to the Trojans, and with the word *interea* and the repetition of *iam* (*Aeneas iam classe . . . iam infelicis Elissae*) he links the events of the past with the present, before finally taking leave of the past in the sad slow lines which conclude the passage (see note on 5 f.).

1 f. 'Meanwhile Aeneas was now in mid-course, unswervingly holding his way with his fleet . . . ' The phrase *medium iter* indicates that he is some distance on his way, 'en pleine route' (Lejay). Not until line 8 is he right out to sea, and it is not therefore appropriate (if indeed it is possible at all) to take *medius* in the sense which it has in *medium aequor*, *medium mare* ('mid-ocean', cf. *Aen.* 3. 664 f., 12. 451 f.), and to regard *medium iter* as equivalent to *iter per medium mare*.

1. The metrical shape of this line, with no third foot caesura (except in so far as the elided syllable of *medium* gives a hint of one), is a favourite with Virgil; it became much rarer with his successors in hexameter poetry, with the exception of his close imitator, Silius Italicus. There are 43 examples of it in Book V; Austin on *Aen.* 4. 278 gives 26 examples (only counting those with elision) in Book IV, Norden (*Aeneid VI*, pp. 429 f.) gives 28 altogether in Book VI, and Winbolt (*Latin Hexameter Verse*, p. 83) says that Virgil has it about once in 35 lines. Most of the instances in Book V are precisely like this one, with strong second and fourth foot caesurae and an elision at the beginning of the third foot. Examples without such elision occur at 127, 260, 303, 418, 639, 662, 675; and there are unusual variations at 407, 664.

2. certus: cf. *Aen.* 4. 554 (of Aeneas) *iam certus eundi*. Servius says 'aut indubitabiliter pergens, aut certus Aeneas, id est sollers, strenuus'. The second of these suggestions can be

rejected, as the word is surely used with some adverbial force
(see on 33); the first one is correct, and to be preferred to the
view of Wagner and others, who argue that the word merely
describes Aeneas' direct course. No doubt this meaning is
present, but the primary reference is to Aeneas' state of
mind. He has at last taken his resolve to leave Dido behind
(cf. the words Ovid gives to Dido, *Her.* 7. 7 *certus es ire tamen
miseramque relinquere Didon?*), and he cannot now be turned
from his purpose.

   atros Aquilone: 'darkened by the north wind'. Servius
has 'atros autem secundum Plinium dicit, qui ait in naturali
historia, non esse maris certum colorem, sed pro qualitate
ventorum mutari'. Aulus Gellius (2. 30) comments to the
same effect: 'Austris spirantibus mare fieri glaucum et
caeruleum, Aquilonibus obscurius atriusque'.

   The word *Aquilo* may be connected with *aquilus* (black),
so that the use of the word *ater* with it is perhaps one of the
many instances in the *Aeneid* of Virgil's fondness for etymological connexions; cf. *Aen.* 3. 693 *Plemyrium undosum*
(Πλημμυρίς) with Page's note, 6. 550 f. *flammis . . . torrentibus
amnis / Tartareus Phlegethon*, 6. 844 *te sulco, Serrane, serentem*,
8. 322 f. *Latiumque vocari / maluit, his quoniam latuisset tutus
in oris*, and see note on *Avernus* (732). A special aspect of
this is concerned with aetiological name associations (like the
capes called after Misenus and Palinurus); see note on 117.
On the subject of etymologies in Virgil see also W. F. Jackson
Knight, *C.R.*, 1934, p. 124 (with references given there), and
Roman Vergil, pp. 197 f., J. Marouzeau, *Virgile linguiste,
Mélanges Ernout*, 1940, pp. 259 f. (reprinted with additions
in *Quelques aspects de la formation du latin littéraire*, 1949,
pp. 71 f.), and J. S. T. Hanssen, *Symbolae Osloenses*, 1948, pp.
113 f.

   The direction of the winds has been much discussed. In
Aen. 4. 310 Dido reproached Aeneas for wishing to leave
Carthage *mediis Aquilonibus*, but in 4. 562 Mercury told
Aeneas that favouring Zephyrs were blowing. S. L. Mohler
(*T.A.Ph.A.*, 1948, pp. 60 f.) ingeniously resolves this apparent
contradiction by citing modern handbooks to show that at
Tripoli and Tunis during the night there is a land breeze
(south or west), and during the day a sea breeze (north-east).
Aeneas would thus have got out of the harbour on the land
breeze, and now would be sailing close-hauled into the north
wind. But with a poet the direction of winds may be a matter
of mood rather than of geography, and Mercury's Zephyrs
more relevant to his persuasive intentions than to meteoro-
logical facts.

3. iam: for the elision of monosyllables see Austin on *Aen.* 4. 570, Norden's *Aeneid VI*, pp. 456 f. (where there is a tabulated list of instances in hexameters). Such elisions occur most frequently in informal verse (Lucilius, Horace's *Satires*); in Virgil they are more frequent in the *Eclogues* than in the *Georgics* and *Aeneid*. The words most often elided are *me, te, se, iam, si, cum*: in this book monosyllabic elisions occur at 8 (*iam*), 274 (*quem*), 693 (*cum*), 733 (*me*).

   infelicis: 'ill-starred', a recurrent epithet of Dido. It occurs as early as *Aen.* 1. 749; she uses it of herself in 4. 596; and here it ends her story. And when Aeneas meets her ghost in the underworld (6. 456) his halting speech to her begins '*Infelix Dido . . .*'

   Elissae: the Phoenician name of Dido. Virgil does not use inflected forms of the word *Dido*: *Elissa* occurs in the genitive at 4. 335 and 4. 610 as well as here.

4. flammis: the flames of the funeral pyre. We are reminded of Dido's last words of all (4. 661–2): 'Hauriat hunc oculis ignem crudelis ab alto / Dardanus, et nostrae secum ferat omina mortis'.

5. latet: 'is unknown to them'; the subject is the interrogative clause *quae causa tantum accenderit ignem.*

5 f. 'but the thought of the bitter agony caused when a great love is desecrated, and the knowledge of what a woman in wild frenzy may do, led the thoughts of the Trojans along paths of sorrowful foreboding.' Observe the metrical art of this passage. The movement, which has already become slow with the spondees in the second half of line 3 and in line 4, is made slower still with the two spondaic words *duri* and *magno*; there is emphasis given by the alliteration first of *d*, then *f*, then *t*, and the assonance of *u* and *-um* in line 7 brings the passage to a sorrowful close. A word of three long syllables after the third foot caesura (*Teucrorum*), so common in Catullus, occurs much less often in Virgil, so that it can sometimes be employed for special effect. Just as the coincidence of ictus and word accent in the fifth and sixth foot gives a rounding-off effect to the line, so coincidence in the fourth as well as in the fifth and sixth may sometimes be used to conclude a group of lines or a paragraph. See W. F. Jackson Knight, *Roman Vergil*, pp. 239 f., *Accentual Symmetry in Vergil*, Blackwell, 1939, *passim*, and *C.Q.*, 1931, pp. 184 f. (with statistics of fourth foot coincidence, showing that Virgil has it appreciably less often than the other major hexameter poets, so that there is the possibility of significant intention when he does use it). For a discussion of the whole subject of accent and ictus, with bibliographical references, see L. P. Wilkinson, *C.Q.*, 1940, pp. 30 f.; and cf. Austin on *Aen.* 4. 132, 185. Various types of fourth foot coincidence at the end of a section may be found in this book at 34, 71, 182, 219, 285, 339, 361, 544, 663, 679, 699, 718, 861, 871. Nine of the twelve books of the *Aeneid* end with a line which has coincidence in the fourth foot. In the same way Milton tends to vary less from the regular stress of the line at the conclusion of sections than he does elsewhere. But it must be emphasized that in matters like this we are speaking of *tendencies*; rhythmic features of this kind may often be due purely to the chance working of the poet's natural desire for variety. The degree of significance to be attached is dependent very largely on other poetic factors, the mood of the passage, the context, the choice of words, the expectation which the poet has aroused in us. On this question of metrical or alliterative 'imitation' of the sense see also notes on 198 and 866.

Notice Virgil's reticence and restraint in this passage. There is no more now to tell of *infelix Elissa*, only a few slow phrases of sorrow and foreboding. And then in line 8 Virgil tears himself away with lines of rapid narrative of a conventional kind which he had in fact already used in practically the same form in *Aen.* 3. 192–5. The transition is most abrupt, not in sequence of narrative but in tone, as Virgil leaves at last a theme on which he could say no more but on which he could never feel that enough had been said. In order to resume his narrative without looking backwards any more, he had recourse to familiar phrases which had come to him before.

5. duri magno sed: postposition of the connecting particle is quite common in Virgil (cf. 55, 87, 217, 225, 320, 344, 410, 415, 764, and notes on 14 *deinde* and 382 *tum*). Postposition to the third place (as here), or to the fourth (as in 733) is of course much rarer. See Austin on *Aen.* 4. 33, with references given there, and Marouzeau, *L'Ordre des mots dans la phrase latine*, iii, pp. 73 f. The usage is not common in early Latin, and perhaps was introduced by the *neoterici* in imitation of Hellenistic usage. It is chiefly for metrical convenience, but it can also serve to emphasize the words brought to the beginning of the sentence. Here great weight is thrown on the adjectives *duri* and *magno*. For the postposition of conjunctions and relatives see note on 22.

6. polluto: 'desecrated'. The word is very strong indeed, and is given added emphasis by being a 'run-on' word before a pause (see on 480 and 840 f.). It denotes the breaking of a sacred tie, cf. *Aen.* 3. 61 *pollutum hospitium*, 7. 467 *polluta* *pace*, and as the word *notum* makes this clause as well as the next one oblique (see next note), I take the word to reflect not the attitude of the Trojans, but their thoughts about Dido's attitude. To Dido her love for Aeneas was a sacred thing, the totality of her life; there was no such conflict in her as there was in Aeneas between his personal feelings and his divine mission. We cannot say how far Virgil identifies himself with Dido's feeling that her love had been wickedly set at naught; certainly he does not mean to blame Aeneas, but what of the blame attaching to the gods? The word *furens*, used of Dido here as so often in Book IV, is frequently applied to people distracted and driven mad by the gods, in whose plight pity rather than anger is our dominant feeling. *Furor* is an evil thing, but its victims (like Dido and Turnus) arouse our sympathy. Compare the *furor* of the Trojan women in 655 f. I cannot think that Warde Fowler is right (*Roman Essays and Interpretations*, p. 189) when he takes *polluto* to mean that Dido's passion had poisoned her love; rather is it that Aeneas' desertion of her meant the ruin and profanation of everything that was of the slightest importance to her.

   notumque: 'and the knowlege of what . . .' The neuter of the participle is used as a noun co-ordinate with *dolores* (which thus means 'the thought of the agony') as the subject of *ducunt*. For the use of the participle as a noun cf. *Geo.* 3. 348 *ante exspectatum*, *Geo.* 2. 398 *cui nunquam exhausti satis est*, and notes on *exstructum* (290) and *serenum* (851). Instances of this type of sentence are rare, but there are a few examples in Livy, cf. 27. 37. 5 *mentes turbavit rursus nuntiatum* (the announcement) *Frusinone natum esse infantem quadrimo parem*, 7. 8. 5 *diu non perlitatum* (the long absence of favourable omens) *tenuerat dictatorem*, 1. 53. 1 *ni degeneratum in aliis* (his degeneracy in other things) *huic quoque decori offecisset*; cf. also Lucan 1. 5 and 1. 70–71 *summisque negatum / stare diu* (the denial of permanence). See Ernout–Thomas, p. 281, Leumann–Hofmann, p. 457, Kühner–Stegmann, ii. 1, p. 769.

7. **augurium**: the word is used here more widely than usual, without direct and specific reference to divine intervention (see Bailey, *Religion in Virgil*, pp. 19–20); but it is wrong to equate it (as Bailey and others do) with so flat a word as 'conjecture'. Essentially it takes our thought back to Dido's prayers to the gods for vengeance, and to her last words (4. 662) *et nostrae secum ferat omina mortis*. Indeed Servius *auct.* may well be right in associating the word with the storm which follows.

8–41. *When they reach the open sea a violent storm comes upon them; Palinurus the helmsman tells Aeneas that it is impossible to continue on their course for Italy, and suggests that they should run with the wind to Sicily. Aeneas agrees, and they land near the tomb of Anchises, and are welcomed by Acestes.*

8–11. These lines, which are modelled on Hom. *Od.* 12. 403–6, are only very slightly varied from *Aen.* 3. 192–5 (see note on 5 f.). Book V has an unusually large number of places where Virgil uses a line or group of lines which occur elsewhere in his works in the same or almost the same form; cf., for example, notes on 144–7, 385–6, 606, 657–8, and see index, s.v. 'repetition'. On this theme see Sparrow, *Half-lines and Repetitions in Virgil*, especially pp. 79 f., where he shows that it is very rarely, if at all, that Virgil uses repetition in the Homeric manner; he aims rather at variety of expression (see note on 42). It is also rare (though there may be some instances) for Virgil consciously to aim at special effect by the repetition of lines already used. In nearly all instances the repetitions were a sort of stop-gap, whether conscious or unconscious. Often they occur in passages which show marks of incompleteness (see on 291–2, 563 f.). We can only conjecture to what extent Virgil would have altered them if he had lived to revise the *Aeneid*, but when we consider his painstaking pursuit of perfection it seems likely that many would have disappeared. The number of repetitions within the *Georgics* is far less proportionately than that within the *Aeneid*.

9. occurrit: sc. *oculis.*

10. olli: an archaic form for *illi*, dative singular. The only other forms used by Virgil are *olli* nominative plural and *ollis*. Quintilian (8. 3. 24 f.) comments on Virgil's use of archaisms: 'cum sint autem verba propria, ficta, translata, propriis dignitatem dat antiquitas. Namque et sanctiorem et magis admirabilem faciunt orationem, quibus non quilibet fuerit usurus; eoque ornamento acerrimi iudicii P. Vergilius unice est usus. *Olli* enim et *quianam* et *moerus* et *pone* et *porricerent* aspergunt illam, quae etiam in picturis est gratissima, vetustatis inimitabilem arti auctoritatem.' (The words *moerus* and *porricerent* in this list are emendations.) *Quianam* occurs in line 13, *porricere* is a variant reading in 238 and 776. The use of archaisms is a very marked feature of the *Aeneid*. There are comparatively few in the *Eclogues* and *Georgics*, and it is clear that Virgil in his epic poetry wished to interweave into contemporary poetic diction some aspects of the diction of Ennius, just as he sometimes echoed him in metre (see on 422) and often recalled him by direct verbal imitation (see on 241). On the Roman attitude towards archaisms see Marouzeau, *Traité de stylistique latine*, pp. 178–81; on archaisms in Virgil see Palmer, *The Latin Language*, pp. 97 f. and especially pp. 111 f., and M. Leumann, *Museum Helveticum*, 1947, pp. 125 f.; see also Austin on *Aen.* 4. 105. The subject is treated at length by A. Cordier, *Etudes sur le vocabulaire épique dans l'Enéide*, Paris, 1939. I have listed in the index (s.v. 'archaisms') some of the many examples in Book V.

The use of the singular *olli* referring to Aeneas (rather than *ollis* to refer to the Trojans) looks back to line 1, and is perhaps also influenced by *Aen.* 3. 192–5 where these lines are in the first person, spoken by Aeneas (*tum mihi caeruleus*, etc.).

caeruleus . . . imber: cf. Hom. *Od.* 12. 405 δὴ τότε κυανέην νεφέλην ἔστησε Κρονίων.

11. **et . . . tenebris**: 'the waves grew rough under its dark onset'. Virgil is still following Homer (*Od.* 12. 406 ἤχλυσε δὲ πόντος ὑπ' αὐτῆς, cf. *Il.* 7. 63 f.). *Tenebris* is instrumental, the context giving it a slight extension of its meaning (= *tenebrosa hieme*); cf. *Geo.* 3. 198 f. (of the sea) *campique natantes/ lenibus horrescunt flabris*. For *inhorrescere* cf. Pacuvius *ap.* Cic. *De Div.* 1. 24 *inhorrescit mare, tenebrae conduplicantur*. The idea of 'roughness' is a basic meaning of the word, cf. *Geo.* 1. 314 *spicea iam campis cum messis inhorruit, Aen.* 10. 711 (*aper*) *infremuitque ferox et inhorruit armos*, and see note on 37. Words connected with *horror* are fairly often applied to the ruffled surface of the sea; cf. Cic. *De Rep.* 1. 63 *subito mare coepit horrescere*, Cat. 64. 269 f. *hic qualis flatu placidum mare matutino / horrificans Zephyrus proclivas incitat undas*, Lucan 5. 564 f. *niger inficit horror / terga maris*, Stat. *Silv.* 5. 4. 5 f. *occidit horror / aequoris*. For the imagery cf. *Aen.* 3. 285 *et glacialis hiems Aquilonibus asperat undas*; there as here a dactylic rhythm is used for the surge and movement of the sea.

12. **ipse**: cf. *Aen.* 3. 201; the word implies that the helmsman is generally the last person to be alarmed in a storm.

13. **quianam**: 'why?', an archaic word used again in *Aen.* 10. 6. See note on 10.

14. **sic deinde**: Virgil often postpones *deinde* in this way, and he avoids using it at the beginning of a line; cf. lines 258, 321, 400, *Aen.* 7. 135, 8. 481, Conway on 1. 195, and Wagner, *Quaest. Virg.* 25. 7. Compare the notes on 5 and 382. *Deinde* (like *proinde*, 11. 383, 400) always scans as a trochee; *dehinc* is sometimes a single syllable, sometimes an iambus (note on 722). For Virgil's use of synizesis see on 352.

15. **colligere arma**: Servius says 'vela contrahere, non penitus
deponere'; this is surely correct, the meaning being 'to
take in the tackle', that is to say to shorten sail, to sail more
close-hauled, by taking in and securing ropes, rigging, etc.
Some commentators have suggested an entirely different
meaning: 'to get together their equipment', i.e. to make
ready for rowing, *arma* being a vaguer term for *remi*, and
the second half of the line a variation on the first. In support
of this view it is argued that in *Aen*. 3. 532 *vela legere* means
to take in the sails altogether, and that *colligere* must mean
not less than *legere*. But here we have not *vela colligere* but
arma colligere, and this describes the preliminary operation
of shortening sail before the manœuvre mentioned in the
next line *obliquatque sinus in ventum*. A decisive parallel for
Servius' interpretation of *arma* is Stat. *Th*. 7. 88 f., where the
ships are slowly returning to normal after a storm: *nondum
arma carinis / omnia, nec toto respirant pectore nautae*. Virgil
was perhaps the first to use *arma* to refer to the tackle of a
ship (after the Greek ὅπλα, cf. Hom. *Od*. 2. 423 and Gow on
Theoc. 13. 52), although in early Latin the word has various
other non-military meanings. Compare *Aen*. 6. 353 (*navis*)
spoliata armis, 4. 299 *armari classem*, Ov. *Met*. 11. 513.

   validisque incumbere remis: cf. *Aen*. 10. 294 *nunc, o lecta
manus, validis incumbite remis*. Aeneas' ships are essentially
sailing ships, and oars are used only for entering and leaving
harbour and in emergencies; cf. 191–3 and note on 828 f.

16. **obliquatque sinus in ventum**: 'he set the sails aslant into
the wind', i.e. trimmed the sheets in order to luff, that is to
sail nearer to the wind which had now changed from north
to west. The commentators quote Dryden, *Astraea Redux*
(63–66):

> How easy 'tis when Destiny proves kind
> With full spread sails to run before the wind!
> But those that 'gainst stiff gales laveering go
> Must be at once resolved and skilful too.

For rather a different description of tacking see 828 f. (with
notes); for the phraseology here cf. Livy 26. 39. 19 *ad incertos
ventos hinc atque illinc obliqua transferentes vela* and Lucan
5. 427 f. *et flexo navita cornu / obliquat laevo pede carbasa*. The
word *obliquare* does not occur before Virgil; some similar
verbs (formed from adjectives or nouns) which are not found
earlier than Virgil are *soporare* (line 855), *acerbare, crispare,
fecundare, hebetare* (also in Livy), *lentare, sinuare, temerare*
(also in Tibullus), *viduare*. See note on 202 for Virgil's use
of new and rare words.

17. magnanime: this compound adjective (μεγάθυμος) is common in epic (Virgil has it a dozen times in the *Aeneid*, cf. 407), and occurs a few times in Cicero. See Norden on *Aen*. 6. 307 for Ennius' use of the word; for compound adjectives in Virgil see on 452.

17 f. auctor spondeat: 'should pledge it with all his authority', a very emphatic phrase.

18. hoc . . . caelo: 'in weather like this', cf. *Geo*. 1. 51 *varium caeli praediscere morem*, *Aen*. 4. 53 *non tractabile caelum*.

    sperem . . . contingere: for *sperare* with the present infinitive (instead of its normal construction with the accusative and future infinitive) cf. *Aen*. 4. 337 f. *neque ego hanc abscondere furto* / *speravi* (*ne finge*) *fugam*, *Aen*. 4. 305 f. Compare the construction of *iurare* and *promittere* in *Aen*. 4. 425 f. *non ego cum Danais Troianam exscindere gentem* / *Aulide iuravi*; *Aen*. 11. 503 *promitto occurrere turmae*. The usage occurs in early Latin, and there are examples with *polliceri* in Caesar; it becomes quite common in the poets. See Ernout-Thomas, pp. 324–5, Kühner–Stegmann, ii. 1, pp. 689 f., 700 f.

    Italiam: the first syllable is long (as it must be for hexameters), but in *Italus* Virgil nearly always has the *i* short. See note on 571.

19 f. The wind has now changed from north to west; it is not its direction which causes the trouble, but its violence. They cannot make way against it with sails or oars (21), and they have to change course and run before it.

19. transversa: 'across our course', 'crosswise', adverbial accusative. This is an extension of the normal Latin usage (with words like *aliquid, multum*, etc.) which the poets, under Greek influence, greatly affected. Cf. Lucr. 5. 33 *acerba tuens*, *Ecl*. 3. 8 *transversa tuentibus*, *Aen*. 12. 398 *acerba fremens*, Stat. *Th*. 1. 348 *venti transversa frementes*, and compare 381, 866, and 869.

    vespere: the land of the evening, the west, cf. Ov. *Met*. 1. 63, *Tr*. 1. 2. 28.

    vespere ab atro: the elision of a short vowel in the fifth foot is not so rare as is sometimes supposed (see Norden's *Aeneid VI*, p. 455, Platnauer, *Latin Elegiac Verse*, p. 85). There are about a hundred instances in Virgil of short *e* elided in this position in the fifth foot (in this book lines 43, 111, 382, 534, 718, 782, 810), and of short *a* about twenty (in this book lines 428, 804, 846). The only elisions in this position in the fifth foot other than those of short *e* and *a* are *Ilium* (three times) and *omnium egenos* (*Aen*. 1. 599).

20 f. Notice the heavy spondaic movement of this line and the next.

20. in nubem cogitur aër: 'the air thickens into cloud'; cf. *Cic. Nat. De.* 2. 101 (*aër*) *tum fusus et extenuatus sublime fertur, tum autem concretus in nubes cogitur.*

21 f. 'We cannot possibly battle against the storm, or make enough way against it'; I take *tendere* in its sense of 'making one's way', 'holding one's course', cf. *Aen.* 1. 205 *tendimus in Latium*, 1. 553 f. *si datur Italiam . . . / tendere*, and lines 286, 670. Some take it to mean 'strive', 'struggle' (cf. *Aen.* 12. 553 *vasto certamine tendunt*), but it then adds nothing to *obniti*. *Contra* goes with both verbs; on the so-called ἀπὸ κοινοῦ construction Conway has a good note (on *Aen.* 1. 75): 'To ask which of two possible constructions must be chosen for any one word is often like enquiring whether a particular figure in a picture is to be regarded as belonging to the left- or the right-hand side.' *Tantum* is elliptical for *tantum quantum opus est*, cf. *Aen.* 9. 806 f. *ergo nec clipeo iuvenis subsistere tantum / nec dextra valet.*

21–22. obniti . . . sufficimus: for the infinitive after *sufficere* (not found before Virgil) cf. Lucan 5. 154, Sil. 14. 603. The poets, partly because of its metrical neatness, greatly enlarged the function of the infinitive in comparison with prose usage; in this they were in a way archaizing, as in early Latin the infinitive performed many of the functions for which prose gradually substituted other modes of expression (such as final subjunctives or prepositional phrases with gerunds and gerundives). See Page on *Aen.* 2. 64 and 7. 393, Kühner–Stegmann, ii. 1, pp. 673–4, Palmer, *The Latin Language*, p. 319, and compare lines 29, 69, 155, 194, 342, 509–10.

22. superat quoniam: the postposition of a conjunction or a relative from the head of its clause was common in early Latin (e.g. Naevius' epitaph *immortales mortales si foret fas flere*, Ennius, *Ann.* 565 V *cum legionibus quom proficiscitur induperator*), and it is quite normal in Classical prose for emphatic words to precede the conjunction (see Kühner–Stegmann, ii. 2, p. 615, Marouzeau, *L'Ordre des mots dans la phrase latine*, iii, pp. 122 f.). But for the verb to precede its subordinating word gives a much more artificial effect; this occurs only in poetry, and is comparatively rare. Marouzeau (pp. 127–8) gives a number of examples of this type of word order, and finds about eighty examples in Virgil of clauses beginning with their verb immediately followed by the subordinating word. Instances in this book where the verb precedes are 51, 74, 121, 126, 355, 563, 698, 713, 810; and other noteworthy instances of postposition of the sub-

ordinating word are 38–39, 119, 597, 705. Compare the note
on line 5 about postponed particles.

   Fortuna: for Virgil's conception of Fortune see on 604.

23. longe: supply *abesse*, or simply *esse* (cf. *Aen.* 12. 52 *longe
illi dea mater erit*, and for a discussion of the phrase *longe
esse* see Westendorp Boerma on *Catalepton* 1. 4). The ellipse
of the verb with *longe* is particularly frequent in Statius,
e.g. *Th.* 5. 25 *neque enim tibi numina longe*, *Th.* 10. 21 *nec
enim lux crastina longe*, *Ach.* 1. 176 *par studiis aevique modis,
sed robore longe* (where see Dilke's note).

24. fraterna: epexegetic of *litora fida*, the sense being *nec
reor litora fida longe abesse, fraterna litora Erycis*. For this
use of *fraternus = fratris* cf. 630 *hic Erycis fines fraterni*.
Eryx, son of Venus and Butes, was Aeneas' half-brother;
he gave his name to the well-known mountain and town in
Sicily (see on 718 and 759). For the variation in vowel length
between *Sĭcānus* (cf. 293) and *Sĭcănius* (*Aen.* 3. 692, 8. 416)
see note on 571.

25. 'if only I remember correctly as I plot our way back again
by the stars I watched before', i.e. when they set out from
Sicily and were driven by a storm to Carthage (3. 692 f.,
1. 34 f.). For *servare* cf. *Aen.* 6. 338 *dum sidera servat.
Remetiri astra* probably means rather more than to calculate
position again by the stars: on the analogy of phrases like
Aen. 2. 181 *pelagoque remenso, Aen.* 3. 143 f. *remenso . . . /
mari* it contains the idea of making a return journey by
calculation.

26. pius: this epithet of Aeneas contains most of the essential
difference between Aeneas and Homer's Achilles. Achilles
is first and foremost an individual, with no feelings of
obligation except to be true to himself and his personal τίμη:
Aeneas is a man shouldering heavy responsibilities, fulfilling
a mission laid upon him by the gods, and observing the claims
of his duty towards the gods, towards his country, his
family, his companions. The word *pius* is not used as a stock
epithet in the Homeric fashion; Aeneas often has no epithet,
often is called *pater* or *magnanimus*. When he is called *pius*
there is always a particular reference to the context, sometimes one packed with significance (see Austin on *Aen.* 4.
393, W. B. Anderson, *C.R.*, 1930, pp. 3 f., and Bailey, *Religion
in Virgil*, pp. 79 f.). Here the word does not have powerful
overtones, but relates mainly to Aeneas' position of responsibility in taking the right decision for his men, and to the
opportunity of revisiting his Trojan friend Acestes and his
father's grave.

26–27. 'Yes, I have been feeling for some time now that the winds are forcing us to it, and that your efforts to make way against them are vain.' *Iamdudum* probably goes with *cerno*, though it could be taken with *poscere*. Observe the intricate order, with *cerno*—which governs both clauses— set in the middle of the second clause; in this book compare lines 28 f., 82–83, 181, 220–1, 229–30, 867–8, and see Conway on *Aen.* 1. 13 and his index s.v. 'interwoven order', and Mackail on *Aen.* 1. 195–6. Quintilian (8. 2. 14) comments on *Aen.* 1. 109 *saxa vocant Itali mediis quae in fluctibus Aras* as a *mixtura verborum*. Virgil rarely or never uses hyperbaton of the violent kind which we find sometimes in Catullus (e.g. 44. 8 f. *quam mihi meus venter / dum sumptuosas appeto, dedit, cenas*), and not infrequently in Ovid (e.g. *Tr.* 3. 9. 12 '*hospes*' *ait* '*nosco Colchide vela venit*' = *hospes Colchide venit, nosco vela*); see Platnauer, *Latin Elegiac Verse*, pp. 104 f.

28 f. Notice again the intricate order, with *tellus* postponed from its adjective *ulla*: *an sit mihi ulla tellus gratior, quove* (= *vel ad quam*) *magis optem . . . quam ea tellus quae . . .* Day Lewis translates:

> What land could be more welcome,
> Where would I rather get these battered ships to port,
> Than the place where my Trojan friend, Acestes, is still living
> And the bones of my father, Anchises, lie in the lap of earth.

28. sit: potential, equivalent to *esse potest*, or *esse possit*.

29. optem demittere: the infinitive with *optare* (on the analogy of *cupere*, *velle*) is common in poetry; cf. *Aen.* 2. 635 and note on 21–22.

demittere: 'bring to harbour'; for the nautical use of *de-* cf. line 57 *delati*, line 212 *decurrit*, 'races shorewards', and the Greek κατάγειν. The chief MSS. and Servius *auct.* have *dimittere*, which could be defended in the slightly personified sense of 'dismiss', i.e. 'disembark from', cf. *Aen.* 10. 366 f. *aspera quis natura loci dimittere quando / suasit equos*. But as no confusion is commoner in MSS. than that between compounds of *de-* and *di-* it is perhaps better to accept *demittere*.

30. Acestes was a king of Sicily of Trojan lineage (cf. 1. 550 and note on 38). Aeneas' meeting with him on the outward journey is referred to (1. 195), but not described in the narrative. He plays an important part in the story of the *Aeneid*, foreshadowing in myth the very close bonds between Sicily and Rome (see on 523 f. and 718).

31. Cf. Lucr. 1. 135 (4. 734) *morte obita quorum tellus amplectitur ossa*. The last incident in his journey which Aeneas related to Dido was the death of Anchises at Drepanum (3. 709 f.).

32. haec ubi dicta: the phrases *haec ubi dicta* and *haec ubi dicta dedit* occur a number of times in the *Aeneid*, and some would therefore supply *dedit* to the former; but an ellipse of *sunt* seems much more natural. Parts of the verb 'to be' in the third person are omitted frequently in Virgil (much more frequently than in Ovid) both in main and subordinate clauses. For the rarer omission of the second person see on 192, and of the first person see on 414. For the omission of parts of the subjunctive see on 648 f. The subject is dealt with at length by T. Winter, *De ellipsi verbi esse apud Catullum Vergilium Ovidium Statium Iuvenalem obvia*, Marburg, 1907; see also Wagner, *Quaest. Virg.* 15, Marouzeau, *Traité de stylistique latine*, pp. 214–16.

32–33. secundi . . . Zephyri: the stormy west wind evidently moderates now that the Trojans have taken their decision to run before it. All through this passage (cf. especially 56) there is the undertone of divine intention that the Trojans should revisit Sicily.

33. cita: the adjective fulfils a mainly adverbial function. Such a usage is very common in prose with certain types of adjective, particularly—but by no means exclusively— those expressing position (*extremus, medius, laevus, diversus*, etc.) or order (*primus, solus, ultimus*, etc.) or states of mind (*laetus, gravis, maestus*, etc.). The usage was easily capable of extension, and of all the poets Virgil was especially fond of it. Instances in this book are too numerous to list; examples of various kinds can be found at 278 (note), 280, 387, 460, 513, 567, 764, 838, 868 (note).

gurgite: Henry's note on *Aen.* 1. 122, demonstrating in seventeen pages that *gurges* is not always the same as *vortex*, should not be missed by anyone.

34. Notice how the spondaic rhythm with the heavy elision slows the movement as the Trojans come in to harbour.

notae advertuntur harenae: 'steer in to the beach they know'. The dative of 'place to which' after compound verbs is common in verse; see Conway on 1. 627, and cf. 1. 377 (*nos*) *Libycis tempestas appulit oris*, and in this book lines 93, 346, 434, 805. It is found in prose in certain circumstances and with certain verbs (e.g. *appropinquare, accedere, admovere, inferre*), increasingly so in the Silver Age; see Ernout–Thomas, p. 69, Kühner–Stegmann, ii. 1, pp. 326 f. The extension of the usage to uncompounded verbs is a feature of poetic style, see on 233, 451.

35. ex celso: Servius *auct.* mentions the possibility of reading *excelso*, but *celsus* is a common word in Virgil and *excelsus* does not occur; in addition the preposition makes the sentence clearer, the full meaning being *miratur procul conspiciens ex celso vertice montis adventum sociarum ratium, et occurrit.*

36. adventum sociasque rates: 'at the arrival of the fleet of his friends', a good example of hendiadys, the use of two words or phrases side by side instead of a single complex phrase, cf. *Aen.* 1. 293 *ferro et compagibus artis* 'with tight bonds of iron'. See Page on *Aen.* 3. 223 *in partem praedamque* ('to share the spoil'). Wagner (*Quaest. Virg.* 33. 4.) gives a long list of examples. Compare also note on 410–11.

37. 'a wild-looking figure carrying his javelins and wearing the skin of a Libyan she-bear'. This is a memorable and picturesque line which Tacitus recalled and imitated, *Hist.* 2. 88 *tergis ferarum et ingentibus telis horrentes*; cf. also the imitations in Val. Fl. 1. 485 f. *agnoscit Acastum | horrentem iaculis*, Sil. 8. 569 f. *Hirpinaque pubes | horrebat telis et tergo hirsuta ferarum*, Prudent. *Cont. Symm.* 2. 299 f. The construction *in iaculis* is analogous to the phrase *in armis* (line 550, *Aen.* 3. 595). Servius *auct.* quotes Ennius (*Ann.* 506 V) *levesque secuntur in hastis*, and we may compare Stat. *Th.* 4. 221 f. *procul ipse gravi metuendus in hasta | eminet*, 7. 669 *turbidus aeria Capaneus occurrit in hasta*, Val. Fl. 1. 641 f. *cum subitus trifida Neptunus in hasta | caeruleum fundo caput extulit* (where see Langen), Manil. 2. 241 *Cretaeo fulget Centaurus in arcu*. These examples suggest that syntactically the words *in iaculis* and (*in*) *pelle* should be taken as descriptive phrases parallel with *horridus* rather than closely dependent on it. The word *horridus* in this context partly no doubt conveys its basic sense of 'bristling'; it can naturally with *pelle*, cf. *Aen.* 7. 669 where *horridus* is used of Aventinus in his lion-skin; and it could with *iaculis* too, if Acestes is carrying a number of light javelins—cf. Virgil's imitations of Ennius in *Aen.* 10. 178 *mille rapit densos acie atque horrentibus hastis*, *Aen.* 11. 601 f. *tum late ferreus hastis | horret ager*, and Ov. *Met.* 8. 285, Hor. *Sat.* 2. 1. 13 f., as well as the imitations of Virgil's phrase cited above. But I take the main impact of *horridus* to be in its wider meaning, so as to give a picture of the simple huntsman of an early age and a rustic society (cf. 40 *gaza laetus agresti*). Compare *Aen.* 7. 746 f. *horrida praecipue cui gens adsuetaque multo | venatu nemorum*, Ov. *Am.* 3. 6. 47 (Ilia) *horrida cultu*, Cic. *Pro. Quinct.* 59 *vixit enim semper inculte atque horride . . . id egit ut amicos observantia, rem parsimonia retineret; antiquam offici rationem dilexit cuius splendor omnibus his moribus obsolevit.*

Libystidis: the adjective *Libystis* (for *Libyca*) occurs only here and in 8. 368, the same phrase. Pliny (*Nat. Hist.* 8. 228) says there were no bears in Africa, but Cerda (quoted in the

Valpy Delphin, ad loc.) collected a number of passages
indicating a widespread view in antiquity that there were.
The geographical adjective is used to enrich the content and
associations of the line; see on 306 and 448-9.

38. The story is told by Servius on *Aen.* 1. 550: Segesta (or
Egesta), who gave her name to Acestes' town in Sicily, was
banished from Troy by Laomedon, and in Sicily she became
the mother of Acestes (also called Egestus) by the god of the
river Crimissus (near Segesta). Virgil's form *Crinisus*, which
Servius calls a poetic licence, may be an error in the MSS.
or a mistake on Virgil's part. For the early connexion of the
Trojans with Sicily see on 718.

38-39. For the postposition of the relative see on 22.

39. veterum . . . parentum: 'his ancestors of old', i.e. his
Trojan mother and her forbears. *Parens* quite commonly
means an ancestor further back than one's parents; cf. *Aen.*
9. 3.

40-41. 'showed his delight at their return, and gladly welcomed
them with his rustic treasures, and ministered to them in
their weariness with friendly aid'. Notice how the three
phrases, developing the picture of Acestes' welcome, bring
this section of the narrative to a rounded and serene conclusion. *Gratari* is an archaic form of *gratulari*, used by the
poets for metrical convenience, and sometimes by Livy and
Tacitus. This is the first instance of *gratari* with accusative
and infinitive (*gratatur eos reduces esse*); cf. Tac. *Ann.* 6. 21.
Gaza agresti is almost an oxymoron: Acestes sets his simple
store before his friends as a Persian king might set his
costliest treasures. The theme of regal simplicity is most
sympathetically developed in *Aeneid* VIII when Evander
welcomes Aeneas at the site of Rome.

41. solatur: the word occurs in poetry and post-Augustan
prose, the Classical word being *consolari*. The use by the
poets of the simple verb where prose preferred a compound
gave an archaic flavour (Festus mentions archaic words like
plentur, spectus, spicit); see note on 10. In many cases the simple
verb was metrically convenient, sometimes it was metrically
necessary. Some Virgilian instances of simple verbs where
prose always or nearly always used a compound are: *fidere*
(line 69) = *confidere*, *mittere* (286) = *dimittere*, *suescere* (402,
414) = *consuescere*, *tueri* (575) = *intueri*, *cernere ferro* (*Aen.*
12. 709) = *decernere* (for this cf. Enn. *Ann.* 196 V *ferro non
auro vitam cernamus utrique* and see Seneca's comments in
Ep. 58. 3), *gradi* = *ingredi*, *piare* = *expiare*, *rigare* = *ir-
rigare*, *temnere* = *contemnere*, *vertere* = *evertere* (see Conway

on *Aen.* 1. 20). Words like *firmare* and *linquere*, which prose
uses less often than *confirmare* and *relinquere*, are very frequent; and the commonest verbs of all, like *ferre* (see on 356
and 403), *capere*, *ponere* (see on 681), *premere*, *tenere*, are often
used in contexts where prose would prefer one of the many
compounds available. See Norden on *Aen.* 6. 620; Leumann–
Hofmann, p. 548. This was one of the aspects of poetic
diction of which Tacitus was very fond, especially in the
Annals (see Furneaux, Intro., p. 53).

42–71. *On the next day Aeneas summons an assembly and reminds
the Trojans that it is the anniversary of the death of his father
Anchises. He proclaims a solemn sacrifice at the tomb, which
is to be followed on the ninth day by contests in rowing, running,
boxing, and archery.*

42 f. The detailed and colourful description of the honours paid
to the dead Anchises gives a religious and patriotic setting to
the account of the anniversary games, so that while Book V
provides a lessening of tension between Books IV and VI
it is still closely related to the Roman theme of the poem
(see Intro., pp. xi–xii). The proclamation of games after the
ceremony has of course its literary model in *Iliad* XXIII,
but it is also reminiscent of Roman *ludi funebres*, the games
held after the funeral of important citizens (Livy 23. 30. 15,
28. 21. 10, 31. 50. 4, 39. 46. 2, 41. 28. 11; see note on 64–65).
In the description of the religious ceremony, Virgil (as so
often elsewhere) mingles Roman and Greek traditions.
Essentially Aeneas is celebrating the normal Roman ritual
at the tomb on the anniversary of a father's death (*parentatio*, see on 60); but this simple ritual is given added mystery
and majesty by the interweaving of elements from the Greek
hero-cult. Hellenistic ideas about the deification of dead
heroes had considerable influence in Rome already by Virgil's
time, and a number of features in Virgil's description of the
ceremonies suggest the conception of the deified hero—
divinus (47), *templa* (60), the blood offering (78), *altaria* (54,
93), *adyti* (84), the *suovetaurilia* (96), and the association of
a priest and a sacred grove with Anchises' tomb (760, where
see note). See Bailey, *Religion in Virgil*, pp. 281 f., especially
291–301.

   Virgil emphasizes the significance and importance of these
religious ceremonies by suggesting that Aeneas has been
brought back again to his father's tomb by the will of the
gods, so that it may be revealed that Anchises is more
honoured by them than Aeneas had known (56, 90, 94–96).
Servius several times speaks of the apotheosis of Anchises,

implying that he had become one of the *di superi*; this is of course something very different from the normal worship of the sanctified dead of the family, the *di parentes* or *di manes*. Virgil does not define the nature of Anchises' divinity nearly as explicitly as Servius suggests; he builds up his poetic picture by implication and atmosphere rather than by precise definition. Again, on line 45 Servius compares the deification of Julius Caesar, saying 'frequenter, ut diximus, ad opus suum Vergilius aliqua ex historia derivat: nam sic omnia inducit quasi divini honores solvantur Anchisae, quos constat Iulio Caesari tribuisse Augustum'. No doubt Virgil's Roman readers might transfer what Virgil had said about Aeneas and Anchises to events in their own experience; but the allegory, if such it is, is not in any way pressed or made explicit. As always in the *Aeneid* it is subordinated to the larger theme.

42–43. Postera . . . clara dies: the two epithets fulfil different functions, *postera* being adverbial and *clara* a descriptive adjective. The convenience of scansion causes the poets to use the feminine gender for *dies* in the nominative (except for *ille dies*) without regard for the distinction in meaning between masculine and feminine which is observed in prose. See Austin on *Aen.* 4. 169 for a full discussion with references.

42. primo . . . Oriente: 'at first dawn', cf. *Aen.* 3. 588 *postera iamque dies primo surgebat Eoo. Oriens* is a noun as in 739, *Geo.* 1. 250 *nosque ubi primus equis Oriens adflavit anhelis*.

stellas . . . fugarat: cf. Hor. *Odes* 3. 21. 24 *dum rediens fugat astra Phoebus, Aen.* 3. 521 *iamque rubescebat stellis Aurora fugatis.* Virgil has a large variety of ways in which he describes dawn; compare 64 f., 104 f., and see Austin on *Aen.* 4. 6 f., Sparrow, *Half-lines and Repetitions in Virgil*, pp. 85 f.

fugarat: the epic poets avoided *cum* with the pluperfect subjunctive even when it was metrically tractable, presumably because of its extreme frequency in prose. See Axelson, *Unpoetische Wörter*, pp. 87–88; there are no instances in Virgil or Valerius, one in Silius, three in Lucan, four in Ovid.

44. tumulique ex aggere: 'from a raised mound', as a Roman general would address his soldiers in camp; cf. 113.

45. Dardanus, founder of the Trojan royal line, was a son of Jupiter, cf. *Aen.* 7. 219 f.

divum: for this form of the genitive plural, also sometimes spelled *divom*, see on 174.

46. This is an example of a 'golden' line, one in which two adjectives are followed by a verb and then by the two nouns with which they agree; Dryden's definition runs: 'That which they call golden, or two substantives and two adjectives, with a verb betwixt them to keep the peace'. It is a form of symmetrical arrangement which was practically unknown in Ennius and very rare in Lucretius, but came into great favour with Catullus. Virgil used it more sparingly, and it became commoner again in his successors, notably Ovid, Lucan, and Claudian. Other examples of golden lines in this book are 38 (which is, however, a 'run-on' line), 134, 344, 500, 516, 524, 838 (some of them have very slight variations). Lines which approximate to this pattern, with symmetry of adjectives and nouns, are 113, 225, 297, 559, 819. A less elaborate and commoner symmetry is the 'framing' of a line by means of an adjective at the beginning and a noun in agreement with it at the end, as in 143, 161, 182, 186, etc. See Norden's *Aeneid VI*, pp. 395 f., Winbolt, *Latin Hexameter Verse*, pp. 219 f., Marouzeau, *L'Ordre des mots dans la phrase latine*, iii, pp. 182 f., and especially Marouzeau's comments in his *Traité de stylistique latine*, pp. 320–1, where he points out how the excessive use of this and similar artifices can give the impression that the words are being used less to convey meaning than to make mosaics. The study of Virgil's successors in the hexameter reveals the measure of Virgil's success in avoiding this danger.

46–48. See Intro., p. xxix, for the chronological difficulties involved here.

47. reliquias: the first syllable of this word (as of *religio*) is treated as long in hexameters; we sometimes find the spelling *relliquias*. See Bailey's Lucretius, *Proleg.*, p. 132, Leumann–Hofmann, p. 92, Postgate, *Prosodia Latina*, p. 54.

divini: Servius and Servius *auct.* discuss the word, suggesting that it may mean 'prophetic' (which here seems unlikely), or be a term of very high respect ('god-like') as in *Ecl.* 3. 37, or mean 'divine' in the sense in which the term could be used of the *di parentes*. In the context the last seems the most likely, and the word may have implications beyond this; see note on 42 f.

51 f. 'If I were spending this day as an exile in the Gaetulian Syrtes, or caught in the Argolic sea and (held) in the city of Mycenae, yet I still would be fulfilling . . .', i.e. whether in desolate Africa or hostile Greece, whether at sea or on land. The Syrtes were the great sand-banks near Carthage, called Gaetulian by association with the Gaetuli of that area, cf. *Aen.* 4. 40 and line 192. The Argolic sea could be a vague term applying to any part of the sea round Greece (and so Servius; cf. *Aen.* 3. 283), but is here perhaps a specific reference to the *sinus Argolicus* near Mycenae. The sense of line

52 is not clearly expressed, and it is difficult to determine it precisely. Three possible meanings are advanced for *deprensus*: (i) caught, surprised by the anniversary; (ii) caught by the Greeks; (iii) caught by a storm. Of these the first is unsuitable for *deprensus* and rather inept in meaning. Servius is perhaps right in supporting the third as a sailors' technical term; he says 'occupatus, et proprie navigantum est, ut *deprensis olim statio tutissima nautis*' (*Geo.* 4. 421). Compare also Lucr. 6. 429 f. *et quaecumque in eo tum sint deprensa tumultu / navigia*, Cat. 25. 13 *deprensa navis in mari vesaniente vento*, Hor. *Odes* 2. 16. 1 f. *in patenti / prensus Aegaeo*, Ov. *Her.* 19. 79 *hic puto deprensus nil quod querereris haberes*, Stat. *Th.* 1. 370 *hiberno deprensus navita ponto*. But in whatever sense we take *deprensus*, the phrase *et urbe Mycenae* is elliptical and abrupt, and we may well conjecture that it is one of the *tibicines*, stop-gaps, which Virgil would have rewritten in his final revision.

51. For the postposition of *si* see on 22.

52. We do not often find in Virgil a trochaic caesura in both the fourth and the fifth foot, no doubt because of the feeling that the line ending is anticipated. See Austin on *Aen.* 4. 58, where he cites nine examples from that book and says that there are only about a hundred instances in the whole *Aeneid*. In this book there are ten (55, 167, 480, 517, 749, 766, 820, 853, 871). Virgil was sparing (much more sparing than Ovid, for example) of a trochaic caesura in the fourth foot at all; it occurs in less than five per cent. of the lines in this book. A marked sense pause in this position is particularly rare; see on 166–7.

urbe Mycenae: so *M*, *P*, and Servius, an appositional genitive like *Aen.* 1. 247 *urbem Patavi*. There is a good deal to be said for the reading of *R*, *Mycenis*: Virgil does not elsewhere use the singular form of *Mycenae*, and for the construction cf. *Aen.* 10. 168 *urbem liquere Cosas*. But *Mycenae* was more likely to be changed by a scribe to *Mycenis* than vice versa.

53. sollemnisque ordine pompas: 'and the ritual processions in proper array'; cf. *Geo.* 3. 22 f. *iam nunc sollemnis ducere pompas / ad delubra iuvat*. The word *sollemnis* is very frequent in religious contexts, and conveys the idea of regularly recurring observances; for *ordine* see on 102.

54. suis: 'due' (= *propriis*). *Suus* is used sometimes in prose and frequently in verse to refer with special emphasis to a prominent word which is not the subject of the sentence. See Page on *Aen.* 3. 469, Austin on *Aen.* 4. 633, and line 832.

55. ultro: the word indicates something beyond what is expected, something which surpasses the immediate probability of the context. See Page on *Aen.* 2. 145, and compare 446. Day Lewis conveys it with

But now—and I'm quite sure it's with the design and
    approval of heaven—
We're actually close to the spot where my father's ashes and
    bones
Are buried.

    cineres: the use of the plural is poetic; see on 81.

    ipsius et: for postponed *et* see on 5.

56. equidem: if *reor* is taken parenthetically (as with the Oxford Text punctuation), *equidem* goes with the whole sentence; it is compounded of *e* and *quidem* (not *ego* and *quidem*), and can be used with any person, not only the first. But there is much to be said for punctuating so that the whole line is parenthetical.

57. portus . . . amicos: 'have reached land and come to a friendly haven'. The poetic plural *portus* is common, cf. 612, 813, Norden on *Aen.* 6. 366, and note on 98. For *delati* see on 29. The present tense *intramus* is influenced by *adsumus*; it is conceivable, though unlikely, that it is contracted for *intravimus*.

58. 'Come then and let us all perform the sacrificial rites with gladness.' The word *laetus* continues the impression built up in this passage (see note on 42 f.) that the anniversary rites are to be performed not only in mourning for the dead, but also in joy for the evident concern of the gods for Anchises. The word *honos* is frequent in poetry in the sense which it has here, both in the singular and the plural; cf. line 94, *Aen.* 1. 632, 3. 118.

59. poscamus ventos: 'let us ask Anchises for favouring winds'. Some commentators regard the phrase as equivalent to *vocemus ventos* (cf. *Aen.* 3. 253), but this seems abrupt in a context concerned with Anchises, especially when he is the unexpressed subject of *velit* in the next line. Henry has a typically long and powerful note in the course of which he cites Eur. *Hec.* 525 f., where Pyrrhus makes sacrifices to the shade of Achilles so that he may grant favourable winds; and Lact. *Div. Inst.* 1. 15, where Lactantius quotes these words and says of Anchises *cui non tantum immortalitatem verum etiam ventorum tribuit potestatem.* A few pages later on, however, Henry retracts in favour of the other view. Heyne argues in favour of the meaning *deos poscamus ventos secundos*, but adds 'habent tamen *venti* aliquid a loco alienum'. But the relevance of asking for winds becomes clear if we give the proper emphasis to the words *urbe posita* in Aeneas' prayer (see next note).

59–60. 'and may he grant me to pay these rites each year in a temple dedicated to him when my city is founded'. Virgil here looks forward to the Roman festival of the *Parentalia*, described by Ovid (*Fast.* 2. 543 f.) as having been instituted by Aeneas in honour of Anchises. The significant phrases in the prayer are *urbe posita, templis sibi dicatis*: Aeneas asks that when in future he pays these yearly ceremonies it may be in his own city, in the temple he will have built. *Templa* is a poetic plural; see on 98, and cf. *Aen.* 3. 84, 6. 840, 9. 626.

60–63. Notice the alternating rhyme of the line endings *dicati* , *Acestes, penatis, Acestes*; see on 385–6.

61–62. boum . . . capita: cf. Hom. *Il.* 23. 260 βοῶν τ' ἴφθιμα κάρηνα, *Aen.* 3. 391 *triginta capitum fetus*, and our 'so many head of cattle', 'so much per head'. It is a formulary phrase with numerals, which probably accounts for the redundant *numero* here.

62–63. The Trojans are to bring their household gods with them (see on 632), and it is naturally assumed that Acestes (like Dido, *Aen.* 1. 704, Evander, 8. 543) will have his own.

64 f. Two different explanations of Aeneas' meaning have been current since antiquity: (i) 'if the ninth day is fine'; (ii) 'when the ninth day brings its light'. Servius (followed by many) supports the first: 'non de die, qui certus est, dubitat, sed de serenitate: unde paulo post (104) *serena iam luce*'. Servius *auct.* gives the second explanation as an alternative to this: 'aut pro confirmativa posita est, ut *vestro si munere tellus* (*Geo.* 1. 7), ut sit *si* pro *cum*, id est *cum venerit*'. The grounds for accepting the second explanation are strong: for Aeneas to say 'We shall have games after the ceremony if it is a fine day' seems inappropriate for epic; it may well be that the ship-race could not take place in bad weather, but an epic poet may take the weather for granted. In addition the word *almus* with *dies* is a permanent epithet, cf. Hor. *Odes* 4. 7. 7, *Ecl.* 8. 17; it is used in this way with *lux* in *Aen.* 1. 306, 3. 311, 8. 455, 11. 182. Finally the phrase *radiisque retexerit orbem* (see on 65) refers to the advent of daylight, not to the advent of a fine day. For this use of *si* cf. Cat. 14. 17 *nam si luxerit* with Ellis's note, where he rightly says that originally the mode of expression may have been connected with some superstitious fear.

64–65. nona . . . Aurora: the solemnities at a Roman funeral lasted for nine days. Servius quotes Hor. *Epod.* 17. 48 *novendiales dissipare pulveres* (on which Porphyrion says 'novendiale dicitur sacrificium quod mortuo fit nona die qua sepultus est'), and adds 'inde etiam ludi qui in honorem mortuorum celebrabantur novendiales dicuntur'. Cf. Apul. *Met.* 9. 31 *nono die rite completis apud tumulum sollemnibus,* *Geo.* 4. 552 f., Stat. *Th.* 6. 238 f. In the *Iliad* (24. 784) the preparations for Hector's funeral last nine days, and the pyre is lighted on the tenth.

65. radiisque retexerit orbem: 'reveals the world with his rays', cf. *Aen.* 4. 119 (the same phrase), 9. 461 *iam sole infuso,* *iam rebus luce retectis,* Ov. *Met.* 8. 1 f. *iam nitidum retegente* *diem noctisque fugante | tempora Lucifero.*

66 f. Day Lewis translates:

I shall hold a Trojan Games: a regatta, first, for the ships;
Then let the champion runners, and those who take the arena
Confident in their skill at throwing the javelin or archery,
Those, too, that boldly challenge with the rawhide boxing
    gloves—
Let them all come forward, eager to win the palm of the
    victor.

66. citae . . . classis: 'a contest for swift ships'. The genitive is regularly used of the contestants or the nature of the contest, cf. *Geo.* 2. 530 *velocis iaculi certamina ponit in ulmo,* Ov. *Met.* 10. 177 *latique ineunt certamina disci,* Livy 10. 2. 15 *sollemni* *certamine navium.*

67–70. Notice the informal construction of this sentence; cf. 548 f.

67 f. The phrase *viribus audax* goes with both the following lines: Aeneas proclaims, in addition to the ship-race, a foot-race and (for those who trust in their strength) a contest in throwing and shooting or boxing.

68–69. For the co-ordination *aut . . . seu* cf. *Aen.* 12. 684 f. *ac* *veluti montis saxum de vertice praeceps | cum ruit avulsum* *vento, seu turbidus imber | proluit aut annis solvit sublapsa* *vetustas.*

68. No javelin contest in fact takes place. Servius, in his anxiety to explain the discrepancy, takes *iaculo sagittisque* as a hendiadys equivalent to *iactu sagittarum.* This is most unlikely. Mackail is correct in regarding the line as 'a for-mulary one . . . the coupling of javelin-throwing and archery being common form, as for instance 9. 178'.

69. fidit . . . committere: this is a marked extension of the normal use of *fidere.* Here it has the sense of *audere,* hence the following infinitive (see note on 21–22). Cf. the imitation in Sil. 7. 599 *fisumque manus conferre Mahalcen.*

    caestu: see on 364. The spondaic line is appropriate for the announcement of the heavy-weight contest.

70–71. Notice that these two lines, bringing the speech to a

close, have coincidence of ictus and accent in the fourth foot;
see note on 5 f.

70. palmae: the palm as a prize for victory came late into
Greece, not before about 400 B.C. (see W. H. Willis,
T.A.Ph.A., 1941, p. 413). According to Livy it was introduced into the Roman world in 293 B.C. (Livy 10. 47. 3
*palmaeque tum primum translato e Graeco more victoribus
datae*). Aulus Gellius (3. 6) refers to an entertaining suggestion found in Plutarch that it is the quality of resilience which
is characteristic both of the palm tree and of the successful
athlete.

71. ore favete: 'utter no ill-omened word', a religious formula
spoken by the priest to the people before a sacred ritual,
requiring them to say nothing unfavourable; it tended to pass
into the meaning of 'observe a holy silence'. Cf. Hor. *Odes* 3.
1. 2 *favete linguis*, Prop. 4. 6. 1 *sacra facit vates, sint ora
faventia sacris*, Tib. 2. 2. 2 *quisquis ades lingua vir mulierque
fave*; and compare the Greek εὐφημεῖτε.

72–103. *The Trojans proceed to the tomb of Anchises, where
Aeneas offers libations and addresses his father's shade. Suddenly a huge snake comes forth from the tomb, tastes the offerings,
and then disappears. Aeneas recognizes that this indicates the
presence of the* manes *of Anchises at the ceremony, and the
sacrifice is renewed, and followed by a ritual feast.*

72 f. For the religious significance of this passage see on 42 f.

72. materna . . . myrto: the myrtle was sacred to Venus,
Aeneas' mother, cf. *Ecl.* 7. 62, *Geo.* 1. 28. It was also sometimes associated with the dead, cf. schol. on Pind. *Isth.* 4. 117
μυρσίνη γὰρ στεφανοῦνται διὰ τὸ εἶναι τῶν νεκρῶν στέφος.

tempora: the repetition of one or more words from the
previous line in a similar metrical position is a feature of
style much more in the Ovidian manner than the Virgilian
(see Austin, *C.Q.*, 1929, p. 54); there are, however, a few
striking examples in Virgil, cf. *Aen.* 7. 653–4, 8. 271–2.

73–74. Mackail comments that the three proper names are
chosen to indicate that the sports will be for all ages: Helymus
enters for the foot-race, Acestes for the archery, and Ascanius
is the leader of the *lusus Troiae*. Helymus was traditionally
associated with Sicily (Dion. Hal. 1. 47, 1. 52) as having
given his name to the Sicilian people called the Elymi (Thuc.
6. 2. 3, cited on 718, where see note).

73. hoc: the syllable is long (although the vowel is short)
because *hoc* is contracted from *hod-ce*; cf. *Aen.* 6. 129 *hoc
opus hic labor est*. *Hic* (nominative) is short in Plautus, but
later was scanned as a long syllable by analogy with *hoc*;

it is occasionally allowed to remain short (*Aen.* 4. 22, 6. 791)
as a deliberate archaism.

   aevi maturus: genitive of 'sphere in which' or 'respect',
cf. *Aen.* 2. 638 f. *integer aevi | sanguis*, Hor. *Odes* 1. 22. 1
integer vitae, and see Ernout–Thomas, pp. 56–58, Kühner–
Stegmann, ii. 1, pp. 443–6, Löfstedt, *Syntactica*, i, pp. 163 f.
It is a usage proper to Latin (we find phrases like *animi
lassus* and *nec sermonis fallebar* in Plautus), which was
greatly extended by the poets, probably under Greek
influence. It was encouraged by the similar usage, occurring
in Classical prose, of the genitive with words indicating
abundance or the opposite, like *plenus, fertilis, inanis, inops*.

74. sequitur quos: for the postponed relative see on 22.

   pubes: in Virgil the word can be very general, sometimes
(as here) meaning simply 'people' without reference to age.
Cf. *Aen.* 2. 797 f. *matresque virosque | collectam exsilio pubem,
miserabile vulgus*, and *Geo.* 1. 343.

75–76. The alliteration of *m* and *c* is extremely marked, perhaps
to give an air of solemnity and archaic ritual at the beginning
of the description of the rites. Alliteration of initial letters
was common in formulae of an archaic kind (e.g. *quod bonum
faustum felix fortunatumque sit*, cf. Cic. *De Div.* 1. 102); it
played an important part in the Saturnian metre, and was
often very prominent indeed in early Latin poetry (e.g. Enn.
Ann. 140 V *at tuba terribili sonitu taratantara dixit*, Enn.
Ann. 359 V *nec cum capta capi nec cum combusta cremari*).
Thus very marked alliteration could be used by later poets
to convey a flavour of the archaic. See Marouzeau, *Traité de
stylistique latine*, pp. 45 f., and Bailey's Lucretius, *Proleg.*,
pp. 146 f. For 'imitative' alliteration see on 866; and for
some examples of the many varied ways in which Virgil
employs the repetition of consonants and vowels see index,
s.v. 'alliteration' and 'rhyme'.

75. ibat: 'set out', ingressive imperfect.

77–78. 'Here in due libation he poured on the ground two gob-
lets of unmixed wine, two of fresh milk, two of sacrificial
blood.' Notice the formulary repetition of *duo*: offerings
were double on especially important occasions, see Warde
Fowler, *C.R.*, 1917, pp. 163 f., Bailey, *Religion in Virgil*, pp.
299 f. For the pouring of libations at *inferiae* to the dead cf.
Hom. *Il.* 23. 219 f., *Ecl.* 5. 67 f., *Aen.* 3. 66 f., 301 f.; the
spirit of the departed was supposed to partake of the
offerings.

   For the various uses of *libare* see on 92; here it means
'pour out in libation', cf. *Aen.* 1. 736 *in mensam laticum
libavit honorem*, *Geo.* 4. 380 f., *cape Maeonii carchesia*

Bacchi: / *Oceano libemus*. For *carchesia* (καρχήσια) see Rich, *Dict. Antiq.*, s.v. The phrase *mero Baccho*, dependent on *carchesia*, is an example of the extended use of the ablative of description which Virgil not infrequently uses; cf. the much more remarkable instance in *Aen.* 3. 618 *domus sanie dapibusque cruentis*. See Mackail's appendix A (on the Virgilian ablative), and compare the notes on 450, 609, 663.

The metonymy of *Bacchus* = *vinum* is very common; cf. *Ecl.* 5. 69 with Forbiger's collection of parallels ad loc. So we find *Ceres* = *frumentum* (*Aen.* 1. 177), *Thetis* = *mare* (*Ecl.* 4. 32), *Neptunus* = *mare* (*Geo.* 4. 29), *Vulcanus* = *ignis* (*Geo.* 1. 295—cf. line 662, a much easier use—), *Minerva* = *tela* (*Aen.* 8. 409). Lucretius (2. 655 f.) comments on this usage; see Bailey and Munro, ad loc. Statius (*Silv.* 3. 1. 41) has a remarkable extension of it when he says of Hercules *multo fratre* (= *Baccho* = *vino*) *madentem*.

79. purpureosque iacit flores: cf. *Aen.* 6. 884 *purpureos spargam flores*, spoken by Anchises as a token of mourning for Marcellus. There, as here, the word means 'purple' or 'red'. Servius *auct.* on *Aen.* 3. 67 discusses *sanguineus color* as one of the ritual colours for offerings to the dead, citing the present passage and *Aen.* 6. 221 f. (at the funeral of Misenus) *purpureasque super vestes, velamina nota,* / *coniciunt*. We cannot tell what flowers are meant in our passage; in *Aen.* 6. 883 f. they are purple lilies, Ovid (*Fast.* 2. 539) mentions violets at the *Parentalia*, Propertius (1. 17. 22) wishes for roses at his funeral. Some suggest taking *purpureus* here in its widest sense, 'bright', 'radiant', as in *Aen.* 1. 591, 6. 641, but this is unlikely in a context where there is point in the more specific meaning.

80. Salve: it is comparatively rarely that the first foot of a Virgilian hexameter is composed of a single spondaic word. There are twenty-four instances in Book IV (Austin on 4. 185); in this book there are twenty-six. Certain words tend to this position without gaining much emphasis, such as *talis, qualis*, parts of *ille* (*olle*) and *ipse*; but in other instances a special stress or solemnity may be given to the word (cf. 471, 813, 815) especially if it is followed by a sense pause, as here and in 807 (compare 195); cf. *Aen.* 6. 590 (*demens*), 4. 185 (*stridens*), 4. 190 (*gaudens*). For *salve* in this position cf. *Geo.* 2. 173 *salve magna parens frugum Saturnia tellus*, and *Aen.* 8. 301 *salve vera Iovis proles*; for further discussion and references see Austin on 4. 185 and 453, and Winbolt, *Latin Hexameter Verse*, pp. 16 and 107 f. It is noticeable that a single dactylic word in the first foot, though of course much more common than a single spondee, is not as frequent a rhythm with Virgil as (for example) with Ovid, and occurs in only about twelve per cent. of his hexameters. On the other hand one of his favourite pauses is after an initial dactyl; see on 480.

Servius punctuates after *iterum* (and so Donatus and many modern editors), and explains that Aeneas had first said *salve* at the time of burial. Henry's argument, however, that such a punctuation destroys the cadence of the line, is undoubtedly true. The meaning that Servius requi es could still be gained with the punctuation before *iterum*; but I think the other meaning (again I say 'hail') is preferable. Henry cites Aesch. *Eum.* 1014 χαίρετε, χαίρετε δ' αὖθις, ἔπη διπλοίζω and Callim. *Hymn.* I. 94 χαῖρε πάτερ χαῖρ' αὖθι, and the Verona scholiast on this passage cites Cat. 64. 23 f. as follows: *salvete deum gens, o bona matrum | progenies salvete iterum* (a citation which provides evidence of a lacuna and corruption in our MSS. of Catullus).

80–81. recepti nequiquam cineres: *nequiquam* partly conveys the feeling that nothing can bring the dead back to life (cf. Cat. 101. 4 *et mutam nequiquam alloquerer cinerem*), partly looks forward to line 82 *non licuit . . .* There have been various interpretations of the difficult phrase *recepti cineres*. Servius takes it to refer to the rescue of Anchises from Troy, and says 'cineres pro ipso patre posuit, ac si diceret, salve pater de Troia liberate sine causa'. This is very strongly supported by *Aen.* 6. 110 f. *illum ego per flammas et mille sequentia tela | eripui his umeris medioque ex hoste recepi*, and 3. 710 f. (at Anchises' death) *hic me pater optime fessum | deseris heu tantis nequiquam erepte periclis*. But *cineres nequiquam recepti* is a strange phrase if it is intended to convey *cineres patris quem vivum nequiquam recepi*. In an attempt to avoid this difficulty it is suggested that *recepti* is genitive singular; but this seems unnatural. Servius tells us that some took *iterum recepti cineres* to refer to the story about the violation of Anchises' tomb by Diomedes, with reference to *Aen.* 4. 427; but this is clearly out of the question. The remaining possiblity is to take *recepti* to mean 'found again', 'restored to me', cf. *Aen.* I. 553 *rege recepto*, I. 583 *sociosque receptos*, Hor. *Odes* 2. 7. 27–28 *recepto . . . amico*; but this forces the meaning of *recipere*, and on the whole Servius' explanation seems the best.

81. As Mackail points out, the salutation is addressed to (i) the buried ashes, (ii) the spirit (*anima*) in Elysium, (iii) the ghost (*umbra*) which haunts or revisits this world. Compare note on 722. The plurals *animaeque umbraeque* are to be explained on the analogy of the plural *manes*; they are also helped by

the immediate proximity of the poetic plural *cineres*, first
found in Virgil (cf. line 55 and Austin on *Aen.* 4. 427). For
poetic plurals generally see on 98; for *umbrae* plural in this
sense cf. Prop. 2. 8. 19 *exagitet nostros manis, sectetur et
umbras*, *Aen.* 6. 510 *omnia Deiphobo solvisti et funeris umbris*,
Ov. *Am.* 1. 13. 3; and see Austin on 4. 571. Servius has a
long note on the various elements of the *anima* which Virgil
includes in the plural *animae*; but it seems much more likely
that the unusual use of the plural here is due to analogy.

   animaeque umbraeque paternae: Virgil tends to avoid
similar case endings in juxtaposition (homoeoteleuton). The
nature of the Latin language causes such juxtapositions to
occur very frequently unless particular care is taken to avoid
them; a comparison with prose usage, and with Ennius and
Lucretius, shows that the comparative rarity in Virgil is
due to deliberate avoidance. In this book there are instances
at 293, 311, 332–3, 376, 405, 530, 682, 845 (where see note),
870 (where see note); and less marked instances at 135, 190,
271, 314, 498, 561; see also note on 277. See Quint. 9. 4. 41–2,
Leumann–Hofmann, p. 800, Marouzeau, *Traité de stylistique
latine*, pp. 51 f. By contrast Virgil is very fond of the assonance or rhyme of similar word-endings when they are not in
juxtaposition; see note on 385–6.

82. Supply to this line *tecum quaerere* from the next clause.
The postposition of *tecum* from the first clause is unusual
and throws emphasis on the word. See note on 26–27.

   Italos: for the scansion see on 571.

   fataliaque: 'destined', 'appointed by fate', cf. *Aen.* 4.
355 *quem regno Hesperiae fraudo et fatalibus arvis*, where *et*
is used epexegetically as *-que* is here (see on 410–11). Elision
between the fifth and sixth foot is not common; there are
twenty-three instances (not counting *neque*) in Virgil, four-
teen with *-que*, six with *sine, ibi, ubi*, and three notable ones:
Aen. **3.** 581 *intremere omnem*, 10. 508 *haec eadem aufert*, 12. 26
hoc animo hauri (see Norden's *Aeneid VI*, p. 456). In this
book there are instances with *-que* at 137, 817. It seems likely
(see my note in *Proc. Class. Ass.*, 1950, p. 31) that the word
accent of *fatália* was not affected by elided *-que*, so that the
fifth and sixth foot have the usual coincidence of accent
and ictus.

83. quicumque est: Aeneas knows that the Tiber is his goal
(*Aen.* 2. 782, 3. 500), but it is still a vague and unlocated
goal. Page well draws attention to the artistic contrast of
this phrase with the Tiber's after fame.

   Thybrim: Virgil prefers the Greek form to the Roman
Tiberis, which occurs only twice (*Geo.* 1. 499, *Aen.* 7. 715).

84 f. For the significance of the snake see on 95; for other
passages describing snakes see lines 273 f., *Aen*. 2. 203 f., *Geo.*
2. 153 f. The description here is one of exceptional colour
and brilliance, without the note of fear in the other passages
cited. Notice in lines 84 and 85 the coincidence of accent
and ictus in the fourth foot, helping to convey the smooth
movement. There is marked alliteration, first of *s* (as in the
Laocoon passage, *Aen*. 2. 203 f.; see note on 866) and then
of *l*.

84–85. dixerat haec . . . cum . . . traxit: the inverted *cum* construction is a favourite one with Virgil; cf. in this book 159 f.,
268 f., 327 f., 654 f., 693 f., 835 f., 864 f. It has its origin in
paratactic expressions where the two clauses are co-ordinate
(see note on 858); its characteristic feature is that the
grammatically subordinate clause carries the chief significance of the sentence. The main clause is very often merely an
indication of the time or circumstances under which the
important action of the *cum* clause took place. See Kühner–
Stegmann, ii. 2, pp. 338 f., and E. Adelaide Hahn, *T.A.Ph.A.*,
1956, pp. 147 f. for a full discussion of this construction in
Virgil.

84. adytis . . . ab imis: Servius *auct.* comments that Virgil in
treating Anchises as a god makes his tomb a kind of temple.
See on 42 f.

85. Servius says that the seven coils here represent the seven
years of Aeneas' wanderings, as in Homer (*Il*. 2. 308 f.) the
nine years of unsuccessful war against Troy are represented by
the portent of a snake eating a mother and her eight young
birds. But it seems more likely that seven is chosen as a
mystic number, cf. *Aen*. 6. 38. Some commentators have
maintained (Henry very emphatically, and Page follows him)
that the snake makes seven circuits of the tomb, progressing
in seven coils. This is based on the argument that *gyrus*
means circuit more naturally than coil (cf. *Geo*. 3. 191 f.);
but it produces a grotesque picture, and disregards the position of *ingens*, which makes it plain that *gyri* are the mighty
coils of the snake. *Septena volumina* is then a variation on the
theme *septem gyros*, adding the picture of movement. The
use of the distributive numeral for the cardinal is quite
common: cf. line 96 (*binas* for *duas*), line 560 f. *tres equitum
numero turmae, ternique vagantur | ductores* (where there are
three captains altogether, not nine), *Aen*. 10. 329 f. *septem
numero, septenaque tela | coniciunt* (seven people throw one
javelin each), *Aen*. 1. 265–6, 7. 538, 8. 448.

86. amplexus . . . lapsusque: for the 'timeless' use of the
participles see on 708.

87 f. Day Lewis translates:

Upon its back was a sheen, a dapple of blueish markings
And of gold-glinting scales, like the shimmer of many colours
A rainbow lays on the dark cloud, refractions from the sunlight.

87–88. 'Blue flecks mottled its back, and a sheen of golden
markings lit up its scales.' *Notae* is nominative plural, and
we should supply as its verb something like *distinguebant*,
taken from *incendebat* by a slight zeugma. *Et* is postponed
to second word in its clause; see on 5. For the imagery cf.
Hom. *Il.* 2. 308, Hes. *Scut.* 166 f., *Geo.* 3. 427, Sil. 2. 584 f.

87. terga: prose does not use the plural of *tergum* unless more
than one person is referred to, and even then the singular is
preferred. In poetry, however, the plural is very common;
compare plurals like *ora* (369), *colla* (277), *pectora* (816); see
note on 98 for poetic plurals, and Austin on 4. 673.

88. squamam: the plural is much more common, but cf. *Aen.*
9. 707, Ov. *Met.* 15. 725, Cic. *Nat. De.* 2. 127.

88–89. 'like the rainbow when it catches the sun's rays and
throws a thousand shimmering colours on the clouds'. Line
89 is almost the same as *Aen.* 4. 701 (where see Austin's
note on rainbows); cf. also Lucr. 6. 524 f., and compare line
609. *R* reads *trahit* here (from 4. 701), but for *iacit* cf. 7. 527.
The introduction by scribes of errors due to reminiscence of
similar lines in Virgil is discussed by Sparrow, *Half-lines and
Repetitions in Virgil*, pp. 111 f. *Nubibus*, which is governed
by *iacit*, is probably local ablative (cf. *Aen.* 4. 373) rather
than dative of 'place to which'. I have discussed this usage
with verbs which imply motion in *C.Q.*, 1951, pp. 143 f.;
compare note on 683.

90. obstipuit visu Aeneas: note the powerful effect conveyed by
this extremely short sentence, coming between the two long
sentences describing the snake. The effect is enhanced by the
complete conflict of accent and ictus.

   agmine longo: 'with its long sweep'; Day Lewis has
'dragging its gradual length'. For this rather unusual use of
agmen (which is generally applied to a number of people or
things moving) cf. *Aen.* 2. 212 f. (of snakes) *illi agmine
certo | Laocoonta petunt*, *Geo.* 3. 423 (of a snake) *extremaeque
agmina caudae*, *Aen.* 2. 782 (of a river) *leni fluit agmine
Thybris* (imitated from Ennius). Macrobius quotes the last
(*Sat.* 6. 4. 4.) to illustrate the use of *agmen* 'pro actu et ductu
quodam'. Compare line 211.

91. levia: 'smooth', i.e. burnished, shining, as in 558.
   serpens: this is of course the participle, not the noun.

92. libavitque: the word means 'to take a little of' and hence

'to taste', as here; cf. *Ecl.* 5. 25 f. *nulla neque amnem /
libavit quadripes nec graminis attigit herbam, Geo.* 4. 54 f.
flumina libant / summa leves. It passes into the meaning of
'pour libations', 'make offerings', as in 77 (where see note).
It is also used metaphorically in the sense of 'take a little of'
as in Cic. *De Inv.* 2. 4 *ex variis ingeniis excellentissima quaeque
libavimus.*

   libavitque . . . rursusque: the first *-que* points forward to
the second and has no co-ordinating function of its own; the
meaning is 'both . . . and'. This is a feature of epic style
which does not occur in normal prose usage; there are
instances in this book at 169, 174, 177, 234, 333, 471, 521,
619, 753, 766, 802. It occurs a number of times in Ennius
(*ferroque lapique, frangitque quatitque, urbemque forumque*)
evidently in imitation of the Greek τε . . . τε which occurs
commonly in Homer especially to link single words (e.g.
ἀνδρῶν τε θεῶν τε, cf. Ennius' *divumque hominumque*, Virgil's
hominumque deumque). The hexameter poets were fond of
linking together in this way words of associated type (766
noctemque diemque, 802 *caelique marisque*). Apart from its
stylistic association with epic diction the usage also had
obvious metrical advantages for dactylic verse. For a full
discussion with references see Austin on *Aen.* 4. 83; see note
on 802 for doubled *-que* at the end of the line, and on 467 for
-que . . . et meaning 'both . . . and'.

93. successit tumulo: *succedere* is frequent in Virgil with the
dative of 'place to which', cf. *Aen.* 1. 631 *tectis, iuvenes,
succede nostris*, and note on 34.

   depasta: Virgil uses both the active form (as here, cf. *Geo.*
4. 539) and the deponent form (*Aen.* 2. 215) of this word.
Altaria is used by a slight and natural metonymy for *dapes
in altaribus positas*.

94. hoc magis . . . instaurat: *instaurare* is a favourite word of
Virgil's, meaning 'to renew' or 'to resume' (*Aen.* 2. 451,
669), used especially of religious ceremonies (*Aen.* 4. 63, 145,
6. 530). Most commentators suggest that Aeneas here starts
the ritual over again because he is uncertain whether there
is a *genius loci* to be propitiated, quoting Livy 5. 52. 9
*recordamini, agite dum, quotiens sacra instaurentur, quia
aliquid ex patrio ritu neglegentia casuve praetermissum est*,
and Livy 25. 16. 3. But it is difficult to make any real sense
out of *magis* with this interpretation; *magis* should refer to
something he was doing already which he now does all the
more. It is better then to take *instaurare* in the sense of
'resume' (after the interruption caused by the snake).
Translate then: 'Because of this he resumed all the more

fervently the rites he had begun in honour of his father, not knowing whether to think . . .'

95. **geniumne loci**: according to the pantheistic view of the old Roman religion every natural feature, hill, spring, tree, river, had its *genius*, its local god; cf. *Aen.* 7. 136 and Milton, *Lycidas* 182–3 'Now Lycidas the Shepherds weep no more; / Henceforth thou art the Genius of the shore . . .'

famulumne parentis: 'or the attendant spirit of his father', cf. Val. Fl. 3. 457 f. *angues* / *umbrarum famuli* with Langen's note. The soul of the dead (like the *genius*) was often represented as a snake; see Conington ad loc., Ov. *Met.* 15. 389–90, R. B. Onians, *Origins of European Thought*, p. 159, n. 2, pp. 206 f. There is ultimately little difference between these alternative views of the snake: it represents the spirit of Anchises appearing at his own tomb.

For the double *-ne* see on 702–3.

96 f. The offerings of sheep, pigs, and bullocks suggest the Roman sacrificial lustration *Suovetaurilia* (*sus, ovis, taurus*); cf. *Aen.* 11. 197 f.

96. **binas**: some good MSS. have *quinas* and one *caeditque binas*, which suggests the origin of the error. The offerings in pairs correspond with 77 f. For *binas = duas* see on 85.

bidentis: sheep in their second year, at which age they have two prominent teeth; see Henry on *Aen.* 4. 57.

97. **nigrantis terga**: black is of course the appropriate colour for the gods below; cf. line 736, *Aen.* 6. 153, 243 (where the ritual phrase occurs again). *Terga* is accusative of respect, common in verse with parts of the body (*Aen.* 1. 320 *nuda genu*, 2. 381 *colla tumentem*). It is a Greek construction which came late into Latin; there is an instance in Lucr. 3. 489 *tremit artus*, and Virgil seems to have popularized it in verse. By the time of Tacitus it was fairly well established as a prose usage. It played a large part in the development of the 'retained accusative' construction, for which see on 135; compare also the note on 285. See Austin on 4. 558, Kühner–Stegmann ii. 1, pp. 285–7, Palmer, *The Latin Language*, p. 289.

98. **vinaque**: the plural is always used by Virgil in the nominative and accusative, but the singular in the other cases. Prose writers used the singular, except when the meaning 'different kinds of wine' was particularly stressed: Servius on *Geo.* 2. 7 says 'mustum numero tantum singulari dicimus, sicut vinum'. The use of the plural where prose used the singular became increasingly common in verse, and the term 'poetic plural' is generally used for such instances. A number of different causes combined to make such usages possible

and reasonable, and the metrical convenience encouraged the extension of them so that they became associated with poetry. The metrical convenience is very clear in cases where the words were otherwise intractable (*silentium, solacium, gaudium, proelium, praemium, atrium, otium, Capitolium,* and so on); but there is more in it than that. The Latin language was deficient in short syllables from the hexameter poet's point of view, and the neuter plural provided short syllables not only for the noun but also for words in agreement (compare *vina liquentia fundit* with *vinum liquens fundit*). We may note that in the more spondaic movement of Catullus' hexameters poetic plurals are relatively rare; and that in Virgil some of the commonest words like *tempus, litus, pectus, foedus, munus, vulnus,* and so on are much commoner in the plural for nominative and accusative (a dactyl) but in the singular for the ablative (a dactyl) and of course for the genitive. In words where the plural did not give short syllables it could be used to avoid hiatus or cacophony (e.g. *pugnas,* 419; *aditus* 441).

The metrical convenience then was very great, but there had to be sufficient linguistic grounds to justify the usage. Among these we may notice: (i) the prose use of the plural in abstract words like *irae, laetitiae, dolores, metus, amores,* where *ira* means 'anger' and *irae* 'feelings of anger' (see Austin on 4. 197); (ii) imitation of Greek plurals, e.g. *currus* = ἅρματα, *ortus* = ἀνατολαί, *pectora* = στήθεα; (iii) the possibility that neuter plurals like *vina, mella, ligna,* were felt to have the collective force of a first declension singular (see Löfstedt, *Syntactica,* i, p. 48); (iv) the added impressiveness of meaning associated with the plural of certain types of word, e.g. *regna, sceptra, templa* (line 60), *simulacra, numina*; (v) the operation of analogy: *arae* because of *altaria, colla* because of *cervices,* and so with many words indicating parts of the body, *ora, pectora, corda, vultus.*

There was some opposition to the extension of the usage. Servius (on *Ecl.* 5. 36) points out that the plural *hordea* is unexpected: 'hordea usurpative metri causa dixit, nam triticum, hordeum, vinum, mel, numeri tantum singularis sunt'; and on *Geo.* 1. 210 Servius *auct.* quotes the line of Bavius 'hordea qui dixit superest ut tritica dicat' ('whoever says barleys may as well say wheats'). We also have preserved by Aulus Gellius (19. 8. 2 f.) a record of Caesar's objection to the plural *harenae* (which Virgil uses a number of times; it cannot be said to be a particularly bold use). On the whole subject see Löfstedt, *Syntactica,* i, pp. 27 f., Marouzeau, *Traité de stylistique latine,* pp. 222 f., Norden's

Aeneid VI, appendix V, Leumann–Hofmann, p. 371, with references given there, Austin on *Aen.* 4. 455, 673, and his index s.v. 'plural'. I have listed other examples in Book V in my index.

fundebat . . . vocabat: for the tenses cf. 75.

99. **Acheronte remissos**: 'released from Acheron', to visit the sacrifices; cf. Hom. *Il.* 23. 219 f., *Aen.* 3. 303 f. (Andromache) *manisque vocabat | Hectoreum ad tumulum*. Acheron was one of the rivers of the underworld (*Aen.* 6. 295, Milton, *P.L.* 2. 578 'Sad Acheron of sorrow, black and deep'), and was commonly used to mean the underworld itself (*Aen.* 7. 312 *flectere si nequeo superos, Acheronta movebo*, Milton, *Comus* 603–4 'With all the griesly legions that troop / Under the sooty flag of Acheron').

100. **nec non et**: a pleonastic expression of familiar speech which Virgil introduced into poetry; he has it fifteen times, nearly always at the beginning of a line. See Austin on *Aen.* 4. 140.

quae cuique est copia: 'each according to his means', a 'detached' use of the relative, equivalent to *sicut cuique est copia*, or *quisque pro sua copia*. Compare Plin. *Ep.* 8. 8. 7 *quamquam tu vero, quae tua humanitas, nulla ridebis*.

laeti: a pause before the sixth foot is unusual, see on 624. The effect is to emphasize *laeti*, a key word in this book; see Intro. p. xvii and note on 58. It also has emphasis from its position at the end of the line, as adjectives (with some exceptions like *altus* and *imus*) tend to be placed less conspicuously; see on 733.

101–3. There are six main verbs in the third person plural of the present tense in these lines. It is a general characteristic of Virgil's narrative style that clauses are short, and subordination is avoided by the use of main verbs and parataxis (see Palmer, *The Latin Language*, pp. 115 f., Leumann–Hofmann, pp. 810–11). The contrast with the typical Latin prose sentence, with its complex of subordinate clauses, is very marked indeed. Hardly less marked is the contrast with Lucretius, whose subject-matter (concerned as it is with expounding arguments) causes him frequently to use long sentences with many subordinate clauses. Between Catullus and Virgil the difference in this respect is less, but still very noticeable; Catullus has more participial constructions and descriptive phrases, while Virgil (generally speaking) has more main verbs, more words to the line, more impetus of narrative movement.

Even so these lines are exceptional in their number of short main clauses; perhaps it is not fanciful to say that the effect

is to suggest how the well-known simple ritual acts are performed one after the other. There are very similar lines in
Aen. I. 212–14. Compare note on 580–2, and on the ὕστερον
πρότερον of 316.

102. ordine . . . alii: 'others set out the brazen vessels in their
due places' (not, as some suggest, 'others in their turn . . .').
Ordine suggests ritual correctness, cf. lines 53 and 773, *Geo.*
4. 376.

103. Cf. Hom. *Il.* 9. 213 ἀνθρακιὴν στορέσας ὀβελοὺς ἐφύπερθε
τάνυσσεν. *Prunas* means 'live embers'; Servius on *Aen.* 11.
788 says 'pruna autem quamdiu ardet dicitur . . ., cum autem
exstincta fuerit, carbo nominatur'.

104–13. *The day of the games comes round, and the people
assemble; the prizes are displayed, and the trumpet sounds for
the beginning of the contests.*

104 f. Virgil's long and elaborate account of the games is
modelled, with variations, on the funeral games for Patroclus
described in *Iliad* XXIII; in turn Statius (*Thebaid* VI) and
Silius (*Punica* XVI) imitated Virgil. In deciding to include
an account of athletic contests in the *Aeneid* Virgil had a
number of motives apart from the Homeric precedent: to
relieve the emotional tension between Book IV and Book VI;
to concentrate attention on Anchises and the religious
honours duly paid in filial reverence by Aeneas to his father
(see note on 42 f.); and to serve as a prototype for current
Roman customs and institutions, especially for the revival
of interest in athletics fostered by Augustus. For a discussion
of these aspects see Intro., pp. ix–xii.

In the description of the contests Virgil has aimed at an
effect quite different from that of *Iliad* XXIII. Where
Homer is direct and immediate in appeal, Virgil gives a more
formally organized account, with a contrived balance and
unity, and a careful arrangement of tension, as is appropriate
for his kind of literary epic. There are many similarities of
incident between Homer and Virgil, but the method and
tone of the two descriptions differ completely. The relationship of Virgil's games to those in *Iliad* XXIII, and the literary
pattern and intention of Virgil's version, are discussed in
Intro., pp. xiii–xvi.

A full comparative study of athletic contests in Greek and
Latin epic poetry, with detailed description of the selection
and arrangement of the individual contests and of the prizes
awarded, is given by W. H. Willis, *T.A.Ph.A.*, 1941, pp.
392 f. See also Heinze, *Virgils Epische Technik*, pp. 145 f.,
and Mehl's appendix to Büchner's article on Virgil in *R.E.*

104–5. Notice how the long sonorous phrases set the scene for the festive occasion, and are followed by the description of the joyous gathering and the large display of magnificent prizes. See note on 42 f. for Virgil's many varied ways of describing dawn. Phaethon is here a name of the Sun, Homer's Ἥλιος φαέθων, not the Phaethon of mythology; cf. Val. Fl. 3. 213.

106. fama . . . Acestae: 'the report (of the games) and the name of renowned Acestes' rather than 'the fame and name of renowned Acestes'. Page strangely takes *nomen* as a second object of *excierat*, with the meaning 'kindred', 'race'; possibly his intention was to account for the singular *excierat*, but *fama* and *nomen* can easily be regarded as a single compound subject.

107. Cf. Cat. 64. 33 *oppletur laetanti regia coetu*; 104–7 are reminiscent of Cat. 64. 31–33.

108. pars . . . parati: a very common *constructio ad sensum*, in prose as well as verse; cf. 119–20 and *Aen.* 6. 660. It is wrong to supply, as many commentators do, a balancing *pars* with *visuri*. They all come to see the Trojans, and some to join in the games *as well*.

109. circoque: probably Virgil is thinking of a curving bank on the sea-shore, serving as a place for spectators and enclosing a space which could be called *circus*; cf. 289. The passage is reminiscent of Hom. *Il.* 23. 257 f. αὐτὰρ Ἀχιλλεὺς / αὐτοῦ λαὸν ἔρυκε καὶ ἵζανεν εὐρὺν ἀγῶνα, / νηῶν δ᾿ ἔκφερ᾿ ἄεθλα . . .

110 f. The successful athletes are to receive prizes of material value as well as tokens of honour like garlands. In the games for Patroclus the prizes were of material value; in the great Greek festivals they were not: in the Olympic games, for example, the victor won a crown of wild olive. In lesser Greek games and most Roman games prizes of value were given; at the Actian games Augustus reverted to the practice of the great Greek festivals. On the whole subject see W. H. Willis, loc. cit. on 104 f.

111. palmae: see note on 70. The palm leaves would probably not be made into garlands or wreaths.

112. perfusae: 'dyed', a poetic use, cf. Lucr. 2. 821.

    talentum: there is better MS. authority for *talenta*, which I would prefer to read. No specified quantity has been given for any of the other prizes here listed, and at line 248 (where see note) Aeneas gives a talent of silver to the crew of each ship. Homer (*Il.* 23. 269) has two talents of gold as fourth prize in the chariot-race.

113. et: the word co-ordinates *munera locantur* and *tuba canit.*
   medio . . . aggere: 'from the mound in the middle',
perhaps the one mentioned in line 44.

114–50. *Four competitors enter for the ship-race, Mnestheus in
the Pristis, Gyas in the Chimaera, Sergestus in the Centaurus,
and Cloanthus in the Scylla. The course is out to sea, round
a rock and home again. The competitors draw lots for position;
the starting signal is given, and the ships get under way amidst
applause.*

114 f. Virgil's ship-race corresponds with the chariot-race in
Homer, both in being the first of the contests and in a number
of points of detail, especially at the turning-point (see notes
on 129, 132, 137–8, 144–7, 163, 188 f., 282 f., 284). Aeneas
of course had no chariots, but in any case the maritime nature
of much of the first half of the *Aeneid* makes a race at sea
particularly appropriate. There were ship-races at the
Isthmian games and at various Greek festivals; and Augustus' Actian games included a regatta (see Intro., pp. x–xi).
On the other hand such an event was far from being a regular
and expected feature of athletic contests. No other extant
ancient epic contains an account of a ship-race, though it is
possible that a race was included in the naval manœuvres
(*naumachia*) described by Ennius (*Ann.* 478–86 V); see
E. Norden, *Ennius und Vergilius*, pp. 163 f. On ship-
races in the ancient world see P. Gardner, *J.H.S.*, 1881,
pp. 90 f. and 315 f., E. N. Gardiner, *Athletics of the Ancient
World*, pp. 95–96, and the same author's *Greek Athletic Sports
and Festivals*, pp. 229, 240, and Mehl and Willis cited on 104 f.
   In the introductory section to this first contest (114–50)
Virgil allows himself plenty of space to set the scene. There
is the description of the four competitors and their ships
(116–23); of the course and the arrangement for the turning-
point (124–31); of the drawing of lots for position, and the
appearance of the captains and the crews (132–5); of the
moment of waiting for the start (136–8); of the animated
scene at the actual start, with the simile from the more
familiar spectacle of chariot-racing (139–47); and of the
excitement of the spectators (148–50). Thus the interest is
built up for the long description of the race itself, which is
full of incident, with all four ships playing major parts in it.

114–15. 'For the first event four ships entered, well matched
with their heavy oars, and especially chosen out of the whole
fleet.' *Gravibus remis* is ablative dependent on *pares
carinae*; the ships are not all of the same size (see 119, 153),
but they are all of the same class (i.e. triremes) with an equal

number of rowers. Triremes did not exist in Homeric times; these are contemporary Roman ships (see on 828 f.).

116 f. The competitors have all been briefly introduced to us earlier in the poem, cf. 1. 222, 510, 612, 4. 288. Their characters as revealed in the race are discussed in Intro., pp. xiv–xv.

116. acri: a spondaic word in this position, with diaeresis both before and after the fourth foot, is rare in Virgil and generally gives emphasis to the word in question. It is one of the very marked differences between Lucretius and Virgil that Lucretius has it often, but Virgil goes out of his way to avoid it, writing *Arma virumque cano Troiae qui* and not *qui Troiae* (cf. for example in this book 190, 563, 597, 599). Other examples of a spondaic word filling the fourth foot are 156, 178, 191, 701, 751, 754, but in none of them is the preceding word so separate as in this line. See Conway on *Aen.* 1. 26, and compare note on 80 (initial spondees).

remige: collective singular, common with military terms like *miles, eques, pedes*.

Pristim: 'Leviathan'. This is a word of vague meaning, indicating some sort of sea monster, cf. *Aen.* 10. 211. There is also the form *pistrix* (*Aen.* 3. 427). The ships would have figure-heads representing their names; cf. *Aen.* 10. 195 f.

116–17. For the repetition of the name Mnestheus see note on 565–70.

117. A considerable number of Roman families traced their origins back to the Trojans: Servius (on 5. 389, 704) tells us that Hyginus and Varro wrote works *De Familiis Troianis.* Cf. 568, and see Mayor on Juv. 1. 100. The Roman *gentes* whose ancestors figure in the ship-race were not among the most highly distinguished: the best-known of the Memmii was the propraetor of Bithynia whom Catullus accompanied, and to whom Lucretius dedicated his poem; the most famous of the *gens Sergia* was Catiline; and we know relatively little of the Cluentii, one of whom was defended by Cicero. Servius tells us that the *gens Gegania* (of whom a number appear in the pages of Livy) was descended from Gyas; it is suggested that Virgil omitted mention of them because the family had died out by his time.

The philological justification for connecting the Memmii with Mnestheus seems particularly slight; evidently Virgil was thinking of μεμνῆσθαι and *meminisse*. Virgil's fondness for aetiological name associations was encouraged by the use made of them in Hellenistic poetry, and sometimes it is a reflection of simple antiquarian interest; but much more often it is directly related to the national theme of the *Aeneid*, to the

pride in Roman tradition which links the names and places
of the present with the events of the distant past. Compare
Atys and the Atii in 568, Acestes and Segesta in 718; and
Iulus and Ilium (1. 267, 288), Caieta (7. 2), Capys (10. 145),
Misenus (6. 233), Palinurus (6. 381; see note on 827 f.), and
the whole series of name associations in 8. 337 f. See Heinze,
Virgils Epische Technik, p. 373; and compare note on line
2 (etymologies).

genus . . . Memmi: 'from whose name comes the race of
Memmius'. *Memmi* is the normal form of the genitive
singular; cf. Lucr. 1. 42 *Memmi clara propago*, Hor. *Sat.*
1. 6. 12 *Laevinum, Valeri genus*, Manil. 1. 795 *Claudi magna
propago*. Others render 'from whom comes the race called
Memmii by name', but this seems clumsy, and gives an
unusual contracted form of the nominative plural.

118. ingentemque . . . ingenti mole: Wagner found it necessary
to justify this by explaining that *ingentem* refers to the ship's
overall size, and *ingenti mole* to its height. But the repetition
is a deliberate literary device, reminiscent of Hom. *Il.* 16. 776
κεῖτο μέγας μεγαλωστί; cf. line 447 *ipse gravis graviterque*,
Aen. 10. 842 *ingentem atque ingenti vulnere victum* (= *Aen.*
12. 640), Lucr. 1. 741, and note on 565–70. Henry and Page,
comparing Lucr. 4. 902 *(ventus) trudit agens magnam magno
molimine navem*, take *moles* in the sense of *molimen*, Henry
with *Chimaeram* and Page with *agit*. Page however adds
'Or perhaps *magna mole* is descriptive abl., "with its mighty
mass" ', and this is far more natural. Others take it with
Gyas, but cf. 223.

It is on this line that Henry has his famous note on *ingens*,
'our author's maid of all work'. Conway has some interesting
remarks on *Aen.* 1. 114, where he discusses the word and
stresses the idea of strangeness prominent in its meaning;
see also Austin on *Aen.* 4. 89.

Chimaeram: this fabulous tripartite dragon occurs first
in Hom. *Il.* 6. 179 f., a lion in front, a serpent behind, and
a she-goat in the middle. Servius *auct.* (ad loc.) tells the
story of how Bellerophon slew it.

119. urbis opus: a most remarkable phrase, which appears to
mean 'the size of a city'; Servius says 'ita magna ut urbem
putares'. Ovid imitates the phrase (*Fast.* 6. 641 *urbis opus
domus una fuit*) and so does Statius (*Silv.* 2. 2. 30 f. *inde per
obliquas erepit porticus arces, / urbis opus*). Henry argues
that the meaning is 'as intricate as a city', i.e. a city in
miniature, and this explanation would fit either of the
quoted passages. On the other hand in Stat. *Th.* 6. 86 (where
the reading *opus* must be correct) we have *montis opus*

cumulare pyram, and it is perhaps best to follow Servius. For the idea cf. Cic. *Verr.* 2. 5. 89 (*navis*) *quae si in praedonum pugna versaretur, urbis instar habere inter illos piraticos myoparones videretur.*

versu: 'tiers', 'banks' (of oars), cf. Livy 33. 30. 5 (*navis*) *quam sedecim versus remorum agebant.* For the much discussed question of the arrangement of oars in a trireme see *O.C.D.*, s.v., with references given there, and add J. S. Morrison, *The Mariner's Mirror*, 1941, pp. 14–44.

120. Henry hotly attacks Ribbeck for bracketing *terno . . . remi*, pointing out with much justification that it is an example of Virgil's favourite device of theme and variation. For the phraseology cf. Lucan 3. 534 (of biremes) *ordine contentae gemino crevisse Liburnae.* Notice the spondaic line, helping to suggest effort and size; see note on 136–41.

121. For the postposition of the relative after its verb see on 22.

122. magna: as *Centaurus* is the name of a ship, it is feminine.

123. For Virgil's use of apostrophe see on 840. This example, unlike the one in 840, is mainly a metrical device; compare 495.

124 f. The setting of the scene with the words *est procul in pelago saxum*, followed by the link with the narrative (*hic*, 129), is an example of a traditional epic type of descriptive passage (ἔκφρασις). Notable instances in Virgil are *Aen.* 1. 159 f. *est in secessu longo locus*, 7. 563 f. *est locus Italiae medio sub montibus altis*; see Austin on *Aen.* 4. 480 f., 483.

125. olim: 'at times', an archaic use, often (as here) as correlative to *ubi* or *cum*; cf. Plaut. *Trin.* 523, Lucr. 6. 148, *Geo.* 2. 403, 4. 421, 433, *Aen.* 8. 391, and see Page on *Aen.* 1. 289. Compare the use of *quondam* (e.g. *Aen.* 2. 367).

126. condunt ubi: for the order see on 22.

sidera: 'the heavens'; the word can have this meaning without specific limitation to night-time. See note on 627–8 and compare 517 (*astra*).

Cori: according to Pliny (*Nat. Hist.* 18. 338) these are north-west winds bringing storms; the word is sometimes spelled *Cauri*. Cf. *Geo.* 3. 278, 356.

127. tranquillo: 'in calm weather'. The neuter of the adjective is used as a noun (see on 851); the ablative is akin to 'time when' with words like *nocte, luce, hieme*, and also to ablative absolute phrases like *mari tranquillo, caelo sereno.* Cf. Livy 31. 23. 4 *tranquillo pervectus Chalcidem*, Sen. *Ep. Mor.* 85. 34 *tranquillo enim ut aiunt quilibet gubernator est*, Livy 31. 12. 5 *Priverni sereno per diem totum rubrum solem fuisse*; see

Kühner–Stegmann, ii. 1, pp. 778–80. Lejay suggests that *tranquillo* and *sereno* were seamen's technical terms.

127 f. 'and rises up from the still waves as a level expanse, a favourite resort for gulls basking in the sun'. *Saxum* is the subject of *attollitur*, and *campus* and *statio* are its predicates. The rock is pictured as a quite large flat-topped formation, not projecting far above the water. *Apricus* here means 'delighting in the sun': Servius says *apricos dicimus locis apricis gaudentes*, and quotes Persius 5. 179 *aprici . . . senes*; cf. Hor. *Odes* 1. 26. 7 *apricos necte flores*, Ov. *Met.* 4. 331 *hic color aprica pendentibus arbore pomis*. Compare the rare word *apricari*, e.g. Varro *Men.* 328 *licet videre multos cotidie hieme in sole apricari*.

129. metam: the regular word for the turning-point at *either* end of the track in a stadium or circus (hence *meta* can mean 'finish' as well as 'turning-point'). In *Il.* 23. 327 f. Nestor describes the turning-point in the chariot-race as a dry stump six feet high of oak or pine; here Aeneas uses a leafy oak (presumably a branch or young tree which could be wedged into the rock) to make the flat low rock more easily visible from a distance.

130. pater: the order is unusual, and perhaps draws attention to Aeneas' position of responsibility in the making of proper arrangements for the competitors. Page strongly supports this view; I would not myself wish to press it far. Cf. 424 and 521 (with note); and compare the more marked effect given by word order in lines like 841 (*deus*), *Aen.* 12. 412 (*genetrix*), 12. 871 (*soror*).

130–1. 'so that they should know where to make the turn for home, where to come round in their long course'; cf. *Aen.* 3. 429 f. *praestat Trinacrii metas lustrare Pachyni* / *cessantem, longos et circumflectere cursus*. The second phrase is a variation on the first; the first is a localized picture of the turn, the second gives a larger image of the whole race.

132. For the drawing of lots for position cf. *Il.* 23. 352 f. Clearly in any race round a turning-point, and particularly in a ship-race or a chariot-race, the inside position gives an advantage.

133. ductores: 'captains'. Each ship has its captain, its helms-man (*rector* 161), and its rowers.

134. populea . . . fronde: the poplar was sacred to Hercules, patron of athletes, cf. *Ecl.* 7. 61, *Geo.* 2. 66, *Aen.* 8. 276, Theoc. 2. 121. Servius *auct.* also suggests that as Hercules brought the poplar from the underworld it is appropriate to funeral games.

135. See E. N. Gardiner, *Athletics of the Ancient World*, p. 78, on the use of oil by athletes before exercise.

umeros . . . perfusa: the 'retained' accusative with a
passive verb, a construction of which Virgil is very fond, has
two quite separate roots. One is the ability of a passive verb
to govern a direct object in the manner of the Greek middle. We
find this in Plautus (e.g. *Men.* 511 f. *non ego te indutum foras /
exire vidi pallam?*), and it seems to have been inherent in the
Latin language, although no doubt it was Greek influence
which encouraged the poets to use and extend such a middle
construction. Compare *Aen.* 2. 275 *exuvias indutus*, 2. 392 f.
galeam . . . induitur, *Aen.* 7. 640 *loricam induitur*, Ov. *Met.*
2. 425 *induitur faciem cultumque Dianae*; in line 264 *indutus*
has a middle sense. We find this usage once in Livy (27. 37. 12
longam indutae vestem), and more frequently in Tacitus (e.g.
Hist. 2. 20 *bracas indutus*). For verbs other than *induere* cf.
line 608 *saturata dolorem*, and *Aen.* 4. 137 *chlamydem circumdata*, *Aen.* 12. 224 *formam adsimulata Camerti*. See
Kühner–Stegmann, ii. 1, pp. 288–9, Leumann–Hofmann, p.
378, Ernout–Thomas, p. 29, Palmer *The Latin Language*,
p. 288.

The other root is the Greek accusative of respect, for which
see on 97. In many instances in Virgil (like the present one)
the two Greek constructions merge, e.g. *Aen.* 1. 228 *lacrimis
oculos suffusa*, 1. 481 *tunsae pectora palmis*, 4. 589 *pectus
percussa decorum*, 4. 659 *os impressa toro*, 6. 156 *maesto
defixus lumina vultu*. In other instances the force of the verb
is purely passive, not middle, so that the accusative is one
of respect rather than a direct object, but even in these it is
reasonable to think that the idea of a retained accusative
contributed to making the usage acceptable. See Page's
Appendix to *Aeneid I–VI*, pp. 505–6, Page on *Aen.* 9. 478,
Conway on *Aen.* 1. 320, Maguinness on *Aen.* 12. 64–5.
Examples in this book (as well as 264, 608 mentioned above)
are 269, 309, 511, 774, 869.

136–41. Observe in this passage how the spondaic movement
of the first three lines conveys the pause and sense of waiting
for action, and is released by the rapid movement of 139–41,
where dactyls largely predominate. Very often the inter-
change of dactyls and spondees in Virgil is purely for the sake
of variety and should not be pressed as 'descriptive', that is to
say as a metrical reflection of the meaning of the passage; and
this may sometimes be the case with lines that are wholly
spondaic in the first four feet (72, 112, 183, 245, 282, 353,
366, 665), and even—though less often—with lines that are
wholly dactylic (285, 300, 564). On the other hand, when the
prevalence of spondees or of dactyls is sustained over several
lines (as here, cf. 20–21, 215–17, 468–71, 613–15), or is linked

with other effects like assonance, or sense pauses, or choice of colourful words (3 f., 204, 242, 484, 570, 651, 701, 813, 840), we are justified in seeing a descriptive purpose. See Marouzeau, *Traité de stylistique latine*, pp. 83 f., and compare notes on 5 f. and 866. There are rather more spondees than dactyls in the first four feet over the whole *Aeneid*—about 54 per cent. Ennius, Catullus, and Silius are more spondaic than Virgil, Ovid, Valerius, and Statius more dactylic. Some 7 per cent. of lines have spondees in each of the first four feet (there are 65 in this book, about 7½ per cent.); but only a little over 2 per cent. are wholly dactylic (16 in this book, just under 2 per cent.).

136–7. *Intendere* is here used in two slightly different senses: 'their arms are tensed on the oars, tensely they wait the signal'. Servius comments 'eodem sermone in diversis usus est rebus'. For Virgil's use of repetition see on 565–70.

137. exspectant signum: the sense pause after the third foot is rare (see on 623); here the elision at the sense pause helps to add to the feeling of expectancy which the rhythm and diction of these lines build up.

137–8. 'and the throb of nervous excitement and their eager longing for glory clutch at their leaping hearts'. These powerfully pictorial phrases are repeated from *Geo.* 3. 105 f., and are an elaboration of Hom. *Il.* 23. 370 f. πάτασσε δὲ θυμὸς ἑκάστου / νίκης ἱεμένων. *Pavor* does not mean 'fear', but the feeling akin to trembling experienced by an athlete when he is keyed up; *pulsans* ('throbbing') is suggested probably by Homer's πάτασσε; *haurire* here literally means 'to drain of blood'. Compare the far-fetched imitation of Virgil in Stat. *Th.* 1. 538, 10. 167 f.

139. dedit sonitum: see on 276 for Virgil's use of *dare*.
   finibus: 'starting-places', the *loca* of 132, cf. *limen* in 316.

140. haud mora: the parenthetical phrase is often used in juxtaposition with a main verb, cf. 368, *Aen.* 3. 207, 6. 177.

140–1. 'the shouts of the rowers ring out to the heavens, the waters are churned into foam as they pull right back on their oars'. Cf. *Aen.* 3. 128 *nauticus exoritur vario certamine clamor*, and the imitation by Prudentius, *Cont. Symm.* 2, *Praef.* 11 f. *clamor nauticus aethera / plangens atque ululans ferit*. The phrase *clamor nauticus* is generally explained as a reference to the shouting of time (κέλευμα) by the bo'sun, cf. Aesch. *Pers.* 396 f., Mart. 4. 64. 21. But Page well argues for a more general meaning in *Aen.* 3. 128, and it is therefore better not to confine the meaning here; cf. also Sil. 11. 487 f.

141. Cf. *Aen.* 10. 208 *spumant vada marmore verso. Adductis ... lacertis* means that the arms are brought up to the chest, cf. 507. Commentators discuss whether *versa* comes from *verrere* or *vertere*: the latter is far more likely, especially in the context of the following lines (*infindunt, convulsum*).

142. infindunt: a metaphor from ploughing, cf. *Ecl.* 4. 33 and the imitation of this passage by Valerius Flaccus (1. 687 f.) *volat immissis cava pinus habenis | infinditque solum et spumas vomat ore tridenti.* Compare *sulcare* in 158.

   dehiscit: 'is split open to its depths', a favourite word with Virgil of the earth (*Aen.* 4. 24) and the sea (*Aen.* 1. 106). The long vowel of the prefix *de-* is shortened before the following vowel; cf. *dehinc* (722), *praeeunte* (186).

143. The same verse occurs in *Aen.* 8. 690. *Tridentibus* refers to the three prongs on the prow of a ship, cf. Val. Fl. 1. 688 (quoted on 142) and Rich, *Dict. Antiq.*, s.v. *rostrum.*

144–7. 'Not with such headlong speed do chariots leap forward over the plain in a contest for paired horses, racing away as they come streaming out from the barriers; no, not when the charioteers shake out the rippling reins as they give free head to their teams, and lean right forward to use the whip.'

   Macrobius (*Sat.* 5. 11. 20) cites Hom. *Od.* 13. 81 f., where ships are compared with chariots; Virgil is of course influenced in his choice of simile by the fact that his ship-race is modelled on Homer's chariot-race; cf. *Il.* 23. 362 f. We have had a vivid description of the tenseness of the rowers and the churning of the water as they start; now Virgil adds the notion of speed by means of a simile drawn from a more familiar type of race. The simile has two images, the speed of the chariots (144–5), and the efforts of the charioteers to get more speed (146–7); these are linked by *nec sic*, not to convey a new comparison, but to reiterate and emphasize the idea of speed in the first image. The same two images are used in *Geo.* 3. 103 f., a very similar passage; the words *certamine . . . cursus*, with their very marked alliteration of initial *c*, are exactly the same as in the *Georgics* passage.

144. biiugo certamine: = *certamine bigarum. Bigae* is a contraction of *bis* and *iugum.*

145. corripuere: see on 316. For the variation of tense between the 'instantaneous' perfect and the present (*ruunt*) cf. 140 (with Page's note), 147, 243.

   carcere: this is the technical term for the starting-pens or barriers on a race course; it is more often plural in this sense (*Geo.* 1. 512), but Servius is wrong in saying that the singular is a neologism—Ennius has it twice, and Tibullus once. Ovid uses it quite frequently.

146–7. immissis . . . iugis: *immittere* in this sense occurs often with *habenas* (line 662), *frenos* (*Aen.* 11. 889); cf. also *Geo.* 2.

364, Prop. 3. 9. 58, Lucr. 5. 787. Servius commenting on *iugis* rightly says *pro equis iugalibus*; cf. Cic. *Verr.* 2. 3. 27 *qui singulis iugis arant.*

147. pronique . . . pendent: cf. *Aen.* 10. 586 f. *Lucagus ut pronus pendens in verbera telo / admonuit biiugos.* For *in* expressing purpose cf. lines 375, 402.

148–50. Virgil adds one more picture to the animated scene— the captains (132–3), the rowers (134–8), the churning water at the start (139–43), the speed with which they shoot forward (144–7); and now as the ships are under way, before the description of the race, we linger for a moment with the excited cheering crowd on the shore.

148. virum: for the form of the genitive plural see on 174.

studiisque faventum: 'rival cries of supporters', cf. 450. The archaic form of the genitive plural of present participles is for metrical reasons always used in hexameter verse, cf. Norden's note on *Aen.* 6. 200 *sequentum.*

149–50. 'the sheltered shores re-echo the noise'. The shores are *inclusa* by the foot-hills and cliffs. For *volutant* cf. *Aen.* 1. 725, 10. 98, Ov. *Met.* 12. 55.

150. resultant: 'reverberate'. Virgil seems to have coined this use of the word. Compare *Aen.* 8. 305 *consonat omne nemus strepitu collesque resultant*; the usage is taken up by later writers, cf. Stat. *Th.* 2. 714, Tac. *Ann.* 1. 65. 1. In *Geo.* 4. 50 we have the more logical use where the noise 'rebounds': *vocisque offensa resultat imago.*

151–82. *Gyas gets the lead, followed by Cloanthus, with Mnestheus and Sergestus contending for third position. As they draw near the turning-point, Gyas urges his helmsman Menoetes to steer closer in; but in fear of the danger of fouling the rock he does not do so, and Cloanthus' ship slips past on the inside. In a fury of anger Gyas throws Menoetes overboard; eventually he manages to clamber out on to the rock, while all the spectators are greatly amused by the incident.*

151 f. The description of the race is full of incident, and all four of the competitors play important parts in it, and leave a clear impression of their individuality (see Intro., pp. xiv–xv). We hear all of them speaking, except Sergestus whose situation speaks for itself. In the first part of the narrative all four are mentioned, and attention is concentrated on the first two (Gyas and Cloanthus). In the next section (183 f.) the struggle for position between the other two (Sergestus and Mnestheus) is described. Finally (225 f.) the last part of the race is between Cloanthus and Mnestheus, each the victor over his rival in the earlier stages.

151. primisque . . . undis: 'and sweeps ahead over the waves right at the beginning'. Others take it to mean 'the waves in front (of the other competitors)', but a reference to the beginning of the course is appropriate to the simile in 144 f. Compare *ultima . . . aequora* in 218 f. *Undis* is probably local ablative, rather than ablative of separation; the prefix in *elabitur* (as in *effugit*) means 'away from the other competitors', cf. the Homeric ἔκφερον ἵπποι (*Il.* 23. 376).

152. turbam inter fremitumque: 'amidst all the turmoil and noise' either of the spectators or of the competitors he is now leaving behind. Probably *fremitus* in line 148 makes the former preferable. For the anastrophe of the preposition see on 370.

153. melior remis: 'his crew are better together' (Day Lewis). It is strange that Cloanthus' ship is here said to be heavy by comparison with that of Gyas, which was specially mentioned for its size in 118 f. Observe the marked and retarding alliteration of *p* and *t* in *pondere pinus tarda tenet*.

  pinus: a very common metonymy (or synecdoche) for *pinea navis*; cf. *Aen.* 10. 206, and compare the similar use of *alnus*.

154. post hos aequo discrimine: 'equidistant behind them'.

155. locum . . . superare priorem: 'inter se, hoc est tertium' (Servius). They are trying to defeat each other in order to be third rather than fourth. The use of *superare* is unusual: some explain *locum* as a kind of cognate accusative, but I prefer Mackail's suggestion 'get forward into' (cf. *Aen.* 2. 303), *superare* being extended to mean *tenere superando*.

  tendunt superare: the infinitive with *tendere* is common in verse, and occurs in prose from Livy onwards: see note on 21–22. *Contendere* is used with the infinitive in Cicero and Caesar.

157–8. iunctisque . . . frontibus: 'prow to prow'; -*que* co-ordinates *una* with *iunctis frontibus*.

158. Cf. *Aen.* 10. 197 *et longa sulcat maria alta carina*. For the metaphor cf. 142. This line may appear at first sight to be something of an anticlimax; but it is often Virgil's way to add the pictorial image at the end of the narrative sentence when we might have expected it to be subordinated earlier on. Henry's spirited defence of the line should be read.

159 f. Compare the structure of *Aen.* 9. 371 f. *iamque propinquabant castris murosque subibant* / *cum* . . . For inverted *cum* see on 84–85; for the assonance of -*bant* see on 385–6.

159. tenebant: Mackail here and in 171 gives the verb the meaning 'were making for', which he argues that it has elsewhere in the *Aeneid*. Servius' comment 'nauticum verbum' perhaps supports this. But I think that in both lines in this passage the meaning 'reach' is called for by the context; cf. *Aen.* 6. 358 *iam tuta tenebam*, and *Aen.* 1. 400 *portum tenet*, with Conway's note.

160. medio: 'at the half-way stage'.

162–4. Day Lewis has:

> Why are you keeping so far out to starboard? Steer in! Port rudder!
> Hug the rock's edge! I want the port-side oarblades to graze it!
> Let the rest of them keep to deep water.

162. quo . . . abis: 'Hey! Where are you going to, so far off to the right?' *Quo* is 'whither', as is shown by the balance with *huc*; for *abire* cf. 166 and 318. The ships are making the turn in an anti-clockwise direction, i.e. to the left, as in a Roman chariot-race; cf. Ov. *Am.* 3. 2. 69 f.

mihi: ethic dative, here underlining the indignation of the speaker. Page drily says ' "Pray" and "Prithee" are accepted renderings, but a naval captain would perhaps put it otherwise'. On the ethic dative see Palmer, *The Latin Language*, p. 296. Essentially it indicates the concern of a person with the action defined in a sentence in which he does not otherwise figure. This is clearly seen in instances like Horace's *Quid mihi Celsus agit?* (*Epist.* 1. 3. 15); cf. line 646. Naturally it shades into the dative of 'advantage' or indirect object (cf. 391, 419) in sentences where a syntactical relationship of that kind is possible.

gressum: the best MSS. have *gressum*, but some (including the MSS. of Seneca *De Ben.* 6. 7. 1, where the line is quoted) have *cursum*. The weight of evidence here is interesting. In favour of *gressum* we can say (i) there is strong MS. authority; (ii) it is *lectio difficilior*; (iii) Aulus Gellius (10. 26) discusses the objection taken by Asinius Pollio to the use by Sallust in naval contexts of *transgressus, transgredi*. Against it we can say (i) that it has come in from another Virgilian passage where the context is not naval, such as *Aen.* 1. 401 or the very similar line at *Aen.* 11. 855 *cur, inquit, diversus abis? huc derige gressum.* (ii) that it is *lectio nimis difficilis*; (iii)—*ex silentio*—that the Virgil passage would have been most suitable for Gellius to quote in his discussion (he does quote Cato and Lucretius) if he had read *gressum* in this passage. On balance the grounds for abandoning the reading of the major MSS. are not sufficiently strong.

163. litus ama: 'hug the edge of the island', cf. Hor. *Odes* 1. 25. 3 f. *amatque | ianua limen.* Difficulty has been felt over *litus* applied to the rock, but it is large enough to be called *campus* (128), and Virgil uses a term applicable to an island.

laeva: this reading has better MS. support than *laevas*. The ablative *laeva* is commonly used in the adverbial sense of 'on the left', cf. *Aen.* 6. 486 *dextra laevaque frequentes*.

laeva . . . cautes: 'let the oars on the left graze the rocks'. The idea of passing very close to the turning-point was a familiar one in chariot-racing; cf. Hom. *Il.* 23. 334 τῷ σὺ μάλ' ἐγχρίμψας ἐλάαν σχεδὸν ἄρμα καὶ ἵππους, Soph. *El.* 720 f., and for *stringere* in this sense Ov. *Am.* 3. 2. 12 *nunc stringam metas interiore rota*, Sil. 16. 361 *sed laevo interior stringebat tramite metam.* For the parataxis *stringat sine* cf. line 717 and Livy 2. 40. 5 *sine . . . sciam, Aen.* 2. 669 f. *sinite instaurata revisam / proelia.* This is a somewhat colloquial use of *sinere*; it is found fairly often in Plautus and Terence, nearly always in the imperative. *Palmula* is a collective singular (cf. 116 *remige*); for the word cf. Cat. 4. 4 f. *sive palmulis / opus foret volare sive linteo*, 4. 17 *tuo imbuisse palmulas in aequore*, and for *palma* in this sense Cat. 64. 7 *caerula verrentes abiegnis aequora palmis.* Festus says 'palmulae appellantur remi a similitudine manus humanae'. Diminutives, which are fairly common in the *Eclogues*, are very rare in the *Aeneid*; see Austin on 4. 328 *parvulus Aeneas* for a full discussion with references, and cf. 842.

164. altum: 'the deep', a use of the adjective as a noun which is very common in poetry, and quite common in prose, nearly always in the singular. See also on 508.

165. pelagi . . . ad undas: 'seawards', 'vers le large' (Belles-sort); i.e. still outwards, instead of turning round the rock.

166–7. Servius mentions the possibility, which Mackail accepts, of punctuating so as to take *iterum* with *abis*; but it is much better to take it with *revocabat*, giving the sense of *iterum clamabat revocans.* The broken effect of the rhythm helps to express the haste and anxiety of Gyas, and this is accentuated by the very rare trochaic pause in the fourth foot of line 167; cf. 623, 871, note on 52, and Winbolt, *Latin Hexameter Verse*, p. 44.

166. Menoete: for the Greek vocative see on 843.

168. propiora tenentem: 'holding a course nearer in' (*sc. metae*, not, as Conington says, *Gyae*). The neuter plural of the adjective is here used as a noun of place; cf. 194 *prima*, 317 *ultima*, 335 *lubrica*, 338 *prima*, 825 *laeva*; compare also 180 and 695.

169. navemque . . . scopulosque: for doubled *-que* 'both . . . and') see on 92.

170. radit . . . interior: 'grazed his way through (scraped through) inside on the left'; cf. the passages cited on 163, and for *radere* cf. Ov. *Am.* 3. 15. 2 *raditur hic elegis ultima meta meis.* The phrase *radit iter* occurs in approximately this sense in *Aen.* 3. 700, 7. 10; in line 217 of this book its meaning is rather different.

171. 'and leaving the turning-point behind him reached safe waters'. *Metis* is poetic plural, see on 98; there is no very strong reason here for the preference of the plural. Conceivably Virgil wished to avoid the four *a* endings of *metā tenet aequora tuta relictā*, but cf. line 556. *Tuta* is in contrast to the danger he had been in when he took the turn so fine.

172. 'Then indeed the young man blazed with furious indignation in every fibre of his being.' The picture of the headstrong Gyas is very vividly drawn, especially in contrast with his safety-first helmsman. *Dolor* depicts his angry chagrin and grief at Menoetes' cowardice and its consequences. The word is given more emphasis by being made the subject; the ordinary expression would be *iuvenis exarsit dolore.* Compare *Aen.* 9. 66 *ignescunt irae, duris dolor ossibus ardet.*

173. Compare Hom. *Il.* 23. 385 (where Diomedes weeps when he loses his whip), line 343 of this book, and see Page on *Aen.* 1. 459.

   segnemque: 'timid', 'unenterprising'. Observe how emphasis is given by the word-order; first the object, then a whole line in apposition to the subject before the verbal action is described.

174. decorisque . . . salutis: 'both of his own dignity and of his crew's safety'. Servius drily says 'inhonestum enim irasci, duci praesertim'. For doubled *-que* ('both . . . and') see on 92. For the alliteration see on 866.

   sociumque: this form of the genitive is not a contraction for *sociorum*, but an early form surviving mostly in fixed expressions, through the medium of legal and religious formulae, in numerical phrases or with words denoting a class, e.g. *virum* (148), *deum, divum* (45), *superum, famulum* (*Aen.* 11. 34), *equum, iuvencum* (*Aen.* 9. 609). Virgil also uses it freely with proper names: *Argivum* (672), *Teucrum* (592), *Danaum, Graium, Pelasgum*, etc. He has it with one adjective, *magnanimum* (*Geo.* 4. 476, *Aen.* 3. 704, 6. 307). See note on 622 for the similar form in the first declension.

175. deturbat: 'pitches', a vivid and somewhat colloquial word, cf. Plaut. *Merc.* 116 *deturba in viam* ('kick him out'); Statius imitates Virgil's use in *Th.* 6. 485 *tunc ipsum fracto curru deturbat.* Contrast *proiecit* in 859, a more dignified word.

176. rector . . . magister: 'helmsman' and 'pilot'. The words
are practically synonymous, except that *magister* is a more
important-sounding title for the man at the helm; see Conway on *Aen.* 1. 115. *Magister* can also mean captain (though
it does not in Virgil), but that it means pilot here is made
certain by line 224; cf. also 867 and *Aen.* 6. 353.

   subit: for the dative see on 34 and cf. 346; for *subit* in the
sense of *succedit* cf. *Aen.* 6. 812 f. *cui deinde subibit / otia
qui rumpet patriae*, Ov. *Met.* 3. 648 f. *subit ipse meumque /
explet opus*, Stat. *Th.* 10. 183 *subit ad vidui moderamina clavi.*

177. hortaturque . . . clavumque: for doubled *-que* ('both . . .
and') see on 92.

   clavumque: 'tiller', 'fustem gubernaculi' (Servius). The
commentators make very heavy weather of this, insisting
that we must understand *clavus* as metonymy for *guber-
naculum* or *navis*. Henry says 'to have turned the tiller
towards the shore would have turned the vessel's course
towards the sea'. But the phrase simply means that he turned
the tiller for the shore, to reach the shore, and there is no
need to think of metonymy.

   litora: the shore from which the race had started, not (as
in 163) the rock marking the turning-point, because clearly
Menoetes in his wide arc must be round the rock by now.

178 f. 'But when at long last Menoetes in his sorry state was
returned to the surface from the bottom of the sea—he was
no longer a young man, and was dripping wet with his clothes
sodden—he made for the top of the island and sank down on
the dry rock.' The picture of Menoetes' helplessness is built
up by the epithet *gravis*, the exaggerated *fundo imo*, the
adverbs *vix tandem*, and the passive *redditus* (he could hardly
do anything about getting to the surface himself—he was
disgorged ·by the sea).

179. madidaque . . . in veste: cf. *Aen.* 6. 359 *madida cum veste
gravatum.*

180. summa . . . scopuli: for the adjective used in the neuter as
a noun and followed by a partitive genitive see on 695.

181-2. Notice the similarity of word endings (*-entem, -antem,
-entem*); cf. 220–2, 279, 468–70, 580–2, 852–3, and see note
on 385–6. A remarkable instance of assonance and rhyme
with present participles is *Aen.* 12. 903–4 *sed neque currentem
se nec cognoscit euntem / tollentemve manus saxumve immane
moventem.* For the intricate word-order see on 26–27.

   Virgil was perhaps thinking here (as he was in 357 f.) of
Il. 23. 784, where all the Greeks laugh at Ajax covered in the
slime in which he has slipped.

182. Compare the shipwrecked Odysseus in Hom. *Od.* 5. 322 f.

183–224. *Mnestheus and Sergestus now have new hope of passing Gyas. Sergestus gets slightly ahead and Mnestheus urges his men to put forward all their efforts to avoid the disgrace of coming in last. Sergestus goes in too near to the turning-point and runs aground, breaking his oars on one side. Mnestheus leaves him behind and soon overtakes Gyas too.*

183 f. Virgil now reverts to the two contestants for the third place, Sergestus in the *Centaurus* and Mnestheus in the *Pristis*. Sergestus is half a length ahead and on the inside when Mnestheus calls for a spurt; this causes Sergestus to try to hold him off by taking the turn too close in to the rocks, with disastrous consequences.

184. Mnestheique: this is the Greek form of the dative, (cf. *Orphei, Ecl.* 4. 57, *Geo.* 4. 553). The *e* would probably be slurred in pronunciation by synizesis (see on 352) rather than pronounced along with the *i* as a diphthong in the Greek fashion; cf. the synizesis in genitives like *Oilei* (*Aen.* 1. 41), *Ilionei* (*Aen.* 1. 120). Most of the MSS. give *Mnesthi*, which may be correct as a Latin form of the dative; cf. *Achilli* (*Aen.* 1. 475).

superare: for the infinitive dependent on a noun see Conway on *Aen.* 1. 704 *cura penum struere*, Page on *Aen.* 2. 10 *amor . . . cognoscere*, Kühner–Stegmann, ii. 1, pp. 743 f., and note on 21–22. This use of the infinitive was replaced in prose by the genitive of the gerund, but remained common in verse.

morantem: 'imperitia gubernantis' (Servius). Gyas is not doing so well without his helmsman.

185. capit ante locum: 'gets the lead'. *Ante locum* is equivalent to τὴν πρόσθε χώραν, the adverb being associated with the noun; cf. *Aen.* 1. 198 *neque enim ignari sumus ante malorum* (τῶν πρὶν κακῶν), Lucr. 5. 1371 *infraque locum concedere cultis*. See Leumann–Hofmann, p. 467, Fraenkel's *Horace*, p. 78, n. 1. It cannot mean 'gets the (inside) position first', because there is only half a length between them, and so no possibility of crossing over. Sergestus was in the inside position already, and now gets a slight lead as they approach the turning-point.

186. ille: this pleonastic use of *ille* in the second of two clauses which have the same subject is perhaps an imitation of the Homeric ὅ γε (as in *Il.* 3. 409 εἰς ὅ κέ σ' ἢ ἄλοχον ποιήσεται ἢ ὅ γε δούλην, *Od.* 2. 326 f. ἤ τινας ἐκ Πύλου ἄξει ἀμύντορας ἠμαθόεντος, / ἢ ὅ γε καὶ Σπάρτηθεν). Other examples in this book are 334 and 457 (where see notes); cf. also *Aen.* 1. 3 *multum ille et terris iactatus et alto*, 6. 592 f. *at pater omnipotens* *densa inter nubila telum | contorsit, non ille faces nec fumea taedis | lumina;* 9. 477 f. *evolat infelix . . . | . . . non illa virum non illa pericli | telorumque memor;* and 9. 796, 10. 385. In most of these examples it is clear (as Page says) that the use of *ille* draws marked attention to the subject, but in the line we are discussing it is difficult to see any such point, and the arguments urged by Servius and Henry (cited on 457) about metrical convenience are probably true here.

186–7. He is not a full length ahead; there is no daylight between. The visual image is made clear by the repetition of *prior, praeeunte, prior,* and of *parte, partim;* see on 565–70 for repetition in Virgil.

186. pra͞eeunte: the diphthong *prae* is shortened before the following vowel; cf. *Aen.* 7. 524 *sudibusve praeustis,* Ov. *Fast.* 1. 81 *iamque novi praeeunt fasces.* On the other hand Statius (*Th.* 6. 519) has *domino pra͞eiret Arion.*

    carina: the word properly means (as here and in 158) the hull or keel (which ran the whole length of the ship); it is very often used by metonymy to mean a ship (e.g. 115, 699).

187. partim: a form of the accusative, not the adverb. Some MSS. have *partem. Premit* means 'overlaps', 'is close upon', cf. *Aen.* 1. 324, 467. It certainly does not mean, as is sometimes suggested, 'scrapes against', as if this were a bumping-race.

188. media . . . incedens nave: 'pacing amidships', on the gang-plank or *agea.* Henry quotes Isidore, *Orig.* 19. 2. 4 '*agea* viae sunt, loca in navi per quae ad remiges hortator accedit'. Compare Ap. Rh. 2. 588 f. Εὔφημος δ' ἀνὰ πάντας ἰὼν βοάασκεν ἑταίρους | ἐμβαλέειν κώπῃσιν ὅσον σθένος.

189 f. With Mnestheus' speech compare that of Antilochus to his horses in Hom. *Il.* 23. 402 f., where he tells them that they cannot vie with the horses of Diomedes who is aided by Athene, but they must defeat Menelaus. The whole situation in Virgil is based on the Homeric incident in the chariot-race, when Antilochus tries to get past Menelaus in a narrow place. Antilochus succeeds because Menelaus gives way, and Virgil varies this by making Mnestheus succeed because Sergestus rashly goes in too close. The speech of Mnestheus is of a kind to win our sympathy, in contrast to the peremptory remarks of Gyas (162 f., 166), which did not endear him to us.

189. insurgite remis: cf. *Aen.* 3. 207, 3. 560, 10. 299, and ἐμβαλέειν κώπῃσιν in Ap. Rh. 2. 589 (cf. Hom. *Od.* 10. 129).

190. Hectorei socii: Servius gives two explanations, 'aut fortissimi qualis Hector fuit, aut re vera quondam Hectoris socii'. Most commentators prefer the second, but Heyne supports the first, probably on the ground that *socii* should have here its nautical sense ('my men', 'men of my crew'). I take the meaning to be *socii mei gentis Hectoreae*, and the adjective is used with the emotional overtone of calling for the utmost endeavours.

192 f. These three areas of sea through which Aeneas and his followers had come are in reverse chronological order. For the storm they encountered at the Syrtes (off Carthage) cf. *Aen.* 1. 102 f., especially 111, 146, and see note on line 51: for the storm in the Ionian sea cf. *Aen.* 3. 192 f., especially 211. Cape Malea (on the southern tip of the Peloponnese) is not mentioned in Book III, except that it occurs in the lines cited by Servius *auct.* after 3. 204; presumably they passed that area on their way from Crete to the Strophades. The Syrtes and Malea are coupled in Prop. 3. 19. 7–8 as proverbially dangerous to sailors.

192. The absence of any real caesura in the third or fourth foot of this line gives an unusual rhythm.

usi: *sc. estis.* The omission of the verb 'to be' in the second person is unusual, but cf. line 687, *Aen.* 1. 202, 237, 10. 827, and see Page on *Aen.* 2. 2.

193. Īŏnĭo: the adjective always has this scansion, though the noun is Īŏnĭa. See note on 571.

sequacibus: 'pursuing'. Servius says 'persecutrices', and Lactantius Placidus quoting this line on *Th.* 7. 16 says *ubi unda ita saeva est ut navigantes persequi videatur.* The image seems to be of the relentless ever-presence of the waves as the ship tries to get through the dangerous area. Cf. *Aen.* 8. 432 *flammisque sequacibus iras.*

194. prima: 'victory', see note on 168.

Mnestheus: his own name is introduced with some pathos in the humbling of his pride.

vincere: for the infinitive see on 21–22, and cf. *Ecl.* 5. 9. The usage after *certare* is common in verse.

195. quamquam o!——: the aposiopesis here effectively increases the pathos; cf. *Aen.* 2. 100, Quint. 9. 2. 54 ἀποσιώπησις, *quam idem Cicero reticentiam, Celsus obticentiam, nonnulli interruptionem appellant, et ipsa ostendit aliquid affectus vel irae, ut 'quos ego . . .' (Aen.* 1. 135). The unexpressed wish would have been something like *o si daretur superare;* cf. *Aen.* 11. 415 *quamquam o si solitae quicquam virtutis adesset.*

196. hoc vincite: 'win this victory', i.e. do not come in last; so Servius 'loco victoriae sit ultimos non redire'. That this is the correct rendering of a disputed passage is shown by the use of *vincere* in line 194, and of *hoc* in 195. Mnestheus does not now hope for first place—that must go to those to whom

Neptune has granted it; but not to come in last, let that be our victory. For the cognate accusative after *vincere* in this sense cf. Sil. 4. 429 *et primum hoc vincet, servasse parentem,* Ov. *Pont.* 3. 1. 31 *te magis est mirum non hoc evincere,* Val. Fl. 1. 248 f. Henry in a long and vigorous note maintains the meaning to be 'do better than this', and Page agrees. Others take *hoc* as ablative, which would make the phrase much less forceful.

197. prohibete nefas: 'save us from shame'; so Servius 'modo opprobrium'. Some have emphasized the religious meaning of the term in connexion with the religious significance of the games (e.g. Warde Fowler, *Roman Essays and Interpretations,* p. 190, Gossrau, ad loc.), but it seems more likely that Mnestheus is using the very strong word to exaggerate his feeling of shame. Cf. Hom. *Il.* 23. 408, where ἐλεγχείη is used.

    certamine summo: 'with utmost effort'; cf. *Aen.* 11. 891.

198. The rhythm of this line is unusual, and designed to help to convey the effort and rhythm of the rowers, so powerfully pictured in the phraseology of this and the following lines. There is conflict of ictus and accent in the first three feet, followed by coincidence in the remaining three. The fourth foot consists of a single dactylic word, the most decisive way of making the ictus and accent coincide (see A. M. Woodward, *Phil. Q.*, 1936, pp. 126 f.), and the effect is enhanced because the fifth foot also consists of a single dactylic word. There are only twenty-four instances in this book of a dactylic word filling the fourth foot; half of these are followed by another dactylic word, but only in two instances (this line and 840, where see note) is the third foot dactylic, and in both of them the effect is supported by alliteration (notice the *t* and *s* sounds in this and the following line). By itself of course a dactylic word in the fourth foot need not be intended to convey any imitation of the sense, or to do more than vary the movement of a passage (see note on 136–41); but when our expectation is aroused by the context, and other rhythmic and alliterative effects are present, we are likely to respond to a metrical feature which would not by itself necessarily be striking. For some examples cf. 84, 216, 219, 318–20, 377, 840.

    aerea puppis: cf. Ov. *Met.* 8. 103 *aeratas . . . puppes,* Hor. *Odes* 2. 16. 21, 3. 1. 39. Here as often *puppis = navis*; the reference is probably to the bronze on the beak.

199. subtrahiturque solum: 'the surface of the water slips from under them'; cf. Ov. *Her.* 6. 67 *caerula propulsae subducitur unda carinae.* On *solum* Servius remarks 'unicuique rei quod subiacet solum est ei cui subiacet, unde est solum navis mare, et aer avium'. The word does not seem to be used elsewhere of the sea; it occurs of the sky in Ov. *Met.* 1. 73 *astra tenent caeleste solum*, and cf. *Aen.* 7. 111 where *Cereale solum* is used of the 'tables' of bread on which the feast is set out.

200. sudor . . . rivis: cf. Hom. *Il.* 23. 688–9 ἔρρεε δ' ἰδρὼς / πάντοθεν ἐκ μελέων.

201. ipse . . . casus: 'mere chance', 'actually it was chance'.

202. animi: genitive rather than locative, as appears from Plaut. *Epid.* 138 *desipiebam mentis*. See on 73, and cf. Austin on *Aen.* 4. 203, Palmer, *The Latin Language*, p. 292, Löfstedt, *Syntactica*, i, pp. 172 f.

suburget: the word occurs only here before the fourth century. The prefix is clearly intended to stress the idea of closeness. Words which are found first in Virgil are mainly of a kind constructed along traditional lines: compounded verbs (as here), frequentatives (see on 470) and ingressives (see on 697), verbs formed from common adjectives or nouns (see on 16), adjectives in *-eus* (see on 510), *-alis* or *-ilis* (see on 559), *-bilis* (see on 591), *-osus* (see on 352), negative adjectives (see on 591, 627), some compound adjectives (see on 256, 452, 566), nouns in *-tor*, *-trix*, *-men*, and fourth declension nouns in *-tus* (see on 442). Other instances in this book of compound verbs not found before Virgil are *ingeminare* (227), *advelare* (246), *eiectare* (470), *exosus* (687), *debellare* (731), *superincumbere* (?) (858). Other compounds with *sub* which occur for the first time in Virgil are *subvolvere* (*Aen.* 1. 424), *subrigere* (4. 183), *subremigare* (10. 227). For other instances of rare or new words or usages (apart from those already cited) see on 142, 208, 269, 279, 395–6, 607, 689, 752, 765, 829, 842. Long lists of Virgil's innovations in the *Aeneid* are given by A. Cordier, *Études sur le vocabulaire épique dans l'Énéide*, pp. 143 f.; see also Palmer, *The Latin Language*, pp. 111 f., and M. Leumann, *Mus. Helv.*, 1947, pp. 116 f., and (for the Roman attitude to neologisms) Marouzeau, *Traité de stylistique latine*, pp. 177–8.

It is of course very important that when we find a word first occurring in Virgil we should not automatically assume that it must have been coined by him. It is necessary to reflect on how little pre-Virgilian poetry we possess out of what must have been written, in order to realize the inadequacy of the evidence for determining definitely whether or not any given word existed before Virgil used it.

203. spatioque subit . . . iniquo; 'and approached the danger area'. Sergestus (in the inside position) tries to hold off Mnestheus' spurt by taking the turn too close. *Spatio . . . iniquo* is probably dative after *subit*, cf. 346: it could also be taken as local ablative, *ad saxa* being understood with *subit*.

204. The spondaic movement, together with the unusually long word in the second half of the line, represents rhythmically the sad end of Sergestus' hopes.

205–6. Observe the pattern of alliteration in these lines, with the harsh *c* sounds giving an effect imitative of the sense, and the *p* sounds of 206 giving emphasis to the final words. The elision over the third-foot caesura without a supporting fourth-foot caesura contributes to the effect; see on 408.

205. acuto in murice: 'on the jagged edges'. *Murex* is the purple shell-fish with pointed shell, and the word here is used of pointed rock. Silius (17. 276) imitates Virgil's phrase. Cf. Pliny, *Nat. Hist.* 19 24 (*Cato*) *qui sternendum quoque forum muricibus censuerat*, and Isid. *Orig.* 12. 6. 50, 16. 3. 3 *murices petrae in litore similes muricibus vivis, acutissimae et navibus perniciosae*.

206. obnixi crepuere: 'grated at the impact'; as the rowers pull on the oars they meet the resistance not of water but of rock. Virgil uses *crepare* only here and in *Aen.* 11. 775 (of rustling linen); he prefers *crepitare* (lines 436, 459).

   inlisaque prora pependit: 'the prow, stove in, hung out of the water'; cf. *Aen.* 10. 303 f. (of Tarchon's ship) *namque inflicta vadi dorso dum pendet iniquo / anceps sustentata diu fluctusque fatigat / solvitur*.

207. magno clamore morantur: whatever this means, it cannot mean 'clamouring loudly at the delay' (Fairclough), the sense in which most commentators take it. The verb must be fully co-ordinate with *consurgunt*; they leap up and with loud shouting do something else. Servius gives 'retro agunt', 'back water', and this seems the correct sense. *Morari navem* may have been a technical term meaning to stop a ship, to hold her steady by reversing the oar movement, to prevent her moving any further in any direction. Compare the technical term *inhibere navem*, to row a ship backwards (a term which Cicero got muddled over, thinking it meant 'to stop rowing'; see *Ad Att.* 13. 21. 3, and his incorrect use of it in *De Orat.* 1. 153, cited on 218). Here then the rowers try to hold the ship steady with their oars.

208. trudes: a very rare technical word meaning a kind of pole for pushing off (Tac. *Ann.* 3. 46). Note the quantity *trŭdes*; the verb is *trūdere*, cf. *Aen.* 1. 144 f. *acuto / detrudunt naves scopulo*.

209. expediunt: 'get out', 'bring out', cf. *Aen.* 1. 177 f. *Cerealiaque arma / expediunt*.

210 f. This splendid picture of Mnestheus' ship sweeping

triumphantly onwards over the waves is given vividness by
means of the dove simile, and added emphasis by its position
between the two shorter passages (205–9, 220–2) describing
the disabled wreckage of Sergestus' ship.

210. acrior: 'inspired by', 'flushed by'.

211. agmine . . . celeri: 'with oars sweeping in swift rhythm'.
This is a vivid and unusual use of *agmen*, not exactly paral-
leled elsewhere. It seems to combine the meanings of *impetus*
(so Servius on *Aen.* 2. 782; see note on 90), and *series, ordo
incedentium* (its proper military meaning; see Servius on
Aen. 1. 186).

  ventisque vocatis: there is the same phrase in *Aen.* 3. 253,
8. 707. It is instrumental here, parallel with *agmine celeri*,
and means 'with the aid of the winds he had invoked to help
him'. It is clear from 281 that sails were not used in this
race, but obviously a following wind is advantageous for
rowing, and its effect is described in the lines which follow.
Observe the pattern of alliteration of the first letter of ad-
jacent words in this and the next three lines.

212. 'sets out for his shoreward course and speeds in over the
safe water', i.e. rounds the turning-point and makes for home
per pelagus apertum, with no rocky obstacles. *Prona* combines its literal meaning of 'sloping downwards' and its
metaphorical meaning of 'easy'. Virgil, like other authors,
uses it of a river's flow (*Geo.* 1. 203, *Aen.* 8. 548), and Henry
maintains that the point here is that the race took place
when the tide was coming in. But this is not necessary,
because (as Henry himself illustrates at some length) the
literal meaning of *pronus* here is connected with the feeling
that you sail up towards the high seas (*in altum*), and down
again (*decurrere*) to the shore. See note on 29, and Conway
on *Aen.* 1. 381; for *decurrere* cf. Livy 24. 36. 3 *Syracusas ex
alto decurrere*. Compare Ov. *Her.* 18. 121 f. (Leander to Hero)
ad te via prona videtur; | a te cum redeo, clivus inertis aquae.

213. The point of comparison in this very fine simile is that
Mnestheus' crew take rapid strokes at first and then speed
onwards under the impetus gained, just as the dove flaps
its wings furiously at the beginning of its flight and then
glides through the sky with wings outspread. Cf. the comparison of the Argo with a hawk swooping through the sky
in Ap. Rh. 2. 932 f.

214. latebroso in pumice: 'in crannied lava-rock'; there is the
same phrase in *Aen.* 12. 587.

  nidi: 'nestlings', by metonymy, cf. *Geo.* 4. 17 *ore ferunt
dulcem nidis immitibus escam, Aen.* 12. 475 *pabula parva
legens nidisque loquacibus escas*. The word is twice linked

with *progenies* (*Geo.* 1. 414, 4. 56), and there means 'nests';
here however the plural would not be suitable for the dove's
nest.

215–17. Day Lewis has:

First a loud, terrified clapping
Of wings as she breaks from cover, then through the noiseless
air
She fluently skims her way, gliding without a wing-beat.

For the first phrase cf. lines 505–6. *Tecto* could be ablative
of separation with *exterrita*, but it probably should be taken
as local ablative with *dat*. The word order supports this, and
so does the balance with *aëre quieto*. Notice how the rhythmical texture of this passage corresponds with the sense:
from *plausumque* to *ingentem* there is spondaic movement and
marked alliteration of *p* and *t*; then the rhythm changes to
dactyls, and line 216 (like 219) has its fourth foot composed
of a single dactylic word (see note on 198). With the dactylic
movement of 216–17, conveying the rapid flight of the dove,
there is alliteration of *l* and *r*. See note on 136–41 and
Marouzeau, *Traité de stylistique latine*, pp. 27–29; cf. *Geo.*
1. 409 *illa levem fugiens raptim secat aethera pennis*. Notice
how in dactylic lines which convey the jerkier speed of
running or galloping the alliteration of consonants is harsher
than here, e.g. *Aen.* 8. 596 *quadripedante putrem sonitu quatit
ungula campum*, *Aen.* 2. 731 f. *subito cum creber ad auris /
visus adesse pedum sonitus, genitorque per umbram* . . .

216. lapsa: 'gliding'; for the tense see on 708.
217. radit iter liquidum: 'skims her airy way'. In 170 the
phrase *radit iter* conveys the idea of closeness; here it has
moved a little in meaning to emphasize the light swift movement of the bird rather than its closeness to the ground (like
our word 'skim'). Both ideas can be seen in Ov. *Met.* 10.
654 *posse putes illos sicco freta radere passu*. *Liquidum* is an
epithet of the air (see on 525), here transferred to the bird's
path through the air. The first syllable of the word is always
short in Virgil; see on 238.

celeris neque: for the postposition of *neque* see on 5. It is
possible, but unlikely, that *celeris* is nominative with the
previous clause.
218. ipsa fuga: 'speeding along on her own'; *ipsa* suggests
that she has now no need of oars. Cf. Cic. *De Orat.* 1. 153 *ut
concitato navigio, cum remiges inhibuerunt, retinet tamen ipsa
navis motum et cursum suum intermisso impetu pulsuque
remorum, sic in oratione perpetua* . . . (see on 207 for this use
of *inhibere*). Notice how carefully this line and the next are

constructed to round off the simile: there is the threefold repetition of *sic* (see on 565–70), and in the last phrase there is coincidence of ictus and accent in the fourth foot (see on 5 f.), assonance of initial *i*, and the words at the caesura and the line-ending are in agreement (see on 385–6).

220. in scopulo . . . alto: Henry takes this to refer to the height of the rock from the sea-bed, but probably it simply means 'up on the rock', as even a jutting reef is high (fatally so) by comparison with the water around it.

220–1. The clauses are rather unusually interwoven: the order is *deserit Sergestum in scopulo et vadis luctantem et vocantem*; see note on 26–27. Observe the assonance of the three participial endings (see on 181–2).

222. 'taking a lesson in rowing with broken oars' (Day Lewis), which well renders the derisive humour.

224. spoliata magistro: 'deprived of her helmsman', see on 176, and cf. *Aen.* 6. 353 (*navis*) *spoliata armis, excussa magistro*.

225–43. *Mnestheus now makes a final spurt to catch Cloanthus, and would perhaps have succeeded had not Cloanthus prayed to the gods of the sea. His prayers are heard, and he reaches harbour, the winner of the race.*

225. iamque: for *iamque* postponed to second word cf. *Aen.* 3. 588 *postera iamque dies*, and note on 5. Here the effect is further to emphasize *solus*, already emphatic as a spondaic word filling the first foot (see on 80).

    superest: 'is left' (to overtake).

227 f. These lines are based on Hom. *Il.* 23. 766 f. where all the Achaeans shout for Odysseus who is just behind Ajax in the foot-race.

227. ingeminat: this word, which does not occur in earlier authors, is a favourite with Virgil both intransitively (as here, cf. *Aen.* 1. 747, 4. 531) and transitively as in 434, 457. See on 202.

227–8. cunctique . . . studiis: 'all urge on the pursuer with their shouts of support'; for *instigare* (the same root as *stimulus*) cf. *Aen.* 11. 730.

228. resonatque fragoribus: some MSS. have *resonat clamoribus* (from 227). For *fragor* of the human voice cf. *Aen.* 11. 214 and Quint. 8. 3. 3.

229 f. 'The leading crew think it shame not to hold on to the glory that is theirs and the triumph already won; they are ready to bargain life itself for fame.' For the interwoven word order see on 26–27. *Teneant* is semi-oblique: *putant indignum esse ni teneant*. For the last phrase cf. *Aen.* 12. 49 *letumque sinas pro laude pacisci*.

231. 'the others are given new strength by success; they can
do it, because they think they can'. Cf. Livy 2. 64. 6 *dum
se putant vincere, vicere*, and Dryden, *Ann. Mir.* 190 'And
seeming to be stronger makes them so'.

232. fors: the nominative is used elliptically (there was a
chance, they would have . . .), and the effect is equivalent to
an adverb, cf. *forsitan (fors sit an)*; compare *Aen.* 6. 537 *et fors
omne datum traherent per talia tempus*, 12. 183 *cesserit Ausonio
si fors victoria Turno . . . Fors et* is also used in this way,
cf. *Aen.* 2. 139, 11. 50. The usage is poetic, and relatively
rare. Cf. Milton, *P.L.* 2. 492 'If chance the radiant Sun . . .'

It is commonly thought that this line indicates that the
result would have been a dead-heat, but it is awkward to
supply *utrique* as the subject to *cepissent*, nor does *utrique
cepissent praemia* easily mean 'they would have shared first
prize'. It seems better to continue with the same subject
from *possunt*: 'and perhaps Mnestheus' crew, as they came
up level, would have gone on to win the prize . . .'

233. ponto: the use of the dative after *tendere palmas, tendere
manus* is confined in Classical prose to persons, where it is
a true indirect object: in an example like this one where
motion is implied we see the germ of the much bolder use in
451 (where see note). See also on 806; cf. *Aen.* 2. 688 *caelo
palmas cum voce tetendit*.

234. fudissetque . . . divosque: for doubled *-que* ('both . . .
and') see on 92.

divosque in vota vocasset: 'called on the gods to hear his
prayers'; cf. 514, *Aen.* 12. 780 *dixit, opemque dei non cassa in
vota vocavit*.

235–8. The frequency of elision in this speech is marked,
especially of syllables ending in *-m*. Virgil used elision, particularly heavy elision, more frequently than the other
hexameter poets, and this is one of the ways in which he
avoided monotony of movement. Approximate figures for
the number of elisions (excluding aphaeresis of *est*) per hundred lines are: Virgil 51 (*Eclogues* 27, *Georgics* 48, *Aeneid* 53),
Silius 44, Lucretius 43, Statius 38, Catullus (hexameter
poems) 35, Valerius 29, Ovid, *Met.* 21, Lucan 13, Claudian 6.
Figures for heavy elisions (long vowels or syllables ending
in *-m*) are: Virgil 25, Silius 17, Catullus 16, Statius 15,
Lucretius 13, Valerius 10, Ovid, *Met.* 3, Lucan 3, Claudian
1. These figures are in some instances based on samples, but
they are accurate enough to give the general picture of the
practice of these hexameter poets. See also Winbolt, *Latin
Hexameter Verse*, pp. 179 f. For some examples of pictorial
elision see notes on 404–5, 422, 613–15, 623–35.

235 f. Compare Odysseus' prayer to Athene when he was just behind Ajax in the foot-race (Hom. *Il.* 23. 768 f.).

235. di . . . pelagi: cf. *Aen.* 6. 264 *di quibus imperium est animarum.*

   aequora: accusative of extent of space, a usage which developed from the cognate accusative in phrases like *navigare aequor.* Compare *Aen.* 3. 191, and 1. 524 with Page's note; see on lines 627–8, and cf. 862 *currit iter.*

237. voti reus: 'in discharge of my vow'. The phrase is discussed in Macr. *Sat.* 3. 2. 6. *Voti damnari* occurs several times in Livy; cf. also *Ecl.* 5. 80 (of the god) *damnabis tu quoque votis.* The man whose prayer is answered is under an obligation to pay what he has promised; he is a defendant in regard to it, liable for it. The genitive with *reus*, like the genitive with *accusare, arguere, damnare,* etc., is common in prose; it is a genitive of 'sphere in which', see note on 73.

237–8. Compare the very similar lines 775–6.

238. proiciam: the technical term for offering sacrificial entrails to the gods, cf. Naev. *fr.* 36 (Marmorale) *simul atrocia proicerent exta ministratores,* Livy 29. 27. 5 *secundum has preces cruda exta caesa victima, uti mos est, in mare proiecit.* Macrobius (*Sat.* 3. 2. 2) and Servius (ad loc.) discuss the word and its orthography. Macrobius urges strongly that the correct form in religious contexts is *porricere,* quoting Veranius *exta porriciunto, dis danto, in altaria* . . . In view of this, and in view of the strong possibility that this word is cited by Quintilian as one of Virgil's archaisms (see note on 10), I would prefer to accept the less familiar form *porriciam* in spite of the very strong MS. support for *proiciam.*

   liquentia: Virgil more often has the *i* long in this verb (e.g. *Aen.* 1. 432, 9. 679); it is short here and in 776, and in *Geo.* 4. 442. Lucretius always has it long. On the other hand *liquescere* has a short *i* both in Lucretius and Virgil. The adjective *liquidus* has a variable first syllable in Lucretius (e.g. Lucr. 4. 1259 *crassaque conveniant liquidis et liquida crassis*), but Virgil always has it short (e.g. 217). On these words in Lucretius see Bailey, *Proleg.,* p. 131; see note on 571 for other variations of quantity in Virgil.

239 f. The description of the deities of the sea, who hear Cloanthus' prayer and give him victory, closes the long and exciting account of the race with a pictorial touch of a most attractive kind, a delightful glimpse of strange pageantry.

239. eumque: the word *is* occurs rarely in poetry, especially in the oblique cases. See Axelson, *Unpoetische Wörter,* pp. 70 f., and Austin on *Aen.* 4. 479 *quae mihi reddat eum vel eo me solvat amantem.*

240. Virgil is fond of this kind of descriptive line made up of sonorous names; compare lines 823 f., and note on 822 f. Phorcys, an old man of the sea, and Panopea, one of the Nereids, occur again there in the description of Neptune's retinue.

241. This line is closely modelled on Ennius *Ann.* 569 V (cited by the Verona scholiast on this passage) *atque manu magna Romanos inpulit amnis*; cf. Hom. *Il.* 15. 694 f. (of Hector) τὸν δὲ Ζεὺς ὦσεν ὄπισθε / χειρὶ μάλα μεγάλῃ, and for the whole picture cf. Ap. Rh. 2. 598 f., where Athene pushes the Argo through the Symplegades, and it shoots forward like an arrow. The long lists in Macrobius (*Sat.* 6. 1) give an excellent idea of the large extent to which Virgil used reminiscences of Ennius (cf. 302 and see notes on 10 and 422); see also C. M. Bowra, *C.Q.*, 1929, pp. 65 f., and E. Norden, *Ennius und Vergilius*, Leipzig, 1915, especially pp. 153 f.

Portunus: 'deus portuum portarumque praeses' (Varro, quoted by the Verona scholiast). At first Portunus seems to have been closely associated with Ianus, but later he was identified with Palaemon (Melicertes), as god of harbours; cf. Ov. *Fast.* 6. 547 *quem nos Portunum sua lingua (sc. Graeca) Palaemona dicet*, and see note on 823 f.

242. Observe the rhythm of this line, beginning with a 'run-on' verb before a strong pause (cf. 444 for a similar effect, and note on 480), and continuing with rapid dactylic movement (see note on 136–41).

244–85. *Aeneas distributes prizes to the crews of the three ships and their captains. When this is completed, Sergestus finally manages to bring home his disabled ship, moving slowly like a maimed snake; he duly receives his fourth prize.*

244. satus Anchisa: a fairly frequent phrase for Aeneas (line 424, *Aen.* 6. 331). *Satus* in this sense is poetic, and is generally followed by the ablative of origin without a preposition.

246. advelat: this compound occurs first in Virgil (and not again in Classical Latin). Similar extremely rare compounds first found in Virgil are *adtorquere* (*Aen.* 9. 52), *addensere* (10. 432), *adlacrimare* (10. 628); see also note on 202.

247–8. These are the prizes to be divided among the crew of each ship, namely three bullocks, some wine, and a talent of silver for each crew. Cf. 61–62 *bina boum . . . capita in navis.* *Optare* means three bullocks of their choice (out of the herd).

optare . . . ferre: the use of the Greek epexegetic infinitive after *dare* is here influenced by Hom. *Il.* 23. 512 δῶκε δ' ἄγειν. Virgil is in any case fond of the infinitive after *dare* (and *donare*), both in this sense (cf. 262, 307, 538, 572, and *Aen.*

1. 319 *dederatque comam diffundere ventis*, with Conway's
note), and in the slightly different sense of *Aen.* 1. 66 *mulcere
dedit*, cf. 1. 79 *tu das epulis accumbere divum*, 1. 522 f., 6. 66 f.,
6. 697, 11. 789, and line 689. Kühner–Stegmann (ii. 1, p.
681) gives long lists of this usage, which is very similar to the
infinitive of purpose, an old Latin use which survived in verse
while in prose it was almost wholly superseded. For related
poetic uses of the infinitive see index.

248. magnum ... talentum: there is no special significance in
magnum, as *magnum talentum* is a usual phrase for a talent
(the normal Attic talent, cf. *Aen.* 9. 265). Compare 'a golden
guinea'.

249 f. Virgil considerably varies his method of describing the
prizes for the various contests, and only once exactly coin-
cides with Homer (see on 266). The first prize here is described at some length, as a beautiful work of art; the second
prize is also given prominence, but not so much by its actual
description as by its history. The third prize and the consolation prize for Sergestus have shorter mentions. In the
foot-race Aeneas himself briefly describes the prizes before
the race; in the boxing they are briefly described in the narrative. In the archery they are not specified at all; but the
special prize which Aeneas awards to Acestes is given particular prominence by its association with Anchises and its
early history. Thus in the course of the games our attention
is especially drawn to the first two prizes awarded and to the
last one of all.

250. chlamydem: a cloak of Greek type, here embroidered with
gold: cf. *Aen.* 4. 137 *Sidoniam picto chlamydem circumdata
limbo.* It was a commonly worn garment in fifth-century
Athens, but very rare with the Romans.

250–1. 'round which ran a deep border of Meliboean purple
with its double wavy line'. For the anastrophe *quam . . .
circum* see on 370. *Meliboeus* (from the town in Thessaly) is
used of purple in Lucr. 2. 500: for the formation of the adjective *Meliboeus* from *Meliboea* cf. *Aen.* 1. 686 *laticemque
Lyaeum* (with Conway's note), 3. 689 *Megarosque sinus*,
6. 877 f. *Romula . . . tellus*, and Page and Mackail on 4. 552
cineri promissa Sychaeo. For Virgil's fondness for geographical association in description see on 306. Mackail is inclined
to accept Servius' explanation of *duplex* as *flexuosus*, i.e.
doubling upon itself; but as *Maeandro* itself conveys this,
it seems more natural to take *duplex* to mean that there were
two interweaving wavy lines ('double key-patterned border'
—Day Lewis). The word *Maeander*, from the river proverbial
for its twists and turns (cf. Ov. *Met.* 2. 246, 8. 162), is used

once by Cicero to mean a winding course—*Pis.* 53 *quos tu Maeandros . . . quae deverticula flexionesque quaesisti?*; cf. Aul. Gell. 16. 8. 17 *in illis dialecticae gyris atque Maeandris*. For *cucurrit* cf. Hom. *Il.* 6. 118 ἄντυξ ἣ πυμάτη θέεν ἀσπίδος, and for the whole line *Il.* 23. 561 f. (θώρηξ) ᾧ πέρι χεῦμα φαεινοῦ κασσιτέροιο / ἀμφιδεδίνηται. Compare also the close imitation by Statius (*Th.* 6. 540 f.) *at tibi Maeonio fertur circumflua limbo / pro meritis Admete chlamys repetitaque multo / murice*, where *Maeonio* means 'winding', *Maeonius* being an epithet of the Meander.

252 f. 'Woven on it was the young prince on leafy Ida, hunting down the swift deer with the javelin, speeding eagerly after them, breathless as if in real life.' Ganymede, the young and beautiful son of the Trojan prince Tros was carried off from Mt. Ida by Jupiter's eagle to be cup-bearer to the gods: cf. Hom. *Il.* 20. 232 f., *Aen.* 1. 28, Ov. *Met.* 10. 155 f. This passage is imitated in Stat. *Th.* 1. 548 f., and Val. Fl. 2. 414 f.

254. acer: the pause after a trochee in the first foot with a 'run-on' word is fairly common (cf. 506, 669, 834) though not nearly so common as after the dactyl of the first foot (see on 480). See Winbolt, *Latin Hexameter Verse*, p. 10.

anhelanti similis: i.e. so life-like that you might forget it was a picture, cf. *Aen.* 8. 649 f. (the picture of Porsenna on Aeneas' shield) *illum indignanti similem similemque minanti / aspiceres*, and Claud. *R.P.* 1. 257 f.

254 f. This is of course a second picture of Ganymede on the *chlamys*. Heyne and Wagner find difficulty over it; but it was quite normal to describe works of art containing a number of scenes, so that Virgil has not felt it necessary to say explicitly that this is a different picture from the first. Descriptions of works of art (ἐκφράσεις) occur in poetry from Homer onwards (e.g. Achilles' shield in *Il.* 18. 478 f.), but they were especially favoured in Hellenistic poetry (e.g. Jason's cloak in Ap. Rh. 1. 730 f., the carved cup in Theoc. 1. 27 f., where see Gow). Notable Roman examples are the embroidered coverlet in Cat. 64. 50 f. (where see Ellis), the pictures on Juno's temple at Carthage in *Aen.* 1. 466 f., the pictures on the door of Phoebus' temple in *Aen.* 6. 20 f., and the shield of Aeneas (*Aen.* 8. 625 f.). Compare also the imitation of this passage in Stat. *Th.* 6. 540 f. The instances in Virgil are discussed by Heinze, *Virgils Epische Technik*, pp. 398 f.

254. ab Ida: the repetition of the word *Ida* from 252 seems weak, and suggested emendations are *ab alto* (Burman), *ab aethra* (Schrader, cf. Val. Fl. 1. 156). But, as Henry insists, the prepositional phrase should go with *rapuit*, not with *praepes*;

cf. Hor. *Odes* 3. 20. 15 f. (of Ganymede) *aut aquosa | raptus ab Ida*. Mackail sees in this repetition an indication that the passage was unrevised. The Romans were not as sensitive about unintentional repetitions as we are (cf. Quint. 8. 3. 51, 10. 1. 7), but it is probable that Virgil would have removed instances like this when he noticed them in revising. Compare the repetition of *spatium* in 316–27, of *iubere* in 385–6, of *extulit* in 424–7, of *magnum munus* in 532–7, of *fessus* in 715–17, and see note on 572. On this subject see Mackail, Intro., p. lxxx, Sparrow, *Half-Lines and Repetitions in Virgil*, pp. 60 f., Henry on *Aen.* 1. 29, Austin on *Aen.* 4. 409, Marouzeau, *Traité de stylistique latine*, pp. 261 f., esp. 265–6, where a number of examples are cited. For intentional repetition in Virgil see on 565–70.

255. Cf. Aen. 9. 563 f. *qualis ubi aut leporem aut candenti corpore cycnum | sustulit alta petens pedibus Iovis armiger uncis*; *Aen.* 1. 394, 12. 247. The eagle is *armiger* because it carries the thunderbolt: cf. Hor. *Odes* 4. 4. 1 f. *qualem ministrum fulminis alitem | cui rex deorum regnum in avis vagas | permisit expertus fidelem | Iuppiter in Ganymede flavo . . .*, Ov. *Met.* 12. 555 f., 15. 386. Pliny (*Nat. Hist.* 2. 146) records the belief that eagles are not struck by thunderbolts.

256. Notice how the spondaic movement of this line describing the helplessness of Ganymede's guardians contrasts with the rapid dactyls of the previous line about the eagle.

longaevi: this compound adjective (= μακραίων) occurs 14 times in Virgil but is not found earlier. Norden however (on *Aen.* 6. 141) argues that it occurs in Virgilian passages which may come from Ennius, and that *grandaevus* is found in Lucilius, so that it seems likely to be an archaic word rather than an invention of Virgil's. For compound adjectives see on 452; for new words in Virgil see on 202.

256–7. Cf. Stat. *Th.* 1. 550 f. *stant maesti comites, frustraque sonantia lassant | ora canes umbramque petunt et nubila latrant*.

258. For the position of *deinde* see on 14.

virtute: 'by his prowess'. Servius here affords a good example of how a commentator can press a poet too hard: '*virtute*: quia ille favore vicerat numinum; unde et praemia dantur congrua; illi chlamys, deorum continens fabulam, huic lorica, id est virtutis insigne'.

259. 'interwoven with burnished chain and triple-meshed in gold', i.e. a coat of mail. Cf. *Aen.* 3. 467 (with Page's note), 7. 639 f., 11. 487 f. *Trilix* is from *licium* = thread; the word *bilix* occurs in *Aen.* 12. 375. Servius *auct.* on *Aen.* 3. 467 defines *trilix* as *trino nexu intexta*. See Rich, *Dict. Antiq.*, s.v. *tela*.

259–60. The assonance and half-rhyme (*consertam . . . trilicem loricam quam . . .*) is here rather harsh. See note on 181–2.

260. Cf. Hom. *Il.* 23. 560 θώρηκα τὸν Ἀστεροπαῖον ἀπηύρων. Demoleos is not otherwise known: there is a Trojan Demoleon in *Il.* 20. 395. For the dative see on 845.

261. Simoenta: the two rivers of Troy were Simois and Xanthus (the latter was also called Scamander, cf. Hom. *Il.* 20. 74). Simoenta is the Greek accusative of Σιμόεις; cf. 634 and note on 536.

Ilio alto: in this line with its Homeric subject-matter Virgil uses a line ending reminiscent of Greek rhythm, with the final syllable of *Ilio* shortened in hiatus. Such shortening is regular in the Greek hexameter, but very rarely imitated by the Romans. Instances in Virgil are *Geo.* 1. 281 *ter sunt conati imponere Pelio Ossam*, *Geo.* 1. 437 *Glauco et Panopeae et Inoo Melicertae*, *Geo.* 4. 461 *flerunt Rhodopeiae arces*, *Aen.* 3. 211 *insulae Ionio in magno*, and *Ecl.* 2. 65, 6. 44, 8. 108, *Aen.* 6. 507. For hiatus without shortening see on 735.

262. The old punctuation was *donat habere viro, decus . . .* Schröter's correction is a great improvement because *huic* in 259 is the indirect object of *donat*, and *viro* would be intolerably weak with it. For the trochaic sense-pause in the second foot we may compare 32, 121, 145, 315, and possibly the unfinished line 653; see Winbolt, *Latin Hexameter Verse*, p. 25. For the infinitive *habere* see on 247–8; for the whole line cf. Hom. *Il.* 15. 533 (a breastplate given tò Phyleus) ἐς πόλεμον φορέειν, δηΐων ἀνδρῶν ἀλεωρήν.

263. Sagaris and Phegeus were both killed by Turnus (*Aen.* 9. 575, 765); Trojans called Phegeus also occur in Hom. *Il.* 5. 9 f., *Aen.* 12. 371 f.

264. conixi umeris: the elision of a long syllable before a short is not uncommon with an opening spondee in the first foot (58 *ergo agite*, 380 *ergo alacris*), but it is rare in any other place in the line. In Virgil's successors in hexameter poetry and in the elegiac poets (see Platnauer, *Latin Elegiac Verse*, pp. 73 f.) its rarity outside the first foot is extreme; there are no instances in Lucan, some half-dozen each in Ovid, Silius, and Valerius, twenty-odd in Statius. The *Aeneid* has about forty instances, e.g. 2. 708 *ipse subibo umeris*, 11. 680 *pugnatori operit*, 11. 618 *extemplo turbatae acies*, 9. 367 *interea praemissi equites*, 6. 145 *ergo alte vestiga oculis*.

264–5. indutus . . . agebat: 'but in days gone by Demoleos used to run wearing it, as he went in pursuit of Trojan stragglers'. *Indutus* here has a middle sense, cf. *Aen.* 7. 640 *loricam induitur*, and note on 135. For the postposition of *at* see on 5.

265. Troas: the Greek third declension form of the accusative

plural, with short *-as*, cf. *lebetas* in the next line. Other
words in Virgil of similar form are *crateras, delphinas, thoracas,
Arcadas, Cycladas, Cyclopas, Garamantas*; see on 536 and cf.
613.

266. A shining cauldron was third prize also in Homer's
chariot-race (*Il.* 23. 613). This is the only point of close
similarity of prizes between Homer and Virgil; see W. H.
Willis cited on 104 f. (*fin.*).

267. cymbia: small drinking cups, cf. *Aen.* 3. 66, 9. 263 (a very
similar line). *Aspera signis* is equivalent to *caelata*, 'embossed'; cf. 536 and Ov. *Met.* 12. 235 *signis exstantibus asper*.

268. adeo: intensifying *iamque*, and so emphasizing the transition in the narrative; cf. line 864 and *Aen.* 2. 567.

269. tempora: for the 'retained' accusative see on 135.

   taenis: the Latin form of the Greek ταινία is not common.
It means 'ribbons', and the reference here is to purple
ribbons attached to the *virides coronae* of 110. Servius says
'significat lemniscatas coronas, quae sunt de frondibus et
discoloribus fasciis'. The ablative plural is here contracted;
it is possible that it should be spelled *taeniis* and scanned as
a dissyllable by synizesis (see on 352).

270–2. cum . . . agebat: the imperfect is not common in an
inverted *cum* clause (see note on 84–85). Here it pictorially
represents the slowness and difficulty with which Sergestus
got restarted: 'they were all parading with their prizes when,
look, Sergestus began to bring back his ship . . .', or 'when
there was Sergestus, bringing back his ship . . .' Compare Cic.
Verr. 1. 17, 2. 2. 89, Sil. 13. 1 f., and (slightly differently)
Geo. 4. 429 f., *Aen.* 3. 301 f. Notice how the sentence is built
up with descriptive dependent clauses while the main verb
and the subject are held up until 272.

270. revulsus: 'worked himself off' (Day Lewis). *R* has
revolsam, but the application of the word to Sergestus has
a vivid effect. In any case *debilis* in the next line shows that
revulsus is right. Servius says 'bene ex mutatione conquisivit
ornatum; nam inrideri et sine honore esse hominis est, remis
carere, navis'.

271. ordine debilis uno: this might mean one of the three banks
of oars on the side which had fouled the rock, but it is more
likely that it means all the oars on the one side.

272. 'amidst derision began to bring back his inglorious craft'.

273. For snake similes and descriptions see on 84. The point
of comparison here is the maimed movement, but Virgil
develops the picture of the snake beyond the actual point of
comparison.

   qualis saepe: a condensed expression for *qualis ut saepe*

fit, cf. line 527, *Aen.* 1. 148, 8. 353, 10. 723, and Munro on
Lucr. 5. 1231.

    viae . . . aggere: probably 'on the causeway', referring to
a road raised slightly above the level of the surrounding
countryside. The phrase might also mean 'on the crown of
the road', as Roman roads were sometimes constructed with
a slight slope from the middle to both sides, but this seems
less likely.

274. obliquum . . . transiit: 'has run over as it came from the
side'. The image is of a snake appearing suddenly on the
road from the side; cf. Hor. *Odes* 3. 27. 6 f. (*serpens*) *si per
obliquum similis sagittae / terruit mannos.*

274–5. gravis ictu . . . viator: an unusual transference for *gravi
ictu . . . viator*. The double disyllable at the end of the line,
causing conflict of word accent and ictus in the fifth foot
(see note on 5 f.), puts emphasis on to *gravis*, and helps to
convey something of the feeling of force and violence. Virgil
uses this type of line ending only about once in a hundred
lines: the nature of the effect caused by it depends largely
of course on the importance of the words involved—compare
this line, for example, with 382. See Austin on *Aen.* 4. 336
and 420, Norden's *Aeneid VI*, pp. 446–8, Wilkinson, *C.Q.*,
1940, p. 35. Other instances in this book are 382, 414, 615,
628, 672, 731 (a more striking type, see note there), 756,
808.

275. saxo: Mackail comments on the awkwardness of the two
ablatives *ictu* and *saxo*. Henry, followed by Page, suggests
that *saxo* is local ablative ('half-dead on the road'), but this
greatly strains the meaning of *saxum*. We must take it as
instrumental with *seminecem*, helped a little by *lacerum*.

276 f. 'In vain as it tries to get away does it writhe its body
in great curves, part of it defiant, eyes blazing, hissing head
raised high; but part is crippled by the wound and dragging,
and it twines itself (see on 279) in knots and coils back upon
itself.'

276. dat . . . tortus: a use of *dare* of which Virgil is very fond,
cf. 139, 435, and Virgilian phrases like *dare motus, dare saltum,
dare fragorem, dare amplexus, dare dicta*; see Maguinness on
Aen. 12. 69 *talis virgo dabat ore colores.*

277. sibila colla: a line ending of this kind, where noun and
adjective are in agreement with similar endings, is not very
common in Virgil; cf. 735 *casta Sibylla*, and (with longer
words) 82, 146, 643, 656, 671, 729. See Austin on *Aen.* 4. 96,
and note on 81. For the poetic plural *colla*, very frequent
in poetry, see on 98.

278 f. Observe the alliteration of *a*, *n*, and *s*, and the rhyme

nexantem . . . plicantem (see on 181–2). For the picture cf.
Geo. 3. 420 f., *Aen.* 2. 381 f., 475.

278. arduus: the adjective is used adverbially with the participle (not a prose usage); cf. 567, 764, 838, and *Aen.* 8. 299
arduus arma tenens, 11. 755 *arduus insurgens*, 12. 902 *altior insurgens*, 8. 559 *inexpletus lacrimans*.

279. nexantem: this very rare alternative form of *nectentem*
would mean 'twining (itself)'; but the good MSS. except *R*
(the O.C.T. apparatus is wrong about *V*) read *nixantem*,
which is greatly to be preferred. This is a form of *nitentem*,
'struggling'; cf. Lucr. 3. 1000, 4. 506, 6. 836. For Virgil's
use of frequentative verbs see on 470.

280. tarda: for the adverbial use see on 33.

281. vela . . . velis: for the repetition see on 565–70. For the
phraseology cf. *Aen.* 1. 400 *pleno subit ostia velo*.

282 f. This passage recalls Homer's account of how Achilles
gave a prize to Eumelus who came in last in the chariot-race
because of the accident which befell him, *Il.* 23. 534 f.

284. Cf. Hom. *Il.* 23. 263 θῆκε γυναῖκα ἄγεσθαι ἀμύμονα ἔργα
ἰδυῖαν and *Il.* 23. 704 f.

  olli: see note on 10.

  datur: the final short syllable is lengthened in arsis, that
is to say by the metrical ictus of the foot. Lengthening of
this kind nearly always occurs either before the main caesura
or before a break in sense, or both: in some instances the
vowel involved was (or could be) long by nature in earlier
Latin. Other examples in this book are *Euryalŭs* (337), *patĕr*
(521), *amittebāt* (853); see also note on 451. For examples
parallel to *datŭr* cf. *Geo.* 3. 76, *Aen.* 1. 668, *Aen.* 4. 222, *Aen.*
2. 411; parallel to *Euryalŭs* cf. *Geo.* 3. 189, 4. 453, *Aen.* 12.
232; parallel to *patĕr* cf. *Aen.* 12. 13 and *Ecl.* 9. 66, *Aen.* 6.
254; parallel to *amittebāt* cf. *Ecl.* 1. 38, *Aen.* 7. 174, 10. 383,
12. 772. Instances where Virgil is perhaps reverting to an
archaic long vowel include *amittebāt* (as is evident from
Ennius, *Ann.* 371 V *non enim rumores ponebāt ante salutem*),
and words like *pavōr* and *labōr*, and forms like *subiīt*. Platnauer (*Latin Elegiac Verse*, p. 61) compares the use of
wreath'd or wreathéd, wĭnd or wīnd, in Victorian poetry.
On the whole subject see Austin on *Aen.* 4. 64 and works
cited there, and Nettleship's Excursus in Conington's edition
(iii, pp. 486 f.), where the examples are conveniently set out.

  Minervae: for Minerva as the patron of women's work cf.
Aen. 7. 805, 8. 408 f.

285. genus: Greek accusative of respect, common in Virgil with
parts of the body (see note on 97), but otherwise rare. Cf.
Aen. 8. 114 *qui genus?*, Tac. *Ann.* 6. 9 *clari genus*.

286–314. *Aeneas now leads the assembled company away from the shore to a grassy plain surrounded by hills, suitable for the remaining contests. He invites competitors for the foot-race, and many Trojans and Sicilians enter for it. He promises gifts to all the runners, and announces the prizes which will be awarded to the first three.*

286 f. The foot-race is modelled on *Il.* 23. 740–97, but where Homer has only three competitors (Ajax, Odysseus, and Antilochus), Virgil has seven named and countless unnamed runners. The main feature of the race, the fall of Nisus, is taken from *Il.* 23. 773 f., where Ajax slips in the dung left by sacrificed animals; and there are other reminiscences, noted ad loc. (see on 324, 325, 327 f.). For the foot-race in ancient times see E. N. Gardiner, *Athletics of the Ancient World*, chap. ix; cf. also his *Greek Athletic Sports and Festivals*, pp. 270 f., and his discussion of the subject in *J.H.S.*, 1903, pp. 267 f. For character and incident in Virgil's race see note on 315–19, and Intro., p. xv.

286. pius: Aeneas' epithet here indicates his position of responsibility as being in charge of the ceremonies and the games in honour of Anchises. It has not the powerful overtones with which it is sometimes charged elsewhere, in Book IV for example. See on 26.

   misso : equivalent to *dimisso*, implying that the prize-giving and concluding arrangements of the ship-race have been duly carried out; cf. 545 and Cic. *Ad Fam.* 5. 12. 8 *ante ludorum missionem*. See on 41 for the use of simple verbs instead of compounds in poetry.

287 f. The alliteration of *c* and *q* in the words *campum . . . cingebant* is very considerable, and yet most readers will feel there is no imitative effect here, nor even any special emphasis intended. See note on 866 for a discussion of how alliteration is effective particularly when other circumstances have prepared the reader for its effect; Tennyson is reported to have said that he sometimes had 'no end of trouble to get rid of the alliteration'. Some warnings about over-readiness to see imitative effect in alliteration are given by O.J. Todd, *C.Q.*, 1942, pp. 29 f.

288–9. theatri circus: 'the circle of a theatre'; the hills surrounding the circular plain give the appearance of an enormous natural 'theatre', which can be used as a stadium with the audience on the slopes. It is of course a different place from the *circus* of 109. As Page points out, the word *theatrum* is used in its widest sense (a place for seeing, θεᾶσθαι), not in the special sense in which it differs from *amphitheatrum* or

circus. Virgil is probably picturing in his mind a contemporary Roman circus, perhaps the *Circus Maximus*; and
he uses terms appropriate to its elaborate arrangements for
spectators in 340 and 664.

289–90. 'To this the hero moved off accompanied by many
thousand people, himself in the midst of the concourse, and
took his seat on a platform.' This is a difficult sentence, and
there has been much doubt about the words *consessu* and
exstructo. Servius took them together and said: 'ordo est:
quo se Aeneas medium tulit cum multis milibus et exstructo
consessu resedit'. But (i) such a hyperbaton would be
intolerably harsh and most un-Virgilian; (ii) *consessus*, as
Henry points out, means 'audience' rather than 'auditorium'
(cf. 340, 577), and although in certain contexts these two
words may become roughly equivalent, the nature of the
word *consessus* is such as to make it a most inappropriate
object of the verb *exstruere*. It seems fairly certain that
exstructo is to be taken as equivalent to a noun ('a structure',
'a platform'); cf. *suggestum* (from *suggerere*) used in this sense
by Cicero, and see note on 6. For *consessu* emendations have
been proposed: Klouček suggested *consessum in medium*,
and Gossrau conjectured *consessum* (supine); but the word
medium would be very awkwardly placed in this case. Most
editors retain *consessu* and regard it as dative (for the dative
in *-u* cf. *Geo.* 4. 158, *Aen.* 9. 605); but the notion of 'motion
towards' has already been expressed in this sentence by *quo*.
It is best to take it as ablative, closely with *medium*: 'central
figure in the assemblage', i.e. with the audience of many
thousands about him. We need not feel any difficulty over
the slightly proleptic use of *consessus* applied to a crowd
of people on their way to watch something. Compare the
very similar lines 75–76, and see E. Adelaide Hahn,
T.A.Ph.A., 1956, p. 170.

291–2. This sentence is somewhat loosely constructed; cf.
563 f. The word *animos* is added to the sentence to stress the
enthusiasm and spirit required of intending contestants;
consequently the antecedent to *qui* has to be supplied as
eorum rather than *eos*, which the run of the sentence had led
the reader to expect. The lines are very similar to 486: this
is clearly an unrevised passage, see next note.

294. There are six other incomplete lines in this book, 322, 574,
595, 653, 792, 815. This is slightly above the average—there
are about fifty-nine in the twelve books (the number is not
certain because some half-lines have been apparently filled
up by scribes). It is hardly possible to draw any firm conclusion about the dating or state of revision of individual

books from the incomplete lines: the largest number (ten) is
in Book II which in some respects is one of the most carefully finished books, but clearly was undergoing yet further
revision. For a full discussion see Sparrow, *Half-lines and
Repetitions in Virgil*, and Austin on *Aen.* 4. 44. It is most
probable that Virgil would have completed these lines had
he lived to finish his revision of the *Aeneid*; indeed some of the
complete lines in the *Aeneid* may be said to consist of a half-
line completed by a temporary *tibicen*. But it is also true that
some of the half-lines as they stand are extremely effective,
and it is just possible (though difficult) to maintain that Virgil
would have retained some as a deliberate technical device.
Euryalus, who appears only here and in the ambush scene
in Book IX, is one of the most tenderly drawn characters in
Virgil; here and in line 322 his name occurs in an incomplete
line, and so again in 9. 467—almost as though Virgil found it
hard to get the words he wanted for Euryalus.

295. viridique iuventa: cf. *Aen.* 6. 304 (of Charon) *iam senior,
sed cruda deo viridisque senectus*. In the nominative Virgil
uses the common word for 'youth', *iuventus* (and occasionally *iuventas*): but in the oblique cases he always uses *iuventa*
because of the metrical convenience. The same is true of
senectus and *senecta* (395).

295-6. The construction is *Nisus (insignis) amore pio pueri*.
Servius gives as an alternative *viridique iuventa Nisus
(insignis), amore pio pueri*, with *pueri* as nominative plural.
But clearly *viridique iuventa* is the attribute of Euryalus
(cf. *Aen.* 9. 181), and Nisus is portrayed as an older man, who
calls Euryalus *puer* in *Aen.* 9. 217.

297 f. Diores, son of Priam, was killed by Turnus (*Aen.* 12.
509). Salius and Patron, the two Greeks, presumably both
joined Aeneas when he was with Helenus at Buthrotum in
Epirus (*Aen.* 3. 292 f., 295 *Priamiden Helenum Graias
regnare per urbis*). Dionysius (1. 51) tells us that Patron, an
Acarnanian, was sent by Helenus to accompany Aeneas when
he left Buthrotum. Servius *auct.* (on *Aen.* 8. 285) tells of a
story that the Salii (dancing priests) were founded by Salius,
an Arcadian who joined the Trojans; and Isidore (*Orig.* 18.
50) attributes this story to Varro. The Salius of *Aen.* 10. 753
is different, apparently an Italian.

299. Tegeaeae: some MSS. read *Tegeae de* (with a consequential
alteration to *Arcadia*), and Servius discusses both readings.
But *Tegeaeae* is a word particularly likely to lose a syllable by
haplography and is undoubtedly the correct reading. The
adjective occurs also in *Geo.* 1. 18, *Aen.* 8. 459.

300. Trinacrii iuvenes: Sicily was called Trinacria (393, 555) from its three promontories. For Helymus see on 73; Panopes is not mentioned elsewhere.

Panopesque: Virgil has polysyllabic endings with Greek proper names some fifty times (cf. 448, 492, 761, 826 with note) and twenty-nine times with other Greek nouns (e.g. *hymenaeus, hyacinthus, cyparissus, elephantus*): see Norden's *Aeneid VI*, p. 438. It is not so much that Virgil allows himself this licence when the words are otherwise intractable as that he welcomes the opportunity of introducing the unusual rhythm under the fixed conditions which he imposed upon himself. Except under Greek influence Virgil uses poly-syllabic endings very rarely, and for special effect; see on 320, 589.

302. Macrobius (*Sat.* 6. 1. 61) quotes this line as adapted from Ennius (*Scen.* 49 V): *multi alii adventant, paupertas quorum obscurat nomina*. See note on 241.

305. nemo: the word occurs only four times in Virgil—three times in this book (349, 383), and in *Aen.* 9. 6. The final syllable is always elided or at the end of a line, and Axelson (*Unpoetische Wörter*, pp. 76–77) argues that the rarity of the word in epic was due to metrical considerations, i.e. a feeling of uncertainty about the quantity of the -*o*. It occurs five times in Ovid's *Metamorphoses*, three times in Silius, twice in Statius' *Thebaid*, not at all in Lucan or Valerius Flaccus.

mihi non donatus: Homer's ἀγέραστος. This is a good example of how the dative of the agent (cf. 360, 610) is very often in some other kind of dative relationship to the sentence: here *mihi* is as much ethic ('I will see to it') as agent with *donatus*.

306. Gnosia: the title generally given to geographical adjectives of this kind is 'literary' or 'ornate' epithet. Virgil was very fond of adding colour by local allusion (see note on 448–9, Austin on *Aen.* 4. 70, Page, Intro. to *Bucolics and Georgics*, pp. xxv f.). Here, of course, the local allusion has a specific point in the fame of Cretan archers; cf. *Geo.* 3. 345 *Cressamque pharetram, Aen.* 11. 773 *spicula . . . Gortynia, Ecl.* 10. 59 f. *libet Partho torquere Cydonia cornu / spicula*. The word *spicula* can mean javelins or arrows, but the association with Crete indicates the meaning here.

307. ferre: 'to take away'; for the epexegetic infinitive see on 247–8.

308. hic: for the scansion see on 73.

unus honos: *unus* is used in the sense of *idem*, cf. 616. Virgil always has the nominative form *honos* (not *honor*), cf. 763. See Austin on *Aen.* 4. 4.

309. flavaque: the word describes the yellow-green colour of the olive (cf. Aesch. *Pers.* 617 ξανθῆς ἐλαίας), rather than the yellow pollen whose claim Henry powerfully urges.

caput: for the construction see on 135.

310. phaleris: 'trappings'. The word is used of decorations worn by soldiers (*Aen.* 9. 458, Juv. 16. 60, where see Mayor) or of the trappings which adorned horses' heads (Livy 22. 52. 5, Juv. 11. 103).

habeto: this form of the imperative, sometimes called the future imperative, has a legal and formal ring about it, and is appropriate for Aeneas' proclamation (cf. 314 *abito*). Virgil often uses the similar form for the second person in didactic passages in the *Georgics* (e.g. *Geo.* 2. 408 f.).

311-12. Amazoniam . . . Threiciis: these 'ornate' epithets (see on 306) also have a specific point, in that Penthesilea and her Amazons fought for the Trojans (*Aen.* 1. 490 f.), and the Thracians too were Trojan allies (*Aen.* 3. 13 f.).

312-13. The shoulder belt (or baldric) which held the quiver was studded with gold (cf. Ov. *Met.* 9. 190 *Thermodontiaco caelatus balteus auro*) and fastened with a buckle (*fibula*); cf. *Aen.* 12. 273 f. *teritur qua sutilis alvo | balteus et laterum iuncturas fibula mordet*. For *subnectit* cf. *Aen.* 4. 139 (Dido's brooch) *aurea purpuream subnectit fibula vestem*.

315-39. *Nisus gets well ahead in the foot-race, but as he nears the finish he slips in a pool of blood. While lying on the ground he trips up Salius who was second, so that his friend Euryalus comes up from third place to win.*

315 f. For the sources of the foot-race and other references see on 286 f.

315-19. The punctuation of the O.C.T. is the traditional one, given in all editions of the *Aeneid*. There are, however, strong grounds for believing that the punctuation of line 317 should be altered so that the passage reads as follows:

> Haec ubi dicta, locum capiunt signoque repente
> corripiunt spatia audito limenque reliquunt,
> effusi nimbo similes. Simul ultima signant
> primus abit longeque ante omnia corpora Nisus
> emicat . . .

The reasons for making this change are given by F. H. Sandbach, *C.R.*, 1957, pp. 102-3, where the development of the race is fully and most convincingly explained. With the traditional punctuation not only was the phrase *simul ultima signant* virtually incomprehensible, but the whole picture of the race was abrupt in the extreme. Virgil appeared to give an account of the start and of the final stages of a race without any indication of the passage of time in the middle.

If, however, we punctuate as printed above, making *simul* a conjunction, then the clause *simul ultima signant* indicates the passage of time and shows at what point Nisus went away from the field. I had myself formed this view of the passage, and made the same alteration in punctuation; but whereas Sandbach says for *simul ultima signant* 'as soon as they begin to trample the last stretch', I had taken it to mean 'as soon as they come in sight of the goal', and had considered the race to be round a turning-point. I have discussed this further on 317–18. With the new punctuation Virgil gives us a picture of the start and of the runners sweeping in a body over the first part of the course (*nimbo similes*; like the mass of a storm cloud, i.e. in a tight bunch, see on 317); then as soon as they near the finish Nisus goes away in front and opens up a big gap. The general picture of the race is now like the chariot-race in *Il.* 23. 373 f.; Homer has given only a brief and unspecific account of the first part of the race and he begins to describe it in detail on the way back at the point where the real effort was made. Finally the imitation by Silius (16. 488 f.) shows that he understood the Virgilian race in this way: *extulit incumbens medio iam limite gressum | Eurytus et primus brevibus sed primus abibat | praecedens spatiis.*

316. corripiunt spatia: 'they dash over the course', a poetic use of *corripere*. Cf. 145 and *Geo.* 3. 104, *Aen.* 1. 418, 6. 634. *Rapidus* is, of course, related to *rapere*.

limenque relinquunt: *limen* here means the starting-point. It was probably simply a line drawn across the track, so that the technical term *carcer* (see on 145) would be inappropriate. Henry (on 317) sees in line 316 'another instance of that ὕστερον πρότερον so familiar to Virgil', of which the classic example is *Aen.* 2. 353 *moriamur et in media arma ruamus*. But Page (*C.R.*, 1894, p. 203) has well objected to the baldness of the grammatical term (which seems to imply a perverse reversal of the proper order), and he argues that in these cases the second clause is often explanatory of the first. The clause which is placed first is the one more important in its imagery to the poet. In this book compare 379 and 403. Norden (*Aeneid VI*, pp. 378 f.) has an interesting discussion of the usage, showing how it is one aspect of Virgil's fondness for the juxtaposition of main verbs in preference to subordinate clauses; for this see note on 101–3.

But in any case it is very doubtful whether the present line is an instance of our so-called ὕστερον πρότερον. The meaning of *relinquunt* is probably not 'set out from', but 'leave behind them', 'draw away from', with the idea of

increasing distance; cf. *Aen.* 4. 154 f. *agmina cervi / pulveru-
lenta fuga glomerant montisque relinquunt*; 7. 7 *tendit iter
velis portumque relinquit*; 8. 125 *progressi subeunt luco
fluviumque relinquunt*; Caes. *B.G.* 5. 8 *longius delatus aestu
orta luce sub sinistra Britanniam relictam conspexit.*

317. nimbo: Henry, Page, and others say that the point of the
simile is that the competitors shoot off like raindrops falling
from a cloud; they compare *Geo.* 4. 312 where the bees burst
forth *ut aestivis effusus nubibus imber.* But there is a lot
of difference between *nimbus* and *effusus nubibus imber*; and
in any case the point of the comparison is that the rapidly
moving massed runners are like the rapidly moving mass of
a storm cloud as it comes across the sky (see on 315 f.).
Compare *Aen.* 12. 450 f. *ille volat campoque atrum rapit agmen
aperto. / qualis ubi ad terras abrupto sidere nimbus / it mare
per medium*; 7. 793 f. *insequitur nimbus peditum clipeataque
totis / agmina densentur campis.*

317–18. If the traditional punctuation is retained (see on 315)
no real sense can be made, and Mackail (ad loc.) speaks of an
unintelligible stop-gap. The most common explanation,
which is generally admitted to be unsatisfactory, is 'at the
same time they fix their eyes on the goal'. But this is an
unparalleled use of *signare*, and the phrase would add nothing
to the description of the race from the spectator's point of
view. Other suggestions are (i) 'they (i.e. officials) mark out
the finish'; the nameless officials obtrude strangely here, and
what kind of race is it when the finish is not marked out until
the race has started? (ii) 'At the same time the last trumpets
sound' (Henry)—but this is a most improbable use of *signare*, and do they sound after the race has started? That
would be a ὕστερον πρότερον indeed. (iii) 'They at once
indicate the outcome' (Magoun, *T.A.Ph.A.*, 1901, p. lxxx),
i.e. take up the positions which they would have finally
occupied except for the unfortunate accident to Nisus and its
unfortunate consequences for Salius. But this is extremely
flat, and it is doubtful whether it can be got out of the Latin.
For additional refutation of some of these views see Sandbach, loc. cit. on 315.

The clause *simul ultima signant* is then a subordinate one,
and we may translate 'as soon as they begin to tread the last
stretch, Nisus goes away in front'. The use of *simul* as a
conjunction is, of course, Virgilian; cf. *Ecl.* 4. 26 f., *Geo.* 4.
231 f., *Aen.* 3. 630 f. Much better sense is thus given to *abit*,
which now means 'goes away in front', not 'gets away first';
cf. Sil. 16. 489 (quoted on 315 f.), and line 162 of this book.
In support of his interpretation of *signant* as *signant pedibus*

Sandbach cites Ov. *Am.* 2. 11. 15 *litora marmoreis pedibus signate, puellae,* Hor. *A.P.* 158 f. *pede certo / signat humum,* Stat. *Th.* 4. 257, 6. 904, Sil. 4. 147; and he draws attention to Servius' alternative explanation 'signant vestigiis' which has been generally overlooked because of the absurdity of his associated explanation of *ultima*: 'culmorum scilicet summitatem'. It is true that there is much more point in the notion of 'trampling' in the parallels cited than there is here, and that Virgil has used a word which seems rather too colourful for his purpose, but that is a small point compared with the incoherence of the whole passage in the older interpretations.

Another possibility is that the race was round a turning-point and that *simul ultima signant* means 'as soon as they come in sight of the finish', i.e. just past the turn. *Signare* would then be used in the sense of *discernere*, rather like *Aen.* 2. 422 f. *primi clipeos mentitaque tela / agnoscunt, atque ora sono discordia signant.* If the race was longer than 200 yards (which seems certain), Virgil would most naturally think of the δίαυλος (400 yards out and home). We know that this figured in Augustus' Actian Games (see Reisch, *R.E.,* s.v. *Aktia*). From Virgil's narrative it appears that the runners both start near Aeneas and finish near him. Homer's races were round turning-points, and Virgil perhaps understood the line in the description of the foot-race (*Il.* 23. 758 τοῖσι δ' ἀπὸ νύσσης τέτατο δρόμος) to mean—as it well may, though the point is disputed—'they went full out once they had passed the turning-point'. In this case he could have felt that the picture of a race in which the runners make their effort just after the turning-point was already in his readers' minds, and that the phrase *simul ultima signant* would be understood without explicit mention of a turning-point. But as the evidence is inconclusive I do not press the case for a δίαυλος.

317. ultima: for the use of the neuter plural see on 168.

318–20. These three lines have the same sequence of dactyl, spondee, spondee, dactyl in the first four feet, and in all of them the fourth foot consists of a single dactylic word; the marked coincidence of ictus and accent in the fourth foot gives the impression of speed. See on 198.

318. omnia corpora: Lejay has a good note on this periphrasis for *omnes*. The effect here is to make us think pictorially of the running figures as Nisus goes ahead of the field.

319. For the wings of the thunderbolt cf. Aristoph. *Birds* 1714 πτεροφόρον Διὸς βέλος, and Val. Fl. 2. 97, 6. 56.

320. longo sed: for the postposition of *sed* see on 5. Here the effect is to emphasize *longo*, already very emphatic because it repeats *longe* (318) in the same position in the line.

longo sed proximus intervallo: cf. Cic. *Brut.* 173 *L. Philippus proximus accedebat, sed longo intervallo tamen proximus.*

intervallo: a spondaic fifth foot occurs in Virgil very rarely (some thirty-five times altogether), more often than not with a Greek word (cf. 761). It is always associated with a polysyllabic ending (except for the Ennian phrase *et magnis dis* in *Aen.* 3. 12, 8. 679); see notes on 300 and 589. It is often combined with some other metrical irregularity of a Greek pattern (e.g. *Aen.* 9. 9 *petīt Euandri*, 9. 647 *Dardanio Anchisae*). The *neoterici* affected this rhythm; cf. Cicero's amusing remark (*Ad Att.* 7. 2. 1) *ita belle nobis 'flavit ab Epiro lenissimus Onchesmites'. hunc* σπονδειάζοντα *si cui voles* τῶν νεωτέρων *pro tuo vendito.* Catullus has thirty examples in the 408 lines of his sixty-fourth poem (including three in succession), but Lucretius has only about the same number in more than 7,000 lines. See Winbolt, *Latin Hexameter Verse*, pp. 128 f., for details of its extreme rarity in Silver Age epic, and Platnauer, *Latin Elegiac Verse*, pp. 38 f., for its very limited use in elegiacs.

Virgil was no doubt led to use this particular spondaic ending by the precedent for it in Lucretius (2. 295 *copia nec porro maioribus intervallis*, 4. 187 *quae quasi cuduntur perque aeris intervallum*), and perhaps also because the phrase was a semi-proverbial expression. But it is also possible that Page was right in seeing an onomatopoeic reflection of the idea of distance in the line rhythm, though I do not feel that in this particular instance any such imitative effect is very prominent. Examples of spondaic endings (other than with Greek words and proper names) include *cara deum suboles, magnum Iovis incrementum* (*Ecl.* 4. 49), *saxa per et scopulos et depressas convallis* (*Geo.* 3. 276), *constitit atque oculis Phrygia agmina circumspexit* (*Aen.* 2. 68), *cornua velatarum obvertimus antemnarum* (*Aen.* 3. 549), *aut levis ocreas lento ducunt argento* (*Aen.* 7. 634), . . . *discedens chlamydemque auro dedit intertextam* (*Aen.* 8. 167), *quae quondam in bustis aut culminibus desertis* (*Aen.* 12. 863). The degree to which the rhythm reflects the sense clearly varies a good deal in these examples; at one end of the scale there seems little or no imitative effect in *cornua velatarum obvertimus antemnarum*, while at the other we clearly may say that *agmina circumspexit* conveys something of the heavy hopelessness feigned by Sinon, and *culminibus desertis* the gloomy loneliness of the night scene. See Norden's *Aeneid VI*, pp. 438–46, for full statistics, and Marouzeau, *Traité de stylistique latine*, pp. 85–86, p. 313; compare note on 866 on the imitative effect of alliteration.

321. For the position of *deinde* see on 14.

322. For the half-line see on 294.

323–6. 'Then just behind him, look, Diores flies along, grazing his very heels now, right up to his shoulder; if there were more of the course left, he would shoot in front and pass him . . .'

324. calcemque terit iam calce: the phrase is strange, not to say anatomically impossible. Henry with great gusto defends Virgil by insisting on the metonymy of *calx* for *pes*. This is a better defence than Conington's suggestion that the heel of Diores' front foot comes into contact with the heel of Helymus' back foot! Virgil is thinking (as Macrobius points out, *Sat.* 5. 13. 4) of Hom. *Il.* 23. 763 f. ὣς Ὀδυσεὺς θέεν ἐγγύθεν, αὐτὰρ ὄπισθεν | ἴχνια τύπτε πόδεσσι πάρος κόνιν ἀμφιχυθῆναι; but he has produced a quite different image. He has extended the expression *calcem terere* ('to tread on someone's heels') along the lines of phrases involving repetition such as *immiscentque manus manibus* (line 429, 'hand to hand'), or *haeret pede pes* (*Aen.* 10. 361, 'foot to foot').

325. incumbens umero: the phrase recalls Hom. *Il.* 23. 765, where Ajax feels Odysseus' breath on his neck. For *incumbere* see on 858.

325–6. The present subjunctive used to express a past unfulfilled condition when the narrative is in the historic present occurs several times in Virgil, cf. *Aen.* 6. 292 f., 11. 912 f. The effect is 'graphic', i.e. it makes the reader feel that he is present while these things are happening.

326. ambiguumque relinquat: this is the reading of all the MSS. I would greatly prefer to accept the correction *ambiguumve* (see app. crit.), and translate 'or leave the issue in doubt', 'or leave it uncertain who had won'. In this passage two of the most powerful arguments for determining a textual point in Virgil are arrayed on opposite sides—the consensus of the MSS., and a Homeric source. But the one argument is here at its weakest and the other at its strongest. Confusion between *-que* and *-ve* is extremely common in MSS. of all periods, and the testimony of the MSS. can therefore well be overridden if the grounds for doing so are strong enough. The Homeric passages are these: *Il.* 23. 382 καί νύ κεν ἢ παρέλασσ' ἢ ἀμφήριστον ἔθηκεν and *Il.* 23. 526 f. εἰ δέ κ' ἔτι προτέρω γένετο δρόμος ἀμφοτέροισι, | τῷ κέν μιν παρέλασσ' οὐδ' ἀμφήριστον ἔθηκεν. In both of them the possibility of getting in front is linked *disjunctively* with the other possibility; and the general similarity between Homer's lines

and Virgil's is so marked that no one can reasonably deny
that Virgil had Homer in mind. Thus when we come to the
final criterion of the correctness of a reading—whether it
makes good sense—the defenders of *ambiguumque* are already
in a weak position.

Those who accept *ambiguumque* (as most modern editors
do) either regard it as predicative ('leave him behind doubtful'), or else as describing Helymus' situation before he was
passed, so that the phrase is more or less equivalent to 'out-
pace his close rival'. With regard to the first it would be
very harsh indeed to use *ambiguus* of a person without
indicating the nature of his doubt (contrast lines 655 f.),
and in any case the suggestions offered by commentators as
to what he was doubtful about (the favourite is 'whether to
give up or go on') are not at all appropriate for a runner
beaten on the post. With regard to the second it is almost
imperative that an adjective of this kind governed by *relinquere* should be predicative, indicating in what state a person
is left (cf. *Aen.* 12. 159 f. *reliquit / incertam*), and surely not
the state in which he was and is no longer.

It is better then to accept the correction *ambiguumve*, and
take the word as neuter, with the same meaning as ἀμφήριστον
in the passages from Homer: 'he would pass him or (at the
least) leave the issue in doubt', i.e. come up from behind
so as to be approximately level, and leave the judges a
problem.

327. The unfortunate accident at the end of the race is modelled
on Hom. *Il.* 23. 774 f., where Ajax slips and falls in the dung
left by sacrificed animals. The subsequent disgraceful behaviour of Nisus has no parallel in Homer. It served as a model
for Statius (*Th.* 6. 614 f.) and Silius (16. 517 f.) to go one
better and have the leader held back by his flying locks while
someone else shot past to win. Such departures from seemly
behaviour were censured by Chrysippus quoted in Cic. *De
Off.* 3. 42 *qui stadium currit, eniti et contendere debet quam
maxime possit ut vincat, supplantare eum quicum certet aut
manu depellere nullo modo debet: sic in vita sibi quemque
petere quod pertineat ad usum non iniquum est, alteri deripere
ius non est.*

    fessique: *-que* co-ordinates *fessi* and *spatio extremo*; cf. 447
and 498 with notes.

    ipsam: *finis* is sometimes feminine in early Latin and in
poetry, cf. 384 and *Aen.* 2. 554.

328. levi: 'slippery'.

328–9. cum . . . labitur: for inverted *cum* see on 84–85.

329–30. 'where by chance it had been shed at the sacrifice of bullocks and had soaked the ground and the green grass above'. *Forte* refers to the chance of the course passing over the place of sacrifice; *ut* is probably 'where' (cf. Cat. 11. 3) rather than 'as'; see on 388.

331–2. presso ... solo: perhaps simply 'as he trod on the spot', or possibly 'though he pressed against the ground' (in the hope of regaining his foothold).

332. titubata: 'tottering'; the passive participle is used in an active sense. Compare *iuratus, cretus, adultus, nupta, suetus, potus, pransus*, etc., and see Mackail and Page on *Aen.* 4. 38, Palmer, *The Latin Language*, p. 327. Lejay, however, may be right in arguing that the passive meaning is possible because the verb can take an internal accusative in the active, *titubare vestigia*. In this case compare *Aen.* 3. 14 (with Page's note) *terra ... regnata Lycurgo*, *Aen.* 4. 609 (with Austin's note) *Hecate triviis ululata*.

332–3. Virgil does not often allow so many similar case endings in juxtaposition (five ablatives in *-o*): see on 81.

333. immundoque ... sacroque: for doubled *-que* ('both ... and') see on 92.

334. For this use of *ille* see on 186. Here clearly the effect is to emphasize the devotion of Nisus.

    amorum: this use of the plural *amores* occurs in prose as well as poetry.

335. lubrica: see on 168.

336. spissa ... harena: probably 'firm sand', a phrase very suitable for the treated surface of a permanent race-course, though less appropriate for an improvised course on grass. Servius says 'tenui: quanto enim quid minutius, tanto est densius'. Others take it to mean 'clotted', with the blood of the sacrifice.

    iacuit revolutus: 'went head over heels and there he lay': the use of *iacuit* portrays the suddenness of the whole thing. Nisus gets in his way and the next we know is that he is lying flat on the ground. Jackson Knight conveys this well: 'fell with a somersault to find himself lying on the caked sand'.

337. Euryalus: the last syllable is lengthened in arsis; see note on 284.

338. prima: see on 168.

339. tertia palma: a delightful use of metonymy, abstract for concrete, imitated by Silius (16. 503) *et modo postremus nunc ordine tertia palma*. Diores is now 'third prize', i.e. winner of the third prize. Cf. 498 and note; compare our phrase 'second string'.

340–61. *An objection is now raised by Salius. Aeneas overrules it, but he presents Salius with a consolation prize; Nisus too is given a special prize.*

340–61. This passage is inspired by Hom. *Il.* 23. 540 f., where first Antilochus and then Menelaus object to the award of the prizes after the chariot-race. Homer's account is much longer, and the indignation and subsequent magnanimity of Antilochus is superbly told. Virgil's brief description gives a lively picture of the chief persons involved in the dispute— Salius filled with excited indignation, and loudly protesting; Euryalus silent, winning people's sympathy by his evident fear of the protest being upheld; Diores vehemently opposing Salius' objection, in case he should lose his third prize; Aeneas benevolent and tactful, meeting the situation by awarding an extra prize to Salius; finally Nisus, covered with mud, urging with a theatrical gesture his own very doubtful claim, and Aeneas smilingly accepting it.

340–1. 'At this Salius with loud objections appealed to the whole audience of the great stadium and to the watching fathers in the front.' *Cavea* and *consessus* are terms used of a Roman theatre or circus, cf. 288 f., 664, *Aen.* 8. 636 *consessu caveae*, Lucr. 4. 78 *consessum caveai subter*. The phrase *ora prima patrum* is no doubt influenced by the thought of the Roman senators sitting in their allocated front seats at the theatre or the circus (Livy 1. 35. 8, Suet. *Aug.* 44).

The use of *implet* in this sentence is colourful and unusual. Virgil is very fond of the word in phrases like *loca questibus implet* (*Geo.* 4. 515), *caelum dehinc questibus implet* (*Aen.* 9. 480), *scopulos lacrimosis vocibus implent* (*Aen.* 11. 274), *implevi clamore vias* (*Aen.* 2. 769). In the present passage this use is extended slightly with *consessum*, and considerably with *ora patrum*. For this extension, where the meaning approximates to 'assails constantly', 'importunes', cf. *Aen.* 11. 896 f. *Turnum . . . saevissimus implet / nuntius*. It is a usage taken up by the Silver Age writers, cf. Val. Fl. 2. 167 *tum voce deos tum questibus implent*, 2. 126, 3. 220.

342. reddi: the accusative and infinitive with *poscere, exposcere, imperare, postulare* is not uncommon in verse, especially with a passive infinitive. Cf. *Aen.* 9. 192 *Aenean acciri . . . exposcunt*, *Aen.* 3. 464 f. *dona . . . imperat ad navis ferri*, Hor. *A.P.* 339; see Kühner–Stegmann, ii. 2, pp. 231 f., and note on 21–22.

343. lacrimaeque decorae: 'his modest tears'. The meaning is not so much that Euryalus' beauty is enhanced by his tears, but that (unlike Salius) he refrains from making a great song and dance, which could be considered *indecorum*; he permits himself as much outward show of disappointment as was thought proper in such a situation. For the Roman propensity towards revealing emotion cf. 173.

344. gratior et: for the postposition of *et* see on 5. Here the effect is to emphasize *gratior*.

veniens: an unexpected use, 'coming forward', 'presenting itself'. Seneca (*Ep. Mor.* 66. 2) misquotes the line to make the use of *veniens* much more normal, *gratior et pulchro veniens e corpore virtus*.

345. adiuvat: 'backs him up'.

346. subiit palmae: 'has come into a place' (339 *nunc tertia palma Diores*). The meaning of *subire* is a slight extension of the use in 176, where see note. For the dative see on 34.

346 f. 'and has qualified for the last place all for nothing if the distinction of first place is to be restored to Salius'. There is good manuscript authority for *reddentur* (*P*), *reddantur* (*MR*), and *redduntur* (*M*[1]). *Reddantur* is sometimes supported on the ground that the semi-oblique subjunctive is appropriate to express the thought in Diores' mind; but then *subiit* and *venit* should be subjunctive too, and Conington is not convincing when he says 'we just catch, as it were, a few of the words which he actually utters'. *Redduntur* would be quite acceptable because the following verbs in the present tense, *manent* and *movet*, are similarly future in meaning; but its authority in *M* rests on a correction, and it is better to accept *reddentur* from *P*.

349. The O.C.T. punctuation makes *pueri* a genitive with *palmam*, but it is surely vocative plural. *Pater Aeneas* calls the runners *pueri*, and his opening words *vestra . . . vobis* almost demand a vocative.

350. casus: accusative plural, 'misfortunes', 'bad luck'. But there is enough latent ambiguity for Nisus to take Aeneas up (354) on the literal meaning ('fall'). It was probably in the desire for the literal meaning here that some MSS. have *misereri* for *miserari*, thus making *casus* genitive singular. By *insontis* Aeneas means that Salius was not to blame; if he implies that Nisus was to blame, he could hardly have put it more mildly.

351. tergum: the meaning 'hide', 'skin', is common, cf. 403. For the 'ornate' epithet *Gaetuli* see on 306.

352. For the custom of gilding the claws of a lion-skin cf. *Aen.* 8. 552 f.

onerosum: this adjective does not occur before Virgil (cf. *Aen.* 9. 384). Ernout, however (*Les Adjectifs latins en -ōsus et en -ulentus*, Paris, 1949, s.v.), says that it is no doubt an

older word, comparing *ponderosus* in Plautus. The adjectives
in -*osus* were found useful in poetry to render Greek adjectives, especially those in -όεις, -ήεις, -ώδης: e.g. *nemorosa
Zacynthos* (ὑλήεσσα Ζάκυνθος), *piscosus* (ἰχθυόεις), *lacri-
mosus* (δακρυόεις). Other instances of adjectives in -*osus* in
this book are: 87 *maculosus* (Plautus, Cicero), 214 *latebrosus*
(Plautus, Cicero), 252 *frondosus* (Ennius, Varro), 839 *tene-
brosus* (first in Virgil; see note ad loc.). Other such adjectives
which are not found before Virgil are *palmosus, nimbosus,
undosus, montosus* (*montuosus* occurs in prose). See Palmer,
The Latin Language, p. 111, Ernout, loc. cit., *passim*,
Leumann–Hofmann, p. 231, and note on 202.

  aureis: the word scans as a spondee by synizesis (slurring
of the *e*); it would otherwise be impossible to use it in
hexameters in the oblique cases. Cf. *Aen.* 1. 698 *aureā
composuit sponda*. Among the words with which synizesis
occurs in Virgil are *deinde* (note on line 14), *dehinc, proinde,
aerei, ferrei, baltei, alveo, anteirent, reice, eodem, eadem,* and
a number of proper names (see on 184); see also Platnauer,
Latin Elegiac Verse, pp. 66 f., and notes on 269 and 432.

353 f. 'Then Nisus said "If the losers get prizes like that, and
you feel sorry for people who fall, what in all fairness are
you going to award to Nisus? Why, I earned *first* prize . . ."'

355. merui qui: for the postposition of the relative see on 22.
  laude: 'by my deserts'; *laus* is approximately equivalent
to *virtus*, as often: cf. *Aen.* 1. 461, 9. 252.

355–6. In this type of past unfulfilled condition the true
apodosis is concealed in an ellipse: 'I earned first prize (and
would have got it) if . . .' Cf. *Aen.* 6. 358 f. *iam tuta tenebam
| ni gens crudelis . . . | ferro invasisset.*

356. tulisset: 'snatched me away'. The simple verb is used for
the compound *abstulisset* (see on 41). There is a rather exaggerated air about Nisus' use of it here, because it is normally
used in more important contexts; cf. *Ecl.* 5. 34 *postquam
te fata tulerunt, Ecl.* 9. 51 *omnia fert aetas, Aen.* 2. 554 f. *hic
exitus illum | sorte tulit.* Nisus' argument is a very cool piece
of audacity, but he seems to have convinced Servius, who
says 'bene dolum suum excusat'.

357. simul: the word here may be used for *simul cum*, as it is
in poetry (Hor. *Sat.* 1. 10. 86) and in Tacitus, or it may be
purely adverbial as in *Aen.* 10. 856 *simul hoc dicens attollit . . .*
  faciem: Henry argues powerfully that *facies* here has its
most common meaning of 'appearance', but in the context
'face' is more likely; cf. *Aen.* 10. 698 f. *Latagum saxo . . . |
occupat os faciemque adversam.*

359. Didymaonis artis: Didymaon is not otherwise known. This is a rare meaning of *ars* ('work of art'); cf. Cic. *De Leg.* 2. 4 *me quidem ipsae illae nostrae Athenae non tam operibus magnificis exquisitisque antiquorum artibus delectant quam recordatione summorum virorum*; Hor. *Odes* 4. 8. 5 f. *divite me scilicet artium | quas aut Parrhasius protulit aut Scopas*; Hor. *Epist.* 1. 6. 17. The word is used here in the poetic plural; see on 98. Some MSS. have *artem,* but *artis* is more likely to have been changed to *artem* than vice versa.

360. 'taken down by the Greeks from the sacred portal of Neptune'. *Danais* is dative of the agent, cf. 305, 610. Page (ad loc. and *C.R.,* 1894, p. 300) argues that the meaning is that some Greek hero took it from a Greek temple and lost it in battle; but it is much more likely that the Greeks took it down from a Trojan temple. Virgil does not tell us how Aeneas came into possession of it; Servius suggests that Helenus perhaps gave it to him (cf. *Aen.* 3. 463 f., and note on 297 f.). The point of the line then is firstly that it was an exceptionally fine shield, in fact a dedicated shield; and secondly that it was the Greeks and not the Trojans who were responsible for its removal from the temple.

362–86. *Aeneas now announces a boxing competition. Dares comes forward, but nobody is prepared to fight him. He claims the prize.*

362 f. The boxing competition has a number of reminiscences of the shorter description in Hom. *Il.* 23. 653 f. (see notes on 364, 427, 429, 468 f., 471), and of Ap. Rh. 2. 1 f. (Amycus and Polydeuces). Virgil does not seem to have drawn material from the vivid and detailed description of the fight between Amycus and Polydeuces in Theoc. 22. For boxing in the ancient world see note on 364, and E. N. Gardiner, *Athletics of the Ancient World,* chap. xv, *Greek Athletic Sports and Festivals,* pp. 402 f.; compare also the versions in Val. Fl. 4. 222 f., Stat. *Th.* 6. 731 f.

With the Greeks boxing was a highly skilled art practised at the great festivals, but in Roman times the use of the *caestus* had transformed it into a far more dangerous contest requiring mainly brute force and physical courage. Virgil describes the Roman type of boxing, but having little liking for it in real life he has chosen to handle the narrative on a mythological plane, in a setting of the distant days of heroes and demi-gods; the contestants (unlike those in the other events) play no further part in the *Aeneid,* and are not associated with Roman families (see Intro., p. xv). They are characters drawn on a large scale and in an exaggerated manner (the assonance and alliteration of the verse are often exaggerated to match; see on 431–2, 481). Dares is a huge and terrifying figure of legendary fame (368 f.), bold and impatient (380 f.), but quickly deflated at the sight of Entellus' gauntlets (406). Entellus, the older man, does not come forward until called on by Acestes, and when he does it is with a lamentation for his past greatness (394 f.). He is slow to start, but with his dramatic gesture as he throws his giant gauntlets into the ring, and with his confident and boastful speech (410 f.), the impression grows that although he may not be as good as he was he is still too good for Dares.

Thus the characters are introduced; the scene is then set and the preliminaries described (421–43). The actual events of the fighting are brief and simple: Entellus aims a mighty blow which misses; he falls and is helped to his feet again; his anger is aroused and he drives Dares all round the ring until Aeneas intervenes to stop the fight. The narrative concludes with a picture of each of them: Dares being carried away defeated (468 f.), and Entellus exultant in his pride, making a sacrifice of his prize to his patron Eryx before retiring for ever from boxing.

In its length the boxing contest balances the ship-race, contrasting with the briefer accounts of the foot-race and the archery; but the method of description in the two long events is very different. The ship-race is all excitement with multiplication of incident involving the four competitors; but in the boxing, incident is at a minimum (Virgil's account forms a most marked contrast with the incident-packed description in Theocritus). The interest is concentrated on the *mise-en-scène* and on the two contestants, enormous figures of almost more than mortal strength, figures of a distant world like Lapiths fighting Centaurs, or Titans or Giants from a legendary past.

362. Heyne well comments: 'poetae studium in oratione varianda cognosce etiam in illo quod dicere noluit *confecti cursus et dona peracta*'. The phrase *dona peregit* is rather unusual in the sense of *dona distribuit*, or *donorum distributionem peregit*.

363. 'if anyone has valour and ready courage in his heart'; a passage referred to by Seneca, *Ep. Mor.* 92. 29.

364. evinctis . . . palmis: the *caestus*, which Roman boxers wore on their hands, had an altogether different function from that of the modern boxing-glove. It consisted of hard leather thongs sometimes reinforced with pieces of metal (401–5). The ἱμάντες of Homer's boxing match (*Il.* 23. 684) were for protecting the knuckles rather than for doing more hurt than the bare fist would cause, and this was the type used down to the fourth century B.C., when a more damaging type began to be used. These had hard leather ridges with sharp edges, and were called ἱμάντες ὀξεῖς; the earlier type was distinguished as μείλιχαι (soft). From the ἱμάντες ὀξεῖς developed the Roman *caestus* with its metal attachments. See Gow on Theoc. 22. 80 f., and H. Frère, *Mélanges Ernout*, 1940, pp. 141 f.

attollat bracchia: the phrase recalls Hom. *Il.* 23. 660 πὺξ μάλ᾽ ἀνασχομένω πεπληγέμεν (cf. 686); cf. Ap. Rh. 2. 14, Theoc. 22. 65, and our 'put up your fists'; see on 427.

365. pugnae: the root meaning of the word is a fight with fists, cf. πύξ and *pugnus*.

366. 'crowned with gold and garlands'. The phrase is not a hendiadys, but refers to two separate forms of decoration, garlands and the overlaying of the horns of the bullock with gold—so Servius: 'quia solent habere laminas quasdam', and he compares *Aen.* 9. 627 *aurata fronte iuvencum*. The custom is referred to in Hom. *Od.* 3. 384, and described a little later, 432 f.

368–9. 'immediately Dares in all his mighty strength thrust out his jaw and stood up, bringing a buzz of excitement from the crowd'. Conington suggests that the force of *cum* is rendered by 'he rose with all his bulk about him'; it probably rather serves to attach the descriptive phrase to the noun *Dares* and not to the verb. *Effert ora* is amusingly picturesque: he presents himself as a competitor by getting up with his face thrust forward in an attitude of arrogant defiance.

The alliteration of *vastis . . . viribus, magnoque virum . . . murmure* is very apparent. Virgil draws a powerful and simple picture of the mighty, self-confident Dares.

369. For the genitive *virum* see on 174.

370. The origin of the tradition that Paris was an outstanding boxer is obscure and generally attributed to the cyclic poets; cf. Hyginus, *Fab.* 91 and 273.

Paridem: this form of the accusative occurs only here in Virgil; in *Aen.* 10. 705 he has *Parin*. For a similar variation cf. *Daren* 456 and *Dareta* 460.

Paridem . . . contra: for the anastrophe (here with displacement) of a disyllabic preposition cf. 152 (*inter*), 250 (*circum*), 414 (*contra*), 435 (*circum*). It is frequent in poetry; see Marouzeau, *L'Ordre des mots dans la phrase latine*, iii, pp. 45 f., especially 58; and Kühner–Stegmann, ii. 1, p. 586, p. 588, Platnauer, *Latin Elegiac Verse*, pp. 97 f. Compare note on 663 *transtra per et remos*, and on 512.

371. Very little is known of the tradition of funeral games for Hector—cf., however, Dar. Phryg. 25.

372–3. The punctuation and meaning of these lines is disputed; it seems best to place a comma after *corpore*, and translate: 'the all-conquering Butes, a man of giant stature, who came to the games boasting of his descent from the Bebrycian race of Amycus'. Some commentators take *se ferebat* in the sense of *Aen.* 8. 199 *magna se mole ferebat* (cf. 1. 503, 4. 11, etc.); but this seems weak with *veniens*, nor is it reasonable in the context to take *veniens* as *ortus*. Virgil is probably thinking of the Homeric εὔχομαι εἶναι. Butes (not the same as Butes, father of Eryx; see on 24) is not mentioned elsewhere. Amycus, savage king of the Bebrycian race, compelled all strangers to box with him for their lives; after many victories he was defeated by Polydeuces and killed (according to Apollonius, 2 *init.*) or forced to promise to change his ways (Theoc. 22).

372. qui se: Page well comments that the ending *qui se* suggests heaviness; observe too that the first four feet are spondaic, and that there is a sense pause after the fifth foot (see on 624). The effect of a monosyllabic ending when a monosyllable precedes is not so striking as when a longer word precedes (see on 481), because the word accent is not in such marked conflict with the ictus. For other double monosyllabic endings (of which Virgil has about 40) cf. 624 and 713; see Austin on *Aen.* 4. 224, Norden's *Aeneid VI*, pp. 438 f., 448 f., Winbolt, *Latin Hexameter Verse*, pp. 141 f.

374. perculit: 'struck down'; cf. *Aen.* 11. 310. For the rest of the line cf. *Aen.* 9. 589 *ac multa porrectum extendit harena.* Observe how the rhythm of the line with its fourth foot coincidence of ictus and accent and the rhyme at caesura and line ending gives a rounding-off effect to the long sentence (see on 5 f. and 385–6).

375. prima: many commentators regard this as a transferred epithet for *primus*, but it is better to take *prima in proelia* to mean 'for the beginning of the fray'; the words indicate Dares' eagerness to get started. Cf. *Aen.* 12. 103 f. *mugitus veluti cum prima in proelia taurus / terrificos ciet*, and *Geo.* 4. 314; see on 857. For the poetic plural *proelia* see on 98, and cf. 467.

376. umeros latos: for the juxtaposition of words ending similarly see on 845.

376–7. 'leading with left and right / as he pounded the air and indulged in a bout of shadow-boxing' (Day Lewis). Cf. *Geo.* 3. 233 f. (the goat) *ventosque lacessit / ictibus et sparsa ad pugnam proludit harena*, *Aen.* 10. 892 f. *tollit se arrectum quadripes et calcibus auras / verberat*, 11. 756 (*aquila*) *aethera verberat alis.*

377. Notice how the coincidence of ictus and accent, and of words with feet, in the second half of the line helps to convey the idea of blow following blow. See on 198.

379. caestus: see on 364.

380. alacris: this archaic form of *alacer* occurs again in *Aen.* 6. 685. See on 10.

   excedere palma: 'were withdrawing from (a claim to) the prize', cf. *Aen.* 9. 789 *Turnus paulatim excedere pugna*.

381. plura: adverbial accusative, see on 19; cf. *Aen.* 3. 610 *haud multa moratus*.

382. For *tum* in the main clause after a participial clause see on 720: for the line ending see on 274.

384. quo . . . teneri?: 'How long must I be kept waiting?' For the tmesis of *quousque* see on 603.

385. ducere dona iube: 'Give the word for me to take away my prize.' For the poetic plural see on 98, and cf. 391, 400.

385–6. cuncti . . . Dardanidae: the same words in *Aen.* 1. 559–60. For the repetition *iube . . . iubebant* see on 254. Notice the rhyme of the line endings *fremebant, iubebant*; see Austin on *Aen.* 4. 55 for a full discussion and references, and add Winbolt, *Latin Hexameter Verse*, p. 161. There are no other true rhymes of successive line endings in this book, but compare the similarity of sound between lines 1–2, 60–63, 77–78, 95–96, 149–50, 649–50, 676–7. Similarity of ending between the word at the third-foot caesura and the last word of the line is very frequent: nearly fifty lines in this book have like word endings in these positions (e.g. 13, 70, 76, 159, etc.) and in a large number more the word at the second-foot caesura (93, 180, 269, 279, etc.) or at the fourth-foot caesura (15, 48, 60, 62, etc.) has an ending similar to that of the last word in the line. See also Palmer, *The Latin Language*, pp. 117–18, Marouzeau, *Traité de stylistique latine*, pp. 58 f., 319 f., W. F. Jackson Knight, *Roman Vergil*, pp. 250 f., Maguinness's *Aeneid XII*, Introd., p. 35; and cf. notes on 81, 181–2.

387–423. *Acestes now urges Entellus, who was trained by Eryx, to oppose Dares. He protests that he is now past the prime of his youth, but none the less accepts the challenge and hurls into the ring a pair of huge gauntlets with which Eryx once fought Hercules. The spectators are all shocked and amazed; Entellus makes a taunting speech, but agrees to fight with matched gauntlets.*

387. gravis: 'sternly': Servius says 'gravis autem aetate vel obiurgatione', of which the second is clearly right. The adjective is used with adverbial force; see on 33.

Entellum: known only from this passage. It was a name associated with Sicily, as we see from the city Entella. Servius says that according to Hyginus he was a Trojan and Virgil altered the tradition.

388. proximus ut . . . consederat: 'sitting as he was next to him'. This usage of *ut* links the clause to its main verb in a very general way, sometimes causal, sometimes temporal, sometimes local. Cf. 329, 667, and *Aen.* 7. 509, 12. 488, 623.

389. 'Entellus, you were once the bravest of heroes: but now!' (Day Lewis). *Frustra* conveys that the glories of the past are apparently of no avail now. Servius and Donatus miss the point entirely and take *frustra* with the following line. Heyne quotes a number of similar passages of reproach from Homer, of which the nearest is *Il.* 5. 171 f.

391 f. 'Where now, tell us, is the divine Eryx whom you called your teacher—and all for this?' If we take the words *magister nequiquam memoratus* closely together (as in the O.C.T. punctuation), *nobis* is ethic dative; cf. 162. *Nequiquam* has the same sense as *frustra* in 389; for Eryx see on 24. Many take *nequiquam memoratus* to mean 'idly famed' (Page, Fairclough), but this is a much rarer meaning of the verb unless it is defined in the context by some such word as *fama*; and Acestes is directing the sting of his rebuke against Entellus, not against Eryx.

393. For the hanging up of spoils cf. *Aen.* 2. 504, 7. 183 f., Val. Fl. 4. 181 f.

394. sub haec: Mackail well comments 'there is the same slight distinction between *sub haec* and *ad haec* as between "rejoins" and "replies"'. Entellus' words are strongly reminiscent of those of Nestor in *Il.* 23. 626 f.

   gloria: 'desire for glory'; the subjective touch to the word is commonly found: Lejay compares the similar nuance in words like *veritas, libertas, officium*.

395. sed enim: 'but indeed', 'but in fact'. This intensifying meaning of *enim* is an archaism (so Quint. 9. 3. 14) which is found with *enim* by itself (= δή) in *Geo.* 2. 104, *Aen.* 6. 317, 8. 84, 10. 874, and with *sed enim* in *Aen.* 1. 19 (where see Conway and Page), 2. 164, 6. 28 (where see Norden). The Greek ἀλλὰ γάρ (implying an ellipse) contributed to the survival of the archaism. For archaisms see on 10.

   senecta: see on 295 (*iuventa*).

395–6. 'old age has slowed me, my blood is cold and runs feebly, and the strength of my limbs is worn out and gone'. Compare *Aen.* 2. 638–9, 8. 508–9, 9. 610–11, 12. 905. The word *hebere* is not found before the Augustan Age (see on 202), nor elsewhere in Virgil; Livy (23. 45. 9) has it in its literal meaning 'to be blunt'. For Virgil's meaning cf. Val. Fl. 1. 53 *ardor hebet*, 4. 41 *corpus hebet somno*. *Hebetare* likewise does not occur before the Augustan Age; cf. *Aen.* 2. 605 (*nubes*) *hebetat visus*, 6. 732 *terrenique hebetant artus. Hebescere*, however, is Ciceronian (e.g. *Cat.* 1. 4, *Tusc.* 1. 73).

397 f. For similar reminiscent longings cf. *Il.* 7. 132 f., 11. 668 f., 23. 629 f., and *Aen.* 8. 560 f. Notice the effect gained by the holding up of the subject *iuventas*.

397. fuerat: this usage of the pluperfect instead of the perfect or imperfect seems to have been a colloquialism. We find it in Plautus; it is rare in Classical Latin prose except for Cicero's letters, but it occurs sometimes in poetry and becomes commoner in later prose. Cf. *Aen.* 10. 613 f. *si mihi quae quondam fuerat quamque esse decebat / vis in amore foret*, Ov. *Tr.* 3. 11. 25 *non sum ego quod fueram*, and see Butler and Barber on Prop. 1. 8. 36, Kühner–Stegmann, ii. 1, p. 141, Platnauer, *Latin Elegiac Verse*, pp. 112 f., Palmer, *The Latin Language*, p. 308.

improbus: 'braggart'. *Improbus* is used of anything beyond normal bounds; it is one of Virgil's favourite words, both in serious contexts (*Aen.* 4. 386, 412, 11. 512, 767), and in light-hearted ones (*Geo.* 1. 119, 388). See Austin's note on *Aen.* 4. 386.

399 f. 'I would not have needed the lure of reward and a fine young bull to bring me here, and it isn't prizes I care about.' The negative applies to *pretio inductus* and the sentence is equivalent to *venissem sine pretii inductu*. *Pulchroque iuvenco* is explanatory of *pretio*; see on 410–11.

400. For *moror* cf. Hor. *Epist.* 1. 15. 16 *nam vina nihil moror illius orae*, *Aen.* 2. 287, 7. 253. The meaning is said to have originated from the formula with which the consul dismissed the senate, *nihil amplius vos moramur, patres conscripti*.

sic deinde locutus: for the order see on 14.

401 f. The dramatic gesture gains in force by coming after a speech in which Entellus has regretted the loss of his former greatness; and he follows it up, as they all stand in amazement, by telling them that these gauntlets which Eryx had were as nothing to those which Hercules wore to oppose him.

402–3. 'they were the gauntlets in which fierce Eryx had so often raised his hands for battle, binding his forearms with the hard leather'. For *suetus = consuetus* and *ferre = conferre* see on 41. *Intendere bracchia tergo* is a variation on *intendere terga bracchiis* (cf. *Aen.* 2. 236 f. *et stuppea vincula collo / intendunt*) as in *Aen.* 4. 506 *intenditque locum sertis* and line 829. Page neatly compares the English 'hang pictures on a wall', or 'hang a wall with pictures'. Conington goes too far in suggesting that Virgil by using this construction also implies the meaning of line 136 *intentaque bracchia remis*.

404–5. Observe the pictorial use of elision in these lines, conveying (as often in Virgil) an idea of immensity; cf. the more marked instance in the description of the Cyclops in *Aen.* 3. 658 *monstrum horrendum, informe, ingens*, and see Norden on *Aen.* 6. 186 *aspectans silvam immensam, et sic forte precatur*. Compare line 422 and see note on 235–8. The effect here is emphasized by the assonance of *-um* and by the three consecutive words ending in *-o* in line 405: see note on 81.

404. Servius (followed by Janell) punctuates after *tantorum*, suggesting that *obstipuere animi tantorum* means 'the hearts of these great heroes were amazed'. He says 'hoc est virorum fortium . . . nam stultum est dicere *tantorum boum*, cum dixerit septem'. This well illustrates Servius' readiness to go to any length to explain a real or imagined difficulty. We may guess that one of Virgil's *obtrectatores* (they are discussed at length by H. Georgii, *Die Antike Äneiskritik*, Stuttgart, 1891; see also notes on 521 and 813 f.) had criticized *tantorum* on the grounds that if the gauntlets were made of seven ox-hides the size of the oxen was not particularly relevant. But in fact the word applies in a looser way to the whole sentence: 'so mighty were the seven huge ox-hides stiff with the lead and iron sewn on them'. Virgil is clearly thinking of Ajax's shield of seven ox-hides, *Il.* 7. 220 f. Statius (*Th.* 6. 732 f.) imitates the passage.

406. longeque recusat: Servius here, as fairly often (e.g. on *Aen.* 1. 13, 2. 711) expresses the view that *longe* means *valde*, which it does mean in Apuleius and later authors, but not earlier than Apuleius (the citations from Statius given in this sense by Lewis and Short are incorrect); in Virgil it always has the idea of distance, and here it gives a very vivid effect equivalent to *longe refugit recusans certamen*. The impossibility of Servius' view is seen most clearly on *Aen.* 2. 711 *longe servet vestigia coniunx*, where he explains *longe* as *valde*. Forbiger here maintains that *longe = diu*, but this is a meaning which it has only very rarely except in the comparative.

407. It is rare to find a word of such length as *Anchisiades* in this position across the middle of the line; cf., however, the same word in the same position in 8. 521, 10. 822, and compare *Geo.* 1. 350 *incompositos, Geo.* 3. 226 *ignominiam, Aen.* 8. 490 *circumsistunt,* 9. 416 *circumspiciunt.* See Norden's *Aeneid VI*, p. 431, and compare note on line 1.

407–8. 'turns the enormous heavy folds of the gauntlets over and over'. The hendiadys *pondus et ipsa volumina* is unusual

with *ipsa* in the second part of it. For *versat* of armour cf.
Aen. 8. 619 f. *interque manus et bracchia versat / terribilem
cristis galeam . . .*

408. Notice the elision over the third-foot caesura where there
is no strong fourth-foot caesura. There are some twenty-
four examples of this in Book V, the majority involving
elision of *-que*. Instances of the elision of a long syllable or a
syllable ending in *-m* occur also at 433, 537, 684, 703.

409. senior: 'the veteran', Entellus.

410–11. 'What would you think if any of you had seen the
gauntlets which Heracles himself wore?' For the postposition of *et* see note on line 5. *Et* is epexegetic; i.e. *et arma* does
not add a new idea, but explains and elaborates *caestus*.
This usage is very common indeed in Virgil, and many of the
instances can be called hendiadys, e.g. *Aen.* 1. 61 f. *molemque
et montis insuper altos / imposuit, Aen.* 1. 111 *in brevia et
Syrtis*; see note on 36. Others are slightly different from
hendiadys, not so much coalescing into one meaning as saying
the same thing in a different and explanatory way, e.g. *Aen.*
4. 355 *quem regno Hesperiae fraudo et fatalibus arvis*; and
(with *atque*) 9. 569 f. *saxo atque ingenti fragmine montis /
Lucetium . . . sternit,* 12. 531 *scopulo atque ingentis turbine
saxi*; and (with *-que*) lines 82 and 399, and 12. 945 f. *ille oculis
postquam saevi monimenta doloris / exuviasque hausit . . .*

411. When Hercules was bringing back the cattle of the Gery-
ones, Eryx met and challenged him. In the resultant fight
Eryx was killed.

412. germanus Eryx: see on 24.

414. For the postposition of *contra* see on 370.

    his ego suetus: *his* might be dative, but it is perhaps better
taken as ablative of instrument (like the first *his*) with some
verb like *pugnare* understood; cf. 402. For the rhythm of the
line ending and the emphasis on *ego* see on 274. *Ego* is not
emphatic by position, because the personal pronouns in the
nominative are commonly postponed from the first word in
the sentence (Leumann–Hofmann, p. 612), but the antithesis
makes it emphatic and its position in the fifth foot in conflict
with the ictus strengthens this effect. The omission of the
verb 'to be' in the first person is not very common, but cf.
Aen. 1. 558, 2. 25, 651, 792, 7. 300 and note on 192.

415. melior: 'hotter', cf. the use of *gelidus* in 395.

    aemula: 'jealous'; old age is his 'rival', cf. *Aen.* 6. 173.
For the postposition of *necdum* see on 5: for the colourless
word ending a line see on 733.

416. 'had not yet flecked my brows with white hair'. Compare
Prop. 3. 5. 24 *sparserit et nigras alba senecta comas*; in this

passage by a colourful personification it is old age that is
flecked with white.

417. Observe the interwoven order for *si Dares Troius nostra
haec arma recusat*; it emphasizes the contemptuous antithesis
between himself and Dares.

418. sedet: 'is the decision of', cf. *Aen.* 2. 660, 4. 15.

    auctor: 'my sponsor', i.e. the man who has urged me to
fight (cf. 387 f.).

419. pugnas: the poetic plural *pugnae* referring to a single
combat is comparatively rare; *proelia* (375) is very common
thus, as it is metrically intractable in the singular. See on 98.

    Erycis tibi terga remitto: 'there you are, I forego the thongs
of Eryx'. *Tibi* is ethic dative, and conveys a good deal of
scorn.

421 f. In this section Virgil recalls Homer *Il.* 23. 685 f. and
Ap. Rh. 2. 67 f.; Servius, who is given to exaggeration in these
matters, says 'est autem hic totus locus de Apollonio trans-
latus'.

421. duplicem: 'double-folded'. Virgil is following Ap. Rh.
2. 32 f. (of Amycus, to whom Entellus corresponds) ὁ δ'
ἐρεμνὴν δίπτυχα λώπην / . . . / κάββαλε. The epithets διπλοῦς,
δίπλαξ, are common in Homer of various types of dress. There
does not therefore seem to be sufficient reason for thinking,
as most commentators do, that *duplex amictus* suggests a
coarse type of cloak worn by countrymen, or for identifying
Entellus' garment (as Servius does, quoting Hor. *Epist.*
1. 17. 25) with the *abolla*.

    rēiecit: notice the quantity of the first syllable. The prefix
re- is short except before double consonants or consonantal *i*. See also on 47.

422 f. Compare the description of Odysseus stripping to fight
Irus (*Od.* 18. 66 f.).

422. membrorum artus: Lejay maintains (ad loc.) that the two
words mean the same thing and that there is a redundancy
about the phrase, but it is more likely that *artus* is here used
in its proper meaning of 'joints' rather than in its wider
meaning, 'limbs'. See Marouzeau, *Quelques Aspects de la
formation du latin littéraire*, 1949, p. 76.

    lacertosque: the word means the upper arm and is com-
monly used in contexts concerned with muscular strength.
Macrobius (*Sat.* 6. 1. 43) quotes from Lucilius *magna ossa
lacertique / adparent homini*, where the same hypermetric
elision occurs. Evidently Ennius had examples of hypermetric elision, for we have Seneca's reported words (Aul.
Gell. 12. 2. 10) 'Vergilius quoque noster non ex alia causa
duros quosdam versus et enormes et aliquid supra mensuram

trahentes interposuit quam ut Ennianus populus agnosceret in novo carmine aliquid antiquitatis'. There are also examples of this kind of elision before Virgil in Lucr. 5. 849, Cat. 64. 298, 115. 5. His successors used it very rarely indeed (three instances in Ovid, one in Valerius, none in Lucan, none in Statius). There are twenty instances in Virgil, many of them with *-que*. In some at least of these cases the elision is used with deliberate effect, e.g. *Geo.* 1. 295 *decoquit umorem* (the must boils over), *Aen.* 1. 332 *ignari hominumque locorumque* (the catch of despair in the voice), *Aen.* 4. 629 *pugnent ipsique nepotesque* (Dido's angry curse carries her on beyond the metre—observe that the elision here comes at the end of a speech), *Aen.* 6. 602 *atra silex iam iam lapsura cadentique* (the stone almost rolls over). See Austin on *Aen.* 4. 558, Norden on *Aen.* 6. 602, Marouzeau, *Traité de stylistique latine*, pp. 304–5. In the instance here it is perhaps intended to help to convey enormous size, along with the spondaic movement of the line (see on 136–41), the other elisions in the line (see on 404–5 and 235–8), and the alliteration of *m* and the repetition of the word *magnus*.

423. exuit: the word is often used (as in 420) meaning 'to take off', but sometimes, as here, meaning 'to bare'; cf. *Aen.* 2. 153 *exutas vinclis . . . palmas*, 4. 518 *unum exuta pedem vinclis*, 8. 567. Compare the similar variation with *induere* (note on 674).

ingens . . . harena: notice the concluding impressiveness of these words which end the account of the preliminary arguments. In the climax of his description of the huge Entellus Virgil turns naturally to the adjective *ingens* of which he is so fond; see on 118.

424–60. *Aeneas brings out matching pairs of gauntlets, and the fight begins. After preliminary sparring Entellus aims a mighty blow, which misses and causes him to fall flat on the ground. He is assisted to his feet, and in fury renews the fight, driving Dares all round the arena.*

424. satus Anchisa: see on 244.

pater: see on 130.

extulit: 'brought out', 'produced', cf. *Aen.* 11. 72–73.

426. 'Immediately each took up his stance, poised on his toes'. Cf. Ap. Rh. 2. 90 f. ἔνθα δ' ἔπειτ' Ἄμυκος μὲν ἐπ' ἀκροτάτοισιν ἀερθείς . . ., Stat. *Th.* 6. 750 f.

427. Cf. Ap. Rh. 2. 68 f. αὐτίκ' ἀνασχόμενοι ῥεθέων προπάροιθε βαρείας / χεῖρας . . ., Hom. *Il.* 23. 686 f. ἄντα δ' ἀνασχομένω χερσὶ στιβαρῇσιν ἅμ' ἄμφω / σύν ῥ' ἔπεσον. The use of *extulit* ('raised') is illustrated by these two passages; see also on 364.

For the repetition of the word from line 424 (in a quite different sense) see on 254.

428. 'They held their heads high, well back out of range of blows.' The force of *capita ardua* is that they are drawn up to their full height, not adopting a crouching position where the head is advanced; cf. Stat. *Th.* 6. 751 f. Greek and Roman boxers adopted a stance to guard the head, not the head and body; see Gardiner, *Athletics of the Ancient World*, pp. 204 f. with illustrations given.

429. Cf. Ap. Rh. 2. 78 καὶ χερσὶν ἐναντία χεῖρας ἔμιξεν, Hom. *Il.* 23. 687 σὺν δέ σφι βαρεῖαι χεῖρες ἔμιχθεν.

pugnamque lacessunt: 'sparring for an opening', cf. *Aen.* 7. 165, 11. 254.

430 f. The contrast between the speed of the young Dares (*ille*) and the strength of the older Entellus (*hic*) is imitated and developed by Statius (*Th.* 6. 765 f.), where Alcidamas the young Spartan corresponds with Dares, and Capaneus with Entellus.

431. membris et mole: for the hendiadys (see on 36) Servius compares *Aen.* 1. 61 f. *molemque et montis insuper altos / imposuit.*

431-2. tarda . . . artus: notice how the strong alliteration of *t* in *tarda trementi* continues in the next line. All through this passage the alliteration is deliberately more marked and violent than is usually Virgil's way; see especially 444-5.

432. genua: the *u* is treated as a consonant, so that the word is a trochee; cf. *Aen.* 12. 905 (the same phrase) and compare *tenuia* as a dactyl in *Geo.* 1. 397, 2. 121, and the similar treatment of *i* in *abiete* (line 663), *parietibus* (line 589), *ariete* (*Aen.* 2. 492), and the more unusual instances in *Geo.* 1. 482 *fluviorum, Aen.* 6. 33 *omnia* (where see Norden), *Aen.* 7. 237 *precantia.* See also notes on 352 (synizesis), 571, and 697.

vastos . . . artus: 'his laboured breathing shakes his huge frame'; cf. Ap. Rh. 2. 85 and *Aen.* 9. 814.

433-6. Day Lewis has:

Many punches are thrown by both of them, missing their target;

Many get home on the hollow ribs or beat a tattoo on

The mighty chests: against ear and temple their fists go flickering

Constantly out, and their cheek-bones are rattled by heavy punches.

Notice the sameness of the verb endings in this rapid narrative: see note on 580-2.

433-4. multa . . . multa: 'many of the punches miss, *but* many . . .' Heyne and Conington are surely wrong in thinking that lines 434–6 elaborate 433 (*nequiquam* then meaning 'without decisive effect') : it is more natural to take them in antithesis. For *vulnera* in this extended sense cf. *Aen.* 2. 529, 7. 533 (in line 436 the extension is easier). For the elision over the caesura in 433 see note on 408.

434. Cf. Statius' imitation (*Th.* 1. 418 f.) *iam crebros ictus ora et cava tempora circum / obnixi ingeminant.* For *ingeminant* see on 227; for the dative with it see on 34.

435. dant sonitus: for the use of *dare* see on 276.

tempora circum: for the anastrophe see on 370.

436. malae (cheek-bones) is here used in antithesis to ears and temples; we speak of a blow to the face. Compare Ap. Rh. 2. 82 f. ὡς τοῖσι παρήϊά τ᾽ ἀμφοτέρωθεν / καὶ γένυες κτύπεον. In Hom. *Il.* 23. 688 δεινὸς δὲ χρόμαδος γενύων γένετ᾽ the meaning seems to relate to the grinding of teeth (cf. Ap. Rh. 2. 83 f.) but Cerda is surely wrong in seeing that meaning in our passage.

437–8. 'Entellus stands his ground, solid, unmoving, not changing his poised stance, just avoiding the blows with body-sway, his eyes fixed on his opponent all the time.' The word *nisus* well conveys the idea of tenseness: although he does not move his feet, his muscles are tautened for the effort of dodging. For *corpore* cf. Cic. *Cat.* 1. 15 *tuas petitiones . . . parva declinatione et, ut aiunt, corpore effugi.* *Tela* is perhaps used metaphorically (the darting blows), or perhaps literally of the *caestus*. For *exire* used transitively meaning 'to avoid' cf. Lucr. 5. 1330, *Aen.* 11. 750; the usage became commoner in the Silver Age poets. Compare *evadere*, line 689. Notice the dactylic movement of 438, conveying the swift swaying of the body.

439. molibus: the word could be taken with *celsam* ('towering high with its massive walls') or with *oppugnat* ('attacks with siege-works'). Servius records both possibilities and says the word is ambiguous (*amphibolon*). The order of the words permits of either interpretation. If we take *molibus* with *celsam* it will have its common meaning of 'massive structure' as Hor. *Odes* 3. 29. 10 *molem propinquam nubibus arduis*, *Aen.* 9. 711; if we take it with *oppugnat* it will mean 'great mounds', 'assault-ramps', for there is little reason for believing with Lewis and Short that it can mean 'siege engines'. Phrases like *tota mole belli* (Tac. *Hist.* 1. 61), *alia mole belli* (Livy 2. 17. 5) cannot be used to support this meaning. There is a good deal of force in Page's argument from the context, that the town *celsam molibus* is like Entellus *mole valens*, and on the whole it seems best to join *molibus* with *celsam*.

441. This line occurs in almost the same form in *Aen.* 11. 766, with the same slight zeugma of *pererrare* with *aditus*. For the word *aditus* in this connexion cf. Stat. *Th.* 6. 752 (of the boxers' defences) *aditusque ad vulnera clausi*; for the poetic plural see note on 98, and Austin on *Aen.* 4. 293.

442. adsultibus: this very rare word is first found here, and otherwise only in Tacitus (*Ann.* 2. 21) before the fourth century. Nouns of the fourth declension which are first found in Virgil (some of which may well have existed before) include *adfatus, secessus, suspectus*. See note on 202.

443. ostendit dextram: 'showed his right': the English phrase tends to refer to a feinted blow, but that is not so here. For the whole line cf. Ap. Rh. 2. 90 f. ἔνθα δ' ἔπειτ' Ἄμυκος μὲν ἐπ' ἀκροτάτοισιν ἀερθείς, | βουτύπος οἷα, ποδέσσι τανύσσατο, κὰδ δὲ βαρεῖαν | χεῖρ' ἐπὶ οἷ πελέμιξεν.

The rhythm of this line is very imitative of the sense; the line is spondaic (see on 136–41), has the comparatively rare pause after the fifth trochee (see on 678), here helping to build up the tension, and then the 'run-on' verb in the next line before a heavy stop (see on 480), giving great emphasis to the action. Notice how almost exactly the same rhythmic effect occurs again in 446–8; spondees, a pause at the fifth trochee, and then (after an extra line) the 'run-on' verb.

444–5. 'His nimble opponent saw it / coming all the way, and quickly side-stepped out of trouble' (Day Lewis). The alliteration in these lines, first of *v* and then of *c*, is exceptionally marked (cf. 431–2), and is echoed in the next few lines, 446 (*v*), 448 and 450–1 (*c*). Virgil's use of triple alliteration in the second half of the line (*venientem a vertice velox*) is discussed by Austin on *Aen.* 4. 29. Other instances in this book are 174, 432, 469, 866 (where see note).

446. ultro: 'with his own impetus'; see on 55. For the rhythm of this and the following lines see on 443.

447. gravis graviterque: this is reminiscent of Hom. *Il.* 16. 776 (of Cebriones) κεῖτο μέγας μεγαλωστί. Cf. notes on 118 and 565–70. The effect of -*que*, which is not grammatically necessary, is to emphasize *graviter*; cf. *Aen.* 12. 289 f. *regem regisque insigne gerentem* / *Tyrrhenum Aulesten*, 3. 329 *me famulo famulamque Heleno transmisit habendam*, 11. 673 *praecipites pariterque ruunt*. See Wagner, *Quaest. Virg.* 34. 2, and compare 327 and 498.

448–9. The simile of a man falling like a tree is a common one, cf. Hom. *Il.* 13. 178 f., 389 f., 14. 414 f., 16. 482 f., Ap. Rh. 3. 1374 f., 4. 1682 f., Hor. *Odes* 4. 6. 9 f., and especially Cat. 64. 105 f. (Theseus killing the Minotaur) *nam velut in summo quatientem bracchia Tauro* / *quercum aut conigeram sudanti*

cortice pinum | indomitus turbo contorquens flamine robur |
eruit (illa procul radicitus exturbata | prona cadit, late quaevis
cumque obvia frangens), | sic domito saevum prostravit corpore
Theseus. . . Virgil's simile, like that of Catullus, has a
geographical localization, and in this way the poet takes
advantage of the poetic suggestiveness of proper names (cf.
595, and *Aen.* 12. 715 f. with Maguinness's note), just as he
does with 'ornate' epithets (see on 306) and lists of names
(see on 822 f.).

448. quondam: 'sometimes', cf. *Aen.* 2. 367, 7. 378.

    cava: Servius *auct.* says 'exesa vetustate: et dicendo *cava*
pinus bene respexit ad aetatem'. This is not altogether
satisfactory, since nowhere else do hollow pines appear in
Latin (they do not normally become hollow, being resinous),
and in addition we should expect a hollow tree to break off
rather than be torn up by the roots. Mackail goes so far as
to suggest that there is a double simile: (i) the decayed tree
which snaps off and crashes (on Erymanthus), and (ii) the
uprooted tree (on Ida). But this is simply not in the Latin,
and we must accept that *cava* is an epithet not altogether
appropriate to the context, intended to convey the idea that
the tree is ready to fall.

    Erymantho: for the quadrisyllabic ending see note on 300,
and cf. *Aen.* 6. 802. Erymanthus was the chain of mountains
in Arcadia where Hercules killed the boar; for its forests cf.
Ov. *Met.* 2. 499 *silvas Erymanthidas ambit.* For the forests of
Ida cf. *Aen.* 2. 696.

449. radicibus: some MSS. have *radicitus* (as in the passage
from Catullus quoted above); there is little to choose between
the two, but the authority for *radicibus* is stronger.

450. studiis: 'with rival cries', cf. 148, 228. The ablative
(without an adjective) used in an adverbial sense is typically
Virgilian; cf. *Aen.* 12. 131 *studio effusae matres,* 928 *con-*
surgunt gemitu Rutuli (with Maguinness's note), *Aen.* 4. 164
tecta metu petiere, and see Mackail's appendix A, 2; compare
note on 77–78.

451. caelo: poetic dative of 'place to which' (= *ad caelum*).
Cf. *Aen.* 11. 192 (the same phrase), *Aen.* 2. 186 (= 6. 178)
caeloque educere. For the development of this construction,
here seen in its most striking form, see on 34, 233, 806. For
a full discussion of it see Löfstedt, *Syntactica,* i, pp. 180 f.,
Ernout, *Rev. Ph.,* 1944, pp. 181 f., Marouzeau, *Traité de*
stylistique latine, pp. 208–10.

    primusque: *M*'s original reading was *primus,* which
Sabbadini accepted. But the lengthening in arsis of a
syllable which had never been long in earlier Latin, and which

is not before the main caesura or before a pause, is not so common in Virgil as to give good grounds for preferring it here. See note on 284.

451–2. Apart from the very marked alliteration of *c* in 451 (see on 444–5), there is also a remarkable preponderance of words beginning with *a* (cf. the end of 432 and 456). See Marouzeau, *Traité de stylistique latine*, p. 31, where he says: 'Le heurt des voyelles à l'initiale donne l'impression de quelque chose de tendu. Il exprime l'attention, l'effort, la violence.' Among his examples he cites *Aen*. 2. 303 . . . *ascensu supero atque arrectis auribus adsto*, 4. 279–81 *at vero Aeneas aspectu obmutuit amens,* | *arrectaeque horrore comae et vox faucibus haesit.* | *ardet abire fuga*. . . . For the note of caution which must be sounded in aesthetic appreciation of this kind see on 866, with quotations from Marouzeau.

452. aequaevum: this compound adjective is not found before Virgil. It occurs also in *Aen*. 2. 561, and seems to have been coined by him on the analogy of *longaevus* (see on 256), *grandaevus, primaevus*. Latin was by nature far less rich in compound adjectives than Greek; Lucretius used them boldly and with striking success (see Bailey, *Proleg.* 7. 1 for an excellent discussion of the subject), but Virgil was more sparing. In the Silver Age there was a slight extension of their use, but in general ablatival phrases or other methods of description were always far more common than compound adjectives. See L. J. D. Richardson, *Greece and Rome*, 1943, pp. 1 f. for a stimulating discussion of the comparative resources of Greek and Latin in this respect. Quintilian discusses the matter of compound adjectives in 1. 5. 65–70, quoting the well-known compounds of Pacuvius *Nerei repandirostrum incurvicervicum pecus*, and concludes: 'sed res tota magis Graecos decet, nobis minus succedit'.

Book V of the *Aeneid* does not contain any particularly striking compound adjectives (*aequaevus* cannot be said to be a striking word), but included among the relatively few pictorial compounds which Virgil permits himself we may notice *aeripes, alipes, armisonus, arquitenens, auricomus, caprigenus, cornipes, fatidicus, horrisonus, ignipotens, lucifugus, malesuadus, navifragus, noctivagus, nubigena, turicremus, velivolus*; and some ending in *-fer* and *-ger* (for example *caelifer, fumifer, laniger, olivifer, sagittifer, soporifer*). On the whole subject see Mackail, Intro., p. lxxxi, Palmer, *The Latin Language*, pp. 102 f., Marouzeau, *Traité de stylistique latine*, pp. 134 f., Leumann–Hofmann, p. 250, Norden on *Aen*. 6. 141, J. C. Arens, *Mnem.*, 1950, pp. 241 f. See note on *terrificus* (524), and cf. note on 202 with references there for adjectives of various types which are first found in Virgil.

   ab humo: the poets use *humus* in the ablative of separation both with and (more commonly) without a preposition. Cf. *Aen.* 3. 24 *ab humo convellere silvam*; *Geo.* 3. 9 *tollere humo*.

454. vim suscitat ira: 'grows violent in his anger'. Some commentators take *ira* as nominative, but the change of subject is not natural, and cf. *Aen.* 12. 108 *se suscitat ira*.

455. 'then the thought of his honour fires his strength, and his confidence in his prowess'. *Pudor* is his feeling of shame if he quits, of the humiliation which he has already tasted and will know in full if he admits defeat. Cf. *Aen.* 12. 666 f. (of Turnus) *aestuat ingens* / *uno in corde pudor mixtoque insania luctu* / *et furiis agitatus amor et conscia virtus.*

456 f. Cf. Ap. Rh. 2. 74 f. ὣς ὅ γε Τυνδαρίδην φοβέων ἕπετ᾽, οὐδέ μιν εἴα / δηθύνειν. Statius closely imitates Virgil's phraseology in *Th.* 10. 739 f. *agmina belligeri Capaneus agit aequore toto* / *cornua nunc equitum, cuneos nunc ille pedestres.*

456. aequore toto: 'all over the arena'; in boxing in the ancient world there was no precisely defined ring as we know it. For the ablatival phrase cf. *Aen.* 12. 501 f. *quos aequore toto* / *inque vicem nunc Turnus agit nunc Troius heros*, 10. 540 *quem congressus agit campo*, 11. 599 *fremit aequore toto*, 2. 421 *totaque agitavimus urbe.*

457. ingeminans: see on 227.

   nunc ille: see on 186. In the passages cited there the pictorial and emphatic force given by *ille* can be clearly seen; on the other hand in 186 itself there seems no force in *ille*. In the present instance Page says 'the personal prowess of Entellus is emphasised'; Servius on the other hand remarks '*ille* vacat, nam metri causa additum est'. In his comment on *Aen.* 6. 186 he cites this line as a *tibicen*, meaning that *ille*, like *forte* in *Aen.* 6. 186, is a stop-gap; and on *Aen.* 1. 3 *multum ille et terris iactatus et alto* he says '*ille* hoc loco abundat; est enim interposita particula propter metri necessitatem'. Henry powerfully supports Servius, speaking of metrical ekes and citing among other instances 'The frog he would a-wooing go' and 'So, "Fair and softly", John he cried; but John he cried in vain.' I would think that in this instance the truth lies between the two extremes; *ille* adds something to the sentence (translate perhaps 'with left and right alike'), but not very much.

458 f. 'thick as the hail which storm clouds send rattling on roof tops is the shower of blows . . .' Cf. *Geo.* 1. 449 *tam multa in tectis crepitans salit horrida grando*, *Aen.* 9. 669 f. The comparison is rather loosely expressed, *quam* being picked up with *sic* instead of *tam*. Page draws attention

to the alliteration of *c* and *s* and the juxtaposition of the
verbs with their similar endings.

460. pulsat versatque Dareta: 'battered Dares and sent him
spinning' (Jackson Knight).

Dareta: for the variation of declension from *Daren* (456)
Servius compares *Chremes* (*Chremen, Chremeta*). See on 370.

461–84. *Aeneas intervenes and stops the fight. Dares is carried
away by his friends back to the ships, and Entellus receives the
ox as his prize. With a single blow he kills it as a sacrifice
to Eryx, and announces his final retirement from boxing.*

463. Like a modern referee Aeneas 'stops the fight', as Achilles
stopped the wrestling match in Hom. *Il.* 23. 734 f.

466. non: used in the sense of *nonne*, a word extremely rare
in epic and not used at all in the *Aeneid*. See Axelson,
Unpoetische Wörter, pp. 89–90.

viris alias: 'that this is strength of a different order'
(Jackson Knight). The reference is to the increased strength
of Entellus (454 f.), which is attributed to divine aid, presumably sent by Eryx. The phrase is imitated in Val. Fl.
4. 126 f. *iam iam aliae vires maioraque sanguine nostro /
vincunt fata Iovis.*

467. cede deo: 'yield to the will of heaven'. Henry strangely
argues that the phrase means that Entellus is now a god in
disguise.

dixitque: Servius regarded *-que* as a metrical stop-gap,
and said 'vacat *-que* metri causa, et maluit perissologiam
facere quam uti communi syllaba, quae frequens vitiosa est'.
But there is some point in *-que*: it links the two verbs together
more closely, so that the sense is 'he spoke, and as he spoke
. . .' Co-ordination by means of *-que . . . et* ('both . . . and')
is not a normal prose usage, but occurs in epic not uncom-
monly; cf. *Aen.* 4. 484–5, 506, and compare note on 92
(doubled *-que*).

dirimit: the short first syllable in *dirimere* is because the
word developed from *disemere*; contrast *dirumpere* (*dis-
rumpere*), *divellere* (*disvellere*), etc.

468 f. The whole of this passage is closely modelled on Hom.
Il. 23. 695 f. φίλοι δ' ἀμφέσταν ἑταῖροι, / οἵ μιν ἄγον δι' ἀγῶνος
ἐφελκομένοισι πόδεσσιν / αἷμα παχὺ πτύοντα, κάρη βάλλονθ'
ἑτέρωσε. Notice the very slow movement: lines 468–71 (middle)
contain only two dactyls altogether in their first four feet
(only one if *genua* here scans with consonantal *u*, see on 432),
and the first half of 471 is particularly slow, with a spondaic
word filling the first foot (see on 80 and 136–41). The alliteration and assonance of the passage (three participles in *-ntem*,

the very marked repetition of the *c* and *q* sounds in 469, the assonance of *cruorem ore*) are deliberately harsh and excessive. See notes on 181–2 and 431–2.

468. ast: an archaic form used eighteen times in Virgil (also in this book at 509, 676), always for metrical convenience except in *Aen.* 10. 743 *ast de me*. See Norden on *Aen.* 6. 316 and note on 10.

469. utroque: 'from side to side', adverb; cf. the Homer passage cited above κάρη βάλλονθ᾽ ἑτέρωσε.

470. eiectantem: the word is not found before Virgil. It occurs three times in Ovid, and in the Silver Age remained predominantly a poetic word. Some other frequentatives occurring first in Virgil are *convectare, domitare, insertare*. See on 202.

471. galeamque ensemque: for doubled *-que* ('both ... and') see on 92.

    vocati: i.e. at the herald's summons his friends collect the second prize for him, because he cannot collect it himself. So in Homer (*Il.* 23. 699) αὐτοὶ δ᾽ οἰχόμενοι κόμισαν δέπας ἀμφικύπελλον.

472. palmam . . . taurumque: not hendiadys, but 'the palm (cf. 111) and the bull'.

473. superans animis: 'overflowing with pride'; the Verona scholiast here cites Ennius (*Ann.* 205 V) *aut animos superant*, where *animos* is presumably corrupt for *animo* or *animis*.

474. haec: emphatically introducing the two points he has to make in 475 and 476.

477. contra . . . ora: for the separation of a disyllabic preposition from its noun see on 370.

478–80. 'drawing back his right hand and rising to his full height he poised the cruel gauntlet right between the horns and drove it into the skull, and dashed out the brains'. *Libravit* probably means not 'swung', as most commentators say, but 'poised', measuring the blow. *Duros caestus* is a poetic plural; see on 98. Mackail's suggestion that he uses the discarded gauntlets of Eryx and swings them down by their straps on the bull's head seems most unlikely, as such an action would prove nothing about the power of his punches.

480. arduus: observe the emphasis given to the 'run-on' word followed by a pause. Virgil was particularly fond of a pause after the first dactyl (see on 80), and in nearly all cases it naturally occurs after a 'run-on' word; often a verb (e.g. 41, 171, 242, 444, 448, 619); often a noun (e.g. 125, 219, 307, 698, 856); not so often an adjective (in this book only here and 141, 347). As this pause is fairly common it does not automatically cause the word before it to be greatly emphasized; but when the word is emphatic in meaning (as is generally the case), or in an unusual order, the pause adds to the effect. For effects similar to the present one with adjectives cf. *Aen.* 8. 5 f. *saevitque iuventus | effera*, 12. 950 f. *hoc dicens ferrum adverso sub pectore condit | fervidus*, 4. 71 f. *liquitque volatile ferrum | nescius*. See Austin on *Aen.* 4. 22, Winbolt, *Latin Hexameter Verse*, pp. 13 f., Marouzeau, *L'Ordre des mots dans la phrase latine*, iii, pp. 181 f. See note on 643 for the different effect when the first foot is composed of two words.

481. Day Lewis renders the movement of the line thus: 'sprawling, quivering, lifeless, down on the ground the brute fell'. This line is a well-known example of the violent effect caused to the rhythm by ending a line with a single monosyllable, which gives conflict of ictus and accent in the last two feet (see note on 5 f.). Servius shows himself, here as elsewhere, to be under the tyranny of grammatical and metrical 'rules' when he says 'est autem hic pessimus versus in monosyllabum desinens'. Quintilian (8. 3. 20) shows better perception when, commenting on *saepe exiguus mus* (*Geo.* 1. 181), he says 'et clausula ipsa unius syllabae, non usitata, addidit gratiam'. In the phrase *procumbit humi bos* the effect is very evidently a metrical portrayal of the crash by the breaking of the normal rhythm of the line. The emphasis of the monosyllabic ending is intensified by the rare alliteration of *b*; and quite apart from the metre such a postponement of a monosyllabic subject till the end of the sentence would give a strange effect in prose. We have seen that in many places in the account of the boxing match Virgil has permitted himself exaggerated effects of alliteration and assonance; here he concludes his series of pictures by painting with the whole palette.

Some instances of monosyllabic endings of a subtler kind are *Aen.* 1. 105 *praeruptus aquae mons* (the arching crashing wave), 6. 346 *en haec promissa fides est?* (bitter emphasis), 10. 864 *aperit si nulla viam vis* (violent desire of vengeance). Virgil has 39 such endings in the *Aeneid*, a number of them traditional (e.g. *divum pater atque hominum rex*). Later poets used this effect far less often: Ovid has eleven examples, Lucan one, Statius four. On the whole subject see Austin on *Aen.* 4. 132 *odora canum vis*, Norden's *Aeneid VI*, pp. 438 f., 440 f., 448 f., Marouzeau, *Traité de stylistique latine*, pp. 313–16, W. H. D. Rouse, *C.R.*, 1919, pp. 138–40. Compare line 638.

483. meliorem animam: the vicarious substitute in a sacrifice would naturally be termed *melior* ('more appropriate', 'more

acceptable') whatever the reason for the substitution; compare the Greek phrase δευτέρων ἀμεινόνων used on such an
occasion. Cf. *Aen.* 12. 296, where the substitution is the
other way round as Messapus kills Auletes on the altar: *hoc
habet, haec melior magnis data victima divis.* More specific
interpretations of Entellus' meaning are given by some:
Servius says that the bull is a better offering because it is less
cruel than human sacrifice; others see a sarcastic and contemptuous reference by Entellus to Dares. It is perhaps a
mistake to try to decide between these conflicting explanations; Entellus tersely uses the formula, leaving his implications ambiguous.

484. 'I lay down my gloves and my skill', cf. Hor. *Epist.* 1.
1. 4 f., *Odes* 3. 26. 3 f. Entellus announces his retirement in
the hour of victory; the slow spondees and the simple words
are most effective.

485–518. *Aeneas proclaims an archery contest, the target being
a dove secured to a mast. Hippocoon hits the mast; Mnestheus'
arrow cuts the cord; Eurytion then shoots down the bird as it
flies away.*

485 f. The archery contest is modelled, often quite closely, on
Hom. *Il.* 23. 850 f. (see notes on 487, 506, 523–4 *fin.*). In
Homer there are only two competitors: Teucer cuts the cord
with his arrow, and Meriones kills the dove. Skill with the
bow plays a prominent part in the Homeric poems, and is a
main *motif* of the *Odyssey*, but with the Greeks of the classical
period and with the Romans the bow was much less important. The really skilled archers were generally Cretans or
Asiatics. Consequently archery played no part in the great
Greek games, nor in Roman *ludi*; and Virgil's reasons for
including it here are very largely literary, to recall and
elaborate on the Homeric description, and to lead into the
portent of Acestes' arrow (see note on 519 f.).

485–6. certare . . . invitat: for this use of the infinitive, where
prose would have some such phrase as *ad certandum*, cf. *Geo.*
4. 23 *vicina invitet decedere ripa calori*, and note on 21–22.

486. dicit: this is *P*'s reading, accepted by some editors on the
ground that *ponit* (read by the majority of the MSS.) is a
scribe's alteration based on the similar line 292. But it can
equally be argued that *praemia ponit* is Virgil's expression
for τιθέναι ἆθλα in both places, and I would therefore prefer
here to follow the majority of the MSS.

487. ingentique manu: 'magna multitudine' said Servius, and
Heyne agreed with him. Forbiger expressed the hope 'nemo
autem cum Servio et Heynio de magna multitudine cogi-

tabit', but Henry and Fairclough have disappointed his expectations. There would have to be very strong arguments indeed to prevent us taking it in the natural sense 'with his mighty hand', Homer's χειρὶ παχείῃ; cf. 241, *Aen*. 11. 556 *dextra ingenti librans*, Val. Fl. 3. 609 f. Henry says, 'The picture afforded by Aeneas setting up the mast himself with his own hand while his subordinates looked on had bordered closely on the ridiculous.' But he shared out the stags (*Aen*. 1. 194); he bound on the boxing-gloves (425); he set up the turning-point for the ship-race (130); now he sets up the mast as Achilles had done (*Il*. 23. 852).

de nave: i.e. the mast is removed from Serestus' ship and set up in the ground (as in *Il*. 23. 852). Serestus did not take part in the ship-race, but has been mentioned as a captain in *Aen*. 1. 611, 4. 288.

488. volucrem: Mackail took such strong exception to this epithet that he conjectured and printed *volucre in traiecto fune columbam / quo tendant ferrum . . .* (*volucre* agreeing with *ferrum*); this is in every way unacceptable. The force of *volucrem* ('flying', 'fluttering') is to add the image of the dove's movement when it is secured by the foot to the cord.

traiecto in fune: some take *traiecto* to mean that the rope was passed round the bird's leg (cf. 511), others that it was passed round the mast. On the whole perhaps the second is better as more appropriate for the force of *iacere*.

490. sortem: the singular is used, drawing attention to the method of choice, where the plural would be more usual.

492. exit locus: for *exit* cf. *Il*. 23. 353 ἐκ δὲ κλῆρος θόρε Νεστορίδαο, Hor. *Odes* 2. 3. 27 *sors exitura*. *Locus* is used by an easy metonymy to mean 'the lot giving him first turn'; cf. line 132.

This Hippocoon is not otherwise known. He is presumably the brother of Nisus, son of Hyrtacus (*Aen*. 9. 406). For the polysyllabic line-ending see on 300.

493. modo . . . victor: 'recently a prize-winner'; he was actually second.

494. For the repetition of Mnestheus, giving rhetorical emphasis, see note on 565–70 and cf. 116–17, 194.

oliva: this is not mentioned in the account of the ship-race; Cloanthus the winner was crowned with laurel. In the foot-race olive crowns were promised to the first three.

495. This Eurytion is not mentioned elsewhere. Pandarus son of Lycaon was ordered by Athene (*Il*. 4. 72 f.) to break the truce by wounding Menelaus during the single combat of Menelaus and Paris. He is mentioned here because he was an outstanding archer (*Il*. 2. 827, 5. 95 f.). For Virgil's use of apostrophe see on 840.

498. For the co-ordination of *extremus* and *galea ima* by means of *-que* see on 447, and cf. line 327 and *Aen.* 6. 640.

    Acestes: used by metonymy for *sors Acestae*, cf. 339 and *Aen.* 2. 201 *Laocoon ductus Neptuno sorte sacerdos* ('Laocoon drawn by lot . . .'), 2. 311–12 *iam proximus ardet* / *Ucalegon* (= *domus Ucalegonis*).

499. manu . . . temptare: 'put his hand to'. *Manu* is often used in Virgil simply to denote personal effort, e.g. *Aen.* 2. 434, 4. 344, 11. 505, 12. 627. Here, however, it perhaps has a rather more specific reference, to the skill of the hand in archery.

501. pro se quisque viri: Servius says 'pro qualitate roboris sui'. The same phrase occurs in *Aen.* 12. 552.

503. volucris . . . auras: 'cut through the winged breezes'. For *diverberat* cf. *Aen.* 6. 294 *frustra ferro diverberet umbras*, 9. 411 *hasta volans noctis diverberat umbras*, Lucr. 1. 222, 2. 152. For *volucris* cf. *Aen.* 11. 795 (*voti*) *partem volucris dispersit in auras*.

504. 'and reached its mark and struck home, full in the wood of the mast'.

505. timuitque exterrita pennis: 'was all one terrified flurry of wings' (Day Lewis). The phrase is an unusual one, as Conington points out, because of the connexion of a verb expressing mental action with an ablative of a part of the body; *tremuit pennis* would have been perfectly usual, like Horace's *et corde et genibus tremit* (*Odes* 1. 23. 8). Virgil was perhaps led to the variation because he had already used *intremuit*. Slater's ingenious suggestion *micuitque* (cf. *Geo.* 4. 73) has found support from Mackail.

506. There are two possible interpretations of *plausu*: the noise of the dove's wings, or the applause of the spectators. Servius says 'alii pinnarum (plausu) dicunt, sed melius est spectantum favore: illud enim est incredibile'. Heyne, Forbiger, and Page support the meaning of the beating of wings; cf. 215, 516. But Servius' objection, which I take to be that *sonuerunt omnia* would be an inappropriate exaggeration, has some force, and the decisive argument in favour of the meaning of applause is the phrase in Homer's archery competition (*Il.* 23. 869) ἀτὰρ κελάδησαν Ἀχαιοί.

507. adducto: 'brought to his chest', i.e. with the bow-string drawn back; cf. 141 and *Aen.* 9. 632 *adducta sagitta*, *Il.* 4. 123 νευρὴν μὲν μαζῷ πέλασεν.

508. alta: 'the heavens', cf. *Aen.* 6. 787 *omnes supera alta tenentes*, 9. 564 *alta petens . . . Iovis armiger*. The singular is also used (*Geo.* 2. 210 *altum . . . petiere*). See on 127, 164, 851.

pariterque . . . tetendit: 'took aim with eye and arrow together', a slight zeugma, but not nearly so marked as *Aen.* 12. 930 f. *oculos dextramque precantem / protendens.*

509–10. contingere . . . non valuit: *valere* with the infinitive is common in poetry, and in prose from Livy onwards, cf. Lucr. 1. 108 f., *Aen.* 2. 492, 3. 415; and see note on 21–22.

510. linea: the word occurs first in Virgil (cf. *Aen.* 10. 784). Adjectives of this kind were very convenient for the hexameter; others which are first found in Virgil include *arboreus, frondeus, fumeus, funereus, litoreus, pampineus, pulvereus, rameus, sidereus, spumeus, squameus, stuppeus, triticeus, tureus, vipereus.* See Norden on *Aen.* 6. 281, Leumann–Hofmann, p. 205, and note on 202.

511. quis: an archaic form for *quibus,* occurring ten times in Virgil, considerably less frequently than *quibus.* See note on 10, and Marouzeau, *Traité de stylistique latine,* pp. 127–8.

innexa pedem: for the 'retained' accusative see note on 135, and cf. *Aen.* 6. 281 *vipereum crinem vittis innexa cruentis.*

512. 'she was away in flight towards the south and the high clouds'. I should prefer to read *atra* with the majority of MSS. rather than *P*'s *alta,* which is weak after the use of the word in 508 and 511. For *atra* cf. 516. *Notos* is governed (like *nubila*) by *in*; for similar word order cf. *Aen.* 2. 654, 6. 416, 692, and see notes on 370 and 663.

513–16. 'Then in a flash—for already he had his bow levelled and his arrow drawn back—Eurytion called on his brother to hear his prayers, took aim at the dove, rejoicing now in the freedom of the sky and flapping her wings in flight, and pierced her as she flew beneath a dark cloud.' There is asyndeton between 514 and the following lines, or in other words the two main verbs *vocavit* and *figit* are not joined by a co-ordinating conjunction (in 515 the word *et* links *laetam* and *plaudentem*).

513–14. Cf. *Aen.* 10. 521 *infensam contenderat hastam.* Servius with his love of hypallage laconically comments 'contento arcu tela tenens parata'. *Tela* is a poetic plural (see on 98) of a rather striking kind; the plural of *telum* does not appear to be used in a singular sense before Virgil. Compare *Aen.* 7. 497 *spicula,* 10. 731 *tela.*

514. in vota: cf. 234. Pandarus had met his death at the hands of Diomedes (*Il.* 5. 290 f.).

516. nigra . . . sub nube: perhaps because the dove showed up against the cloud, perhaps to indicate how nearly it escaped.

517–18. vitamque . . . aetheriis: cf. *Geo.* 3. 547 *(aves) praecipites alta vitam sub nube relinquunt.* Schrader objected to *astris* and proposed *auris,* but (like *sidera*) *astra* can have a very vague meaning in the sense of 'the sky'; cf. 838, and note on 126.

519–44. *Acestes, left with no target to aim at, shoots his arrow high into the air. It catches fire, and disappears like a shooting star. Aeneas recognizes this as a good omen, and awards Acestes first prize.*

519 f. In this sequel to the last contest of the games Virgil raises the level of significance of the events he has been describing, and emphasizes the divine background to the action of the *Aeneid*. During the account of the athletic contests the tension of the poem has been relaxed; by concluding the archery with a miraculous portent Virgil restores the high epic tone so as to lead into the patriotic account of the *lusus Troiae* and the eventful narrative which follows. The skill with which he manages the transitions both into and away from the subject-matter of the games avoids the danger that they might give the impression of a detached interlude not integral to the main theme of the poem. See Intro., p. xii and pp. xvi–xvii. For the significance of the portent see on 523–4.

519. 'Now only Acestes was left, with the prize lost' (i.e. already won by Eurytion). For *superare* = *superesse* cf. line 713, *Ecl.* 9. 27, *Aen.* 2. 597, 643, 3. 339.

520. contorsit: the reading *contendit* has equally good support, and may be right; cf. 508 and 513. *Contorquere* is frequent with *telum*; it may not perhaps seem very suitable when *telum* = *sagittam*, but cf. 497. I prefer *contorsit* with its rather exaggerated sense ('sent his arrow whirring') because it fits the context of the next line better (*arcumque sonantem*).

521. 'displaying both his veteran skill and his sounding bow'. For doubled *-que* ('both . . . and') see on 92. For *pater* in apposition to the subject cf. 130 and 424. Here the effect is perhaps more marked because *pater* is in a different clause from the subject. Cf. line 841, *Aen.* 1. 196, and see Page's note on *Aen.* 1. 412. Compare the use of *ille* in this way (see note on 457, where it is shown that the degree of emphasis imparted in cases of this kind can be disputed). Notice the long second syllable of *pater* (see note on 284). Some have suggested that it is influenced by the Greek πατήρ, but there is no evidence to show that the vowel was long by nature in early Latin, and so it is best to regard it as a short syllable lengthened in arsis.

Servius records that Virgil's critics found fault with this line: 'culpat hoc Vergiliomastix: artem enim in vacuo aëre ostendere non poterat: quamquam dicant periti posse ex

ipso sagittariorum gestu artis peritiam indicari'. The
criticism is unjustified, for the line conveys an attractive
picture of the skilled and experienced archer and the sound
of his bow as he uses it in an exhibition shot; we are reminded
of Odysseus lovingly handling and stringing his bow.

522. For the phraseology compare *Aen.* 2. 199 f., introducing
the description of Laocoon's fate.

    subitum: all good MSS. have *subito*, but the co-ordination
of adverb and participle with *-que* would be awkward here
(contrast an instance like 447, where see note), and the
corruption is very easily explained.

522–3. 'and destined to be of great portent'; *magno augurio*
is ablative of description rather than predicative dative.

523–4. 'the great outcome proved it so in later days, when awe-
inspiring prophets sang of the late-fulfilled omens'. This
is a difficult and much disputed passage, both in the actual
meaning of the words and in the identification of the future
events here portended. Servius begins by saying that *sera*
means *gravia* (thinking of a connexion with *seria*), and goes on
'et quod improbant vates Aeneas amplectitur'. His meaning
for *sera* is certainly not possible in the context (if at all),
but it is possible that he is right in taking *vates* to refer to
those present at the time. In this case the meaning will be
'and awe-inspiring prophets sang of omens for later days'.
Heinze supports this view as giving a better meaning for
canere omina; I have preferred the other rendering because
the antithesis between *futurum* and *docuit post* seems naturally to extend into the following line with its similar tense.
For *exitus ingens* cf. Statius' imitation in *Th.* 6. 944 *penitus
latet exitus ingens*; for *sera omina* cf. Hom. *Il.* 2. 324–5 τέρας
. . . ὄψιμον ὀψιτέλεστον.

    Much difficulty has been felt with Servius' rendering (and
to some extent this applies to the other rendering too) over
the apparent contrast between *terrifici vates* prophesying evil
and Aeneas accepting the portent as a good omen. It is
sometimes suggested that Aeneas was mistaken in regarding
it as a good omen (which would surely be absurdly contrary
to the whole tone of the passage); sometimes that the prophets were wrong, and even that Virgil was indicating his
contempt for prophets (see E. Bréguet, *Mus. Helv.*, 1956, pp.
54 f., and the reply by E. Liechtenhan, *Mus. Helv.*, 1957, pp.
52 f.). But there is not really any question of who was right;
it is nowhere suggested that the omen was evil. The word
terrifici refers to the natural awe which prophets inspire when
they proclaim omens, and which on this occasion the Trojans
all felt in any case (529).

We must now ask what in fact this sign did portend; what was the *exitus ingens*? Lejay (ad loc.) argues that it did not portend anything beyond the victory of Acestes, but Virgil's emphasis is such that it surely must have had a precise meaning which his Roman readers would understand. What then was it? If we regard the passage from a literary point of view and consider the impact which it makes as a whole on the reader, there can be no doubt that the events portended must be directly concerned with Acestes; certainly Aeneas thinks and says so. It seems therefore that we must discard the suggestion (accepted by many) that it has anything to do with the comet of 44 B.C., or with the deification of Aeneas, Caesar, or Augustus. See especially D. L. Drew, *The Allegory of the Aeneid*, pp. 43 f. for support of the comet theory. There are some strong arguments in favour of it: the comet (*sidus Iulium*) was seen during the games which Octavian was celebrating in Caesar's honour, and was commonly believed to be the spirit of Caesar rising up to heaven (*Ecl.* 9. 47, *Aen.* 8. 681, Pliny, *Nat. Hist.* 2. 93–94, Suet. *Iul.* 88, Dio 45. 6. 4). Servius (on *Ecl.* 9. 46, *Aen.* 6. 790, 8. 681) speaks of these games as *ludi funebres*, but this does not seem an accurate description; they were actually the *ludi Veneris Genetricis*, also called *Victoriae Caesaris*, which Caesar had himself inaugurated after Thapsus. Against the comet theory it can be argued that a comet is itself an *omen* rather than an *exitus ingens*; that we are here concerned with a shooting star (such as is often seen, 527) not a comet; but above all that Caesar's comet is irrelevant in a context directly concerned with Acestes.

It seems then that the star portends the future greatness of Acestes, in particular with regard to the foundation and fame of his city Segesta (see on 718), possibly with some forward reference to the part Segesta played in the First Punic War, when it immediately made common cause with Rome. At the beginning of the book Acestes is the humble chieftain of a rustic folk (37 f.); at the end he is the ruler of his city (757 *gaudet regno Troianus Acestes*), which is destined to play its part in the imperial sway of Aeneas' own city of Rome. Henry and Mackail go further and think that the deification of Acestes is portended; there is no evidence for this, but it is a reasonable possibility, and would give a good focal point for the meaning of line 524.

For a good discussion of the subject see Heinze, *Virgils Epische Technik*, pp. 165 f. See also R. Pichon, *R.E.A.*, 1916, pp. 253 f., where he argues convincingly for Segesta as the *exitus ingens*, but is much less convincing when he goes

on to connect the dove at which the competitors have been
aiming with a hypothetical ceremony at Segesta involving a
dove. The ancient commentators were troubled about the
dove (see Servius on 517), which they thought an inappropriate target for the archery competition because it was sacred
to Venus. But Servius gives the answer when he says 'sane
sciendum hunc totum locum ab Homero esse sumptum'.
Virgil had a dove as target because Homer did, and he saw
no reason to change.

524. terrifici: for the word (which is poetic and rather rare)
cf. Lucr. 2. 632 *terrificas capitum quatientes numine cristas*,
Aen. 12. 103 f. (the only other instance in Virgil) *mugitus
veluti cum prima in proelia taurus | terrificos ciet*. For com-
pound adjectives see on 452; others of this kind used by
Virgil include *horrificus, luctificus, vulnificus*. For the idea
of the line cf. Lucr. 1. 102 f. *vatum | terriloquis victus dictis*,
Aen. 4. 464 f. *multaque praeterea vatum praedicta priorum |
terribili monitu horrificant*.

525 f. Day Lewis has:

> The shaft, as it sped among the streaming clouds, took fire,
> Blazing a trail in the sky, then burnt itself out and vanished
> Into thin air: thus, often, a star dislodges itself
> From heaven and shoots across it, trailing a long-haired flame.

525. liquidis: Servius says severely: 'nubes pro aëre posuit:
nubes enim liquidae esse non possunt'. We find *liquida
nubila* (*Aen.* 7. 699), and fairly often *liquidus aër* (e.g. 6. 202);
cf. line 217. Servius' comment is too bald a statement of
metonymy; we must understand Virgil to mean that clouds
were present, and they are characterized as the air is characterized: thin, yielding, unsubstantial.

526. signavitque viam flammis: cf. *Aen.* 2. 696 f. (of a shooting
star) *cernimus Idaea claram se condere silva | signantemque
vias*. The meaning there, as here, is 'leaving the trace of its
path', not (as some maintain) 'pointing out the way'.

527. caelo . . . refixa: the stars are thought of as 'fixed' in the
sky (Pliny *Nat. Hist.* 2. 28 *sidera quae affixa diximus mundo*),
and the sky is 'studded' with them, *stellis ardentibus aptum*
(*Aen.* 6. 797). Shooting stars then are 'loosed' from the sky;
for *refixa* cf. Hor. *Epod.* 17. 5 *refixa caelo devocare sidera*.

528. Compare Lucr. 2. 206 f. *nocturnasque faces caeli sublime
volantes | nonne vides longos flammarum ducere tractus ?*, *Geo.*
1. 365 f., and *Aen.* 2. 693 f., where the shooting star is in
itself an *augurium*; cf. Hom. *Il.* 4. 75 f., Ap. Rh. 3. 1378 f.
οἷος δ' οὐρανόθεν πυρόεις ἀναπάλλεται ἀστήρ|ὁλκὸν ὑπαυγάζων,
τέρας ἀνδράσιν.

This line has a quasi-caesura in the third foot without a strong fourth-foot caesura; see on 591, and cf. *Aen.* 2. 9 (= 4. 81) *suadentque cadentia sidera somnos*.

530–1. nec ... omen abnuit: i.e. Aeneas accepted it as an omen, and acted accordingly, regarding it as favourable. Compare Anchises in *Aen.* 2. 699 f., and Tolumnius' words in 12. 260 (after the omen of the eagle and the swans) *accipio agnoscoque deos*.

532 f. In *Il.* 23. 615 f. Achilles presented Nestor with a prize although he did not compete in the games.

533 f. 'for the great king of Olympus, by giving auspices such as we have seen, intended that you should be especially distinguished in the winning of honours'. The phrase *exsortem ducere honores* is a most unusual one, combining in a typically Virgilian way a number of implications of meaning. The basic sense of *exsors* is 'not drawn for by lot', i.e. especially set aside as a mark of distinction; cf. *Aen.* 8. 552 *(equum) ducunt exsortem Aeneae*, 9. 270 f. (of Turnus' horse) *ipsum illum, clipeum cristasque rubentis* / *excipiam sorti, iam nunc tua praemia, Nise*. When *exsors* is applied to people it normally means 'not sharing in', e.g. *Aen.* 6. 428 *dulcis vitae exsortis*; Servius on our passage says 'ἄκληρον, sine sorte'. Virgil combines the two meanings in this line; Acestes was excluded by the lot from competing in the contest, and this is seen to have been a mark of distinction. In the same way the phrase *ducere honores* partly has reference to winning a prize although excluded by the lot from competing, partly to winning great glory because of the indication of distinction given by the divine sign. Some editors accept the reading *honorem*, given by some inferior MSS., in order to take *exsortem* with it, but the rhythm of the two lines is more subtle and *exsortem* itself more forceful if we take it in agreement with *te*.

535. ipsius Anchisae: the bowl had been given as a gift to Anchises, and had been therefore among his personal treasures.

536. cratera: for the Greek form of the accusative compare *Simoenta* (261, 634), *aëra* (839), *aethera*, *aegida*, *lampada*, *Arcada*, *Hectora*, etc.; and see note on 265.

impressum signis: 'embossed', cf. 267, and the elaboration in Stat. *Th.* 6. 531 f.

537. For the elision over the caesura see on 408, and Austin on *Aen.* 4. 54; cf. in particular *Aen.* 2. 548 . . . *Pelidae genitori. illi mea tristia facta* . . .

in magno munere: 'as a great gift'. The unusual use of *in* adds some impressiveness to the phrase, cf. *Aen.* 8. 273 *tantarum in munere laudum*, Cic. *Verr.* 2. 3. 115 *in summo beneficio*.

Cisseus: this Thracian king was in Virgil's version father of Hecuba (cf. *Aen.* 7. 320, where Servius comments that Virgil is following Euripides, and *Aen.* 10. 705). According to Homer Cisseus was the father of Theano, and Hecuba the daughter of Dymas.

538. ferre: for the infinitive see on 247-8.

sui: this is the objective genitive of *se* depending on *monimentum*, not the genitive of *suus* in agreement with *amoris*. The line is almost exactly repeated at 572 (where see note).

541. praelato invidit honori: 'grudge him his preferred position'. *Praelato* agrees with *honori*; it seems unnatural to regard it as a second dative (of the person) after *invidit*. As an epithet of *honos* it is somewhat transferred, but as Wagner remarks 'si quis est praelatus, etiam honos eius dicatur praelatus'. *Invidere* often takes the accusative of the thing grudged (Servius *auct.* here says *id est praelatum honorem*; cf. *Aen.* 8. 509 *invidet imperium*), but the dative is found fairly frequently, e.g. Cic. *De Leg. Agr.* 2. 103 *qui honori inviderunt meo*, Sall. *Cat.* 58. 21 *quodsi virtuti vostrae fortuna inviderit*. *P* has *honore* in the first hand, and this is attractive: such a construction with *invidere* became common in the Silver Age, and Quintilian (9. 3. 1) comments on it as being normal in his time where Cicero would have had the accusative. We find it already in Livy 2. 40. 11 *non inviderunt laude sua mulieribus*. Henry's suggestion that *honos* is used by metonymy for the person is entertainingly rather than convincingly argued.

542. quamvis . . . deiecit: *quamvis* is found with the indicative in Virgil only here and in *Ecl.* 3. 84; the indicative occurs very rarely indeed in prose, but fairly often in verse (Lucretius, Horace, Propertius, Ovid). It is clearly due to analogy with *quamquam*; see Kühner–Stegmann, ii. 2, p. 443.

543. donis: Servius says 'ad dona', but such a dative with *ingredi* seems unparalleled, and it is perhaps best to take *donis* as ablative of respect with *proximus*, equivalent to *ordine donorum*.

545–603. *The final event is an equestrian display by the Trojan boys. They process in three companies, young Priam leading one, Atys another, and Iulus the third, and they give a brilliant display of intricate manœuvres and mock battle. This is the ceremony which Iulus introduced to Alba Longa, and it was handed on to Rome and called the* lusus Troiae.

545 f. The *lusus Troiae* brings the games to an end with the rounding-off effect of a closing ceremony (see Intro., p. xvi), and at the same time links the events of the remote past with

Virgil's own days. We hear of these equestrian manœuvres in the time of Sulla (Plut. *Cat. Min.* 3); they were revived by Julius Caesar (Suet. *Iul.* 39, Dio 43. 23. 6), and established under Augustus as a regular institution, performed by boys of noble birth (Suet. *Aug.* 43 *sed et Troiae lusum edidit frequentissime maiorum minorumque puerorum, prisci decorique moris existimans clarae stirpis indolem sic notescere*; cf. Dio 51. 22. 4, 53. 1. 4, 54. 26. 1). They continued to be held under Augustus' successors (Suet. *Tib.* 6, *Cal.* 18, *Claud.* 21, *Nero* 7, Tac. *Ann.* 11. 11). For the keen interest which Augustus took in the training of the young and for the *collegia iuvenum* see H. Last in *C.A.H.* x, pp. 462 f., H. I. Marrou, *Histoire de l'éducation dans l'antiquité*, 1950, pp. 398 f., L. R. Taylor, *J.R.S.*, 1924, pp. 158 f., M. Rostovtzeff, *Römische Bleitesserae, Klio*, Beiheft iii, 1905, pp. 59 f., especially 64 f.

It seems most unlikely that the *lusus Troiae* was originally connected with Troy. Lejay (on 5. 553) cites Festus' explanation of the archaic verbs *amptruare, redamptruare*, as describing the movements of dancing, which would suggest a noun *troia* meaning 'movement', 'evolution'; and on a sixth-century oenochoe found at Tragliatella there are figures of horsemen and a labyrinth, and the Etruscan word *Truia* (see E. N. Gardiner, *Athletics of the Ancient World*, pp. 126–7). When the legend of Rome's Trojan origins became widespread, the *lusus Troiae* would easily be associated with Troy. Mehl, cited below, has a full account of various theories concerning the antique origins of ritual dance and folklore from which the ceremony may have developed.

The whole description of the ceremony is written with a verve which clearly reflects Virgil's enjoyment of such visual pageantry; and it is painted in the bright and joyful colours appropriate to the hopes that were placed in the promise and achievement of the younger generation, whether of Aeneas' day or Virgil's own. It has often been remarked that the youthful characters in the *Aeneid* are drawn with particular sympathy and vividness, and this is as true of Iulus as it is of those whose destinies are less happy (Euryalus, Lausus, Pallas). Iulus is shown here, as in 4. 156 f., in boyish excitement and pride; a little further on in this book (667 f.) he reacts more quickly than anyone else to the news about the ships; and in the later books, against a grimmer setting, we see him growing up. On this see Warde Fowler, *The Death of Turnus*, pp. 87 f.; on the *lusus Troiae* generally see Heinze, *Virgils Epische Technik*, pp. 157 f., E. Mehl in *R.E.*, suppl. viii (1956), pp. 888 f., K. Schneider in *R.E.* xiii, pp. 2059 f., Daremberg–Saglio, s.v. *Trojae ludus*, and not least the

enthusiastic appraisal by Henry. There is an interesting
imitation of Virgil's account by Claudian (28. 621 f.).

545. nondum certamine misso: see on 286. Here, as the singular *certamine* indicates, the meaning is 'before the archery
contest was duly concluded', rather than 'before the whole
games were concluded'. Servius finds difficulty over the
tenses because he takes it that the archery was already
concluded, but probably *certamine misso* would refer to some
final announcement by Aeneas.

546. Iuli: Virgil uses the name Iulus (which in *Aen.* 1. 267 f.
he associates with Ilium; see note on 117) nearly as frequently
as the original Greek name Ascanius.

547. Epytiden: cf. Hom. *Il.* 17. 324, where Apollo appears to
Aeneas in the guise of Periphas the herald, son of Epytus.
There is a different Epytus in *Aen.* 2. 340, possibly the son of
Periphas.

548 f. 'Away you go now and tell Ascanius, if he has got the
boys all ready with him in their formation and has marshalled
his equestrian display, to bring on the procession in his
grandfather's honour and show himself in his panoply.'
Notice the informal arrangement of this sentence, and the
unusual metrical effect of a heavy pause (at the end of the
speech) after the first syllable of the line. A pause in this
position is not uncommon when it is very light (e.g. 235), and
in this instance the enclitic *ait* somewhat, but not entirely,
smoothes the abruptness. Compare 690, and for a rather
different effect (with elision) cf. 651.

550. ducat avo turmas: *ducat* is jussive subjunctive in parataxis
with *dic*; cf. *Aen.* 4. 635 *dic corpus properet fluviali spargere
lympha*, and note on 163. For the use of the dative *avo* cf. 603.

551. ait: for the redundancy after *fatur* (547) cf. *Aen.* 3. 480,
11. 42.

  discedere: this is the reading of *P*; the other MSS. have
decedere, but *discedere* is more vivid as a description of people
moving outwards and away from the centre of the arena.
As *infusum* in the next line indicates, they had pressed in
closer for the boxing and the archery.

553 f. Notice the careful arrangement of the full description
which sets the scene. First the entrance of the riders is
described in general terms, then their accoutrements, then
their formations and the three leaders; finally the applause
of the audience, and the preliminaries are complete and the
manœuvres begin.

554–5. quos . . . mirata fremit: 'murmurs its admiration for
them'. The accusative is after *mirata*, not as Servius says
after *fremit*. For the tense of *mirata* see on 708.

556. 'Each has his hair bound in ceremonial style with a trimmed garland.' *In morem* (cf. *Aen.* 8. 282 *pellibus in morem
cincti*) probably goes with the whole sentence rather than
with *tonsa* alone; the phrase commonly means 'in the traditional style', but as this was the first celebration of the *lusus*
its significance is 'in the (approved, required) ceremonial
style'.

There is considerable disagreement about the meaning of
tonsa corona. Servius, after apparently taking *tonsa coma*
together (perhaps he read *tonsa est coma*; see next note),
explains *corona* as *galea*. The main difficulty is that in 673
Ascanius takes off the helmet which he had been wearing for
the mock battle; there is no mention elsewhere of helmets,
and how could he wear a garland and a helmet? Hence
Servius' desire to change these garlands into helmets; he
also adds the possibility that the helmets may have been
garlanded ('alii dicunt potuisse eos galeas habere coronatas');
cf. perhaps *Aen.* 7. 751. But it is a plain fact that this line
contains no reference to helmets, and it is impossible to
believe that in the phrase *coma pressa corona* the word
corona could mean a garlanded helmet. We must then
assume that the boys are not at this stage wearing helmets
(lines 575–6 support this), and conclude either that there is
an inconsistency in the narrative, or (as is perfectly reasonable) that helmets were not donned until the mock battle
began. Henry states with considerable pungency the arguments against seeing a reference to helmets in this passage,
but advances a far-fetched suggestion, namely that '*corona*
is neither helmet nor chaplet, nor anything but the crop, the
round crop of the hair, the round crop into which the previously long hair (*coma*) of the boys had been reduced,
restricted, confined (*pressa*) by cutting, by the shears (*tonsa*)'.

tonsa: the word is generally taken to mean 'trimmed', i.e.
with the leaves clipped to a uniform length, or with the larger
leaves removed, and commentators cite *Geo.* 3. 21 *caput
tonsae foliis ornatus olivae* (cf. the same words in line 774
of this book). Nettleship with some force asks what beauty
there could be in such a garland, and would read *tonsa est coma*,
with *tonsa* agreeing with *coma*; but this seems weak. I think
it is perhaps possible that in the *Georgics* passage *tonsa
oliva* means not 'trimmed olive', but simply 'cut olive', so
that *tonsa corona* might mean a garland of cut leaves, as
opposed to a garland artificially made. Compare our somewhat pleonastic expression 'cut flowers'.

557. praefixa: 'tipped'. Virgil uses the word in its other
construction in *Aen.* 7. 817 *praefixa cuspide myrtum*. The

words *praefixa hastilia ferro* occur at the line ending also in *Aen.* 12. 489; cf. *Aen.* 10. 479. Servius records on the authority of Baebius Macer that Augustus used to present boys who took part in the *lusus Troiae* with a helmet and two *hastilia*—'ad quod Vergilium constat adludere'.

558. levis: 'polished', 'burnished', as in 91.

558 f. 'High on their chests and passing round their necks are pliant circlets of twisted gold.' Nearly all MSS. have *et* for *it*, but Servius argues for the verb *it*, and the construction if we read *et* is almost intolerable. *Summum pectus* is explained by Servius as *pectoris et colli confinium*. Suetonius (*Aug.* 43. 2) tells us that Augustus presented a *torques aureus* to Nonius Asprenas, who was hurt while taking part in the *lusus Troiae*.

559. flexilis: this adjective is not found before Virgil. Similar adjectives which do not occur before Virgil are *sutilis, tortilis, armentalis, crinalis, glacialis, iuvenalis, lustralis*. See Palmer, *The Latin Language*, p. 111, Leumann–Hofmann, p. 235, and note on 202.

560 f. There are thirty-six boys plus three leaders (thirteen to each group). For *terni = tres* see note on 85. Each group is in two files of six, and each is accompanied by its trainer. Servius suggests that there are three groups because of the original three centuries of Roman knights (Livy 1. 13).

560. vagantur: 'weave their way', a colourful word describing the wheeling movements of the ride-past.

562. agmine partito: 'in divided column', probably making more explicit the double file picture already suggested by *bis seni*. Others take it to mean that the three groups are separated by spaces.

paribusque magistris: 'each alike with its trainer'. *Paribus* suggests that the groups have their trainers stationed in corresponding positions (presumably at the side). Fairclough and others think that *magistri* are the same as *ductores*, but (i) in 669 *magistri* clearly means trainers, (ii) with the words *quemque secuti* the description must shift from the leaders to those who are following. It would be inelegant to say 'There was an officer at the head of each company, and the men behind them were a splendid sight in double file with their officers leading them'.

563 f. This sentence and the next are somewhat loosely constructed. *Una acies iuvenum ducit quam* . . . leads the reader to expect a verb to which *acies* will be the subject, but in fact the phrase means *primam aciem iuvenum ducit* . . . *Alter Atys* is very condensed for *alter ductor est Atys*. Other marks of incompleteness in the passage (apart from the unfinished line 574) are the omission of any mention of Atys' horse, the almost verbal repetition in line 572 of line 538, and the flatness of lines 573–4. See also Mackail, ad loc.

563. ducit quam: for the postposition of the relative see on 22.

564. Virgil tells of the death of Polites, son of Priam, in *Aen.* 2. 526 f. Servius reports a variant tradition in Cato's *Origines*, according to which Polites came to Italy and founded the town Politorium. It was a common custom to call children after their grandfathers; cf. *Aen.* 12. 348 (Eumedes) *nomine avum referens.* For the use of apostrophe see on 840, and for the vocative form *Polite* see on 843.

565–70. These lines contain a number of instances of deliberate repetition, or anaphora (for unintentional repetition see on 254). The threefold repetition of the word *albus* to link three clauses closely together is a favourite device of Virgil's; cf. *Aen.* 1. 448–9, 2. 97–98, 4. 138–9, 7. 219–20, 473–4, and in this book 73–74, 181–2 (somewhat varied), 218–19, 586–7. Then there is the repetition of the name Atys, and in a different way of Iulus; cf. 116–17, 493–4, and Page on *Aen.* 4. 25. There is the phrase *pueroque puer*, a type common in Greek; cf. *Aen.* 1. 684 *notos pueri puer indue vultus*, 3. 329 *me famulo famulamque Heleno transmisit habendam*, 10. 600 *morere et fratrem ne desere frater.* Other examples of the way in which Virgil uses anaphora will be found at 9 (with chiastic order), 80, 85, 118, 136–7, 186–7, 281, 447, 583–4, 614–15, 698, 724–5. See Marouzeau, *Traité de stylistique latine*, pp. 270 f., Maguinness's *Aeneid XII*, Intro., pp. 16–17 and 35, L. Otto, *De Anaphora*, Diss., Marburg, 1907.

565–6. Cf. *Aen.* 9. 49 f. *maculis quem Thracius albis / portat equus*, and the horses, whiter than snow, of the Thracian Rhesus (Hom. *Il.* 10. 436 f.).

566. bicolor: 'dappled'. The word is found first in Virgil, cf. *Aen.* 8. 276 *Herculea bicolor cum populus umbra.* See notes on 202 and 452.

566–7. 'showing white pasterns and a white forehead held high'. *Vestigia* occurs in poetry with the meaning 'foot', cf. Cat. 64. 162 *candida permulcens liquidis vestigia lymphis*, Ov. *Met.* 8. 571 *nudae vestigia nymphae.* Here *vestigia pedis* is equivalent to *pedes*; cf. *Aen.* 7. 689 f. *vestigia nuda sinistri / instituere pedis, crudus tegit altera pero. Primus pes* refers to the front of the foot, not to the forefoot; cf. Cat. 2. 3 (*primus digitus*), Prop. 2. 26. 11 and Val. Fl. 8. 44 (*prima palma*), Plin. *Nat. Hist.* 11. 172 (*prima lingua*).

567. ostentans arduus: for the adverbial use of *arduus* see on 278.

568. Compare the association of the sea captains with Roman families (lines 116–23). Augustus' mother was a member of the *gens Atia*; thus there is special point in the friendship of these two boys, founders of the *gens Iulia* and the *gens Atia*.

570. Notice how the spondees slow the movement to give emphasis and dignity; see on 136–41. The words *ante omnis pulcher Iulus* occur again in *Aen.* 9. 293.

571. Sidŏnio: the quantity of the *o* varies. Here and in *Aen.* 1. 678, 4. 75, 137, 545, 683 it is short, but we find it long in *Aen.* 1. 446, 613, 9. 266, 11. 74, always in the phrase *Sidonia Dido*. Conway (on *Aen.* 1. 678) is inclined to scan *Sidoniam* as a trisyllable with consonantal *i*, but this seems unlikely (on this theme see Austin's note on *Aen.* 4. 126 *conubio*). Other variations of scansion in Virgil include *Dĭana, Ēous, Ītalus* (82 etc.) but occasionally *Ĭtalus* and always *Ītalia, Lăvinia* (*Lăvinium, Lāvinius*), *Ŏrion, Sȳchaeus*. Compare *Ĭŏnius* (193) and *Ĭōnia, Prĭamus* and *Prĭamides, Sĭcania* and *Sĭcanos* (24); see Platnauer, *Latin Elegiac Verse*, pp. 53 f.

    candida: the word here is nearly synonymous with *pulchra*, with the additional idea of radiance, cf. *Aen.* 8. 138 *candida Maia*, 8. 608 (*Venus*) *dea candida*. It should not be taken, as some take it, in its applied meaning 'sincere', i.e. 'trusting', 'innocent'; such a meaning would be forced in the context, and Virgil does not use the word in this sense.

572. This line is almost an exact repetition of 538; see note on 563 f. We hear of gifts from Dido also on two later occasions, at points in the story where the tension is high: 9. 266, where Iulus promises to Nisus (as he prepares to depart through the enemy lines) a bowl which Dido had given; and 11. 72 f., where Aeneas covers the dead body of Pallas with a cloak which Dido had made.

573. Trinacriis: the best MSS. have *Trinacriae* or *Trinacrii*, neither of which seems reasonable. Even if *equi Trinacriae* were possible Latin for Sicilian horses, which is doubtful, the position of *Trinacriae* would compel it to be taken with *pubes*, which is contrary to the required sense. The conglomeration of *Trinacrii senioris Acestae* would be intolerable.

574. For the incomplete line see on 294.

575. pavidos: 'nervous', *gloriae cupiditate sollicitos* (Servius), cf. 138.

    tuentes: = *intuentes*, see on 41.

577 f. 'After they had joyfully ridden round in front of the whole throng before the gaze of their families . . .' For the zeugma see on 340–1; for *lustrare* in the sense of 'traverse' cf. 611, *Aen.* 3. 385, 11. 190, *Ecl.* 5. 75, and see Warde Fowler, *The Death of Turnus*, pp. 96 f.

578–9. The signal was evidently given first with a shout, and then with the crack of a whip, like the spoken words 'On your marks, get set' before the starter's gun is fired. If, as seems likely from 562, Epytides had taken part in the inaugural parade, he (and presumably the other two trainers) have now taken up their positions at the side of the arena.

580 f. The boys are riding in a long double column down the centre, and at the word of command the right hand rider of each pair wheeled right and the left hand rider wheeled left (*discurrere pares*). The following words explain this further: each of the groups breaks up its column formation (*agmina terni solvere*) as the sections turn away from each other (*diductis choris*). Then at another word of command they wheel about to face one another and charge. Diagrammatically we may represent it like this:

```
↑↑↑↑↑↑        ↑↑↑↑↑↑        ↑↑↑↑↑↑
······        ······        ······
  •             •             •
······        ······        ······
↓↓↓↓↓↓        ↓↓↓↓↓↓        ↓↓↓↓↓↓
```

We are not told what the *ductores* do; presumably they remained in the middle of the field so that at the end of the charge the columns could be re-formed as before.

580–2. Observe in these three lines the four verbs ending with *-ere*; Virgil uses this type of sentence, consisting of a number of short and similarly constructed main clauses, for narrative description in which the events are closely connected (cf. 101 f., 315 f., 433 f.). Sometimes, as in 101 f. and here, the effect is to reproduce the formal regularity of the events; in this passage the repetitions of 583–4 and the threefold repetition in 586–7 (see note on 565–70) add to the idea of symmetry and order. Lines 583–7 also have a large number of main verbs, though not with the same marked similarity of ending as 580–2.

580. olli: in this account of Roman tradition Virgil prefers the archaic form of *illi*; see on 10.

discurrere: the original forms of the third person plural of the perfect appear to have been *-ēre* and *-ērunt*; the form *-ērunt* is probably a conflation of the two. Virgil greatly prefers the form *-ēre*; in this book the figures are 18 *-ēre* and four *-ērunt*. C. F. Bauer (*The Latin Perfect Endings -ere and -erunt*, Philadelphia, 1933) gives figures of 231 *-ēre* endings to 29 *-ĕrunt* in the *Aeneid*, and points out that this is only partly due to the metrical convenience in dactylic verse, because *-ĕrunt* is much more frequent proportionally in the hexameters of Horace and Juvenal. Evidently the ending -*ēre* had an archaic and ritualistic ring, appropriate to the high style as being slightly unusual. Cicero (*Orat.* 157; cf. Quint. 1. 5. 43) speaks of the pleasant sound of *scripsere*, but says '*scripserunt* esse verius sentio'; he uses the ending -*ēre* very rarely. In Caesar it is very rare indeed, perhaps non-existent; in Livy the proportion of -*ēre* to -*ērunt* is far higher in the early books with their archaic and poetic flavour than it is in the later books. See also Löfstedt, *Syntactica*, ii, pp. 295 f., and Marouzeau, *Traité de stylistique latine*, pp. 125–6.

583 f. 'Then they enter upon other movements and counter-movements, keeping corresponding positions, and they weave their circling patterns in and out, and wage phantom battles in their panoply.' In the previous sentence Virgil's account of the first manœuvre was detailed and precise; now he describes the subsequent movements of the pageant in much more general terms, in order to convey the mood and colour of kaleidoscopic pattern. *Adversi spatiis* suggests that one half of the arena was a mirrored reflection of the other; *adversi* may mean 'facing', or simply 'opposed' or 'corresponding' in their spacing. *Alternosque orbibus orbis impediunt* conveys the picture of the intricate interweaving of circular patterns to which Virgil returns in his Labyrinth simile. See on 593, and cf. *Aen.* 12. 743 (Turnus in flight) *et nunc huc, inde huc incertos implicat orbis.* The use of the phrase in *Aen.* 8. 448 f. (of the making of Aeneas' shield) *septenosque orbibus orbis / impediunt* conveys a rather different picture. For a discussion of these patterns of movement see H. v. Petrikovits, *Klio*, 1939, pp. 209 f.

585. pugnaeque cient simulacra: cf. line 674, Lucr. 2. 41 (= 324) *belli simulacra cientes.*

588 f. Virgil uses two similes to illustrate his description of the *lusus Troiae*; the Labyrinth expresses the idea of complicated figures, and the dolphins convey the picture of swift and joyful movement.

588–91. 'It was like the Labyrinth in lofty Crete long ago, of which the story tells that it had a weaving path between blind walls and a bewildering riddle of a thousand ways, where the insoluble and irretraceable maze would break the tokens of the trail.'

588. The Labyrinth at Cnossos was said to have been built by Daedalus for King Minos; the Athenians had to pay human sacrifice to the Minotaur which lived in the Labyrinth until Theseus killed it, and returned out of the maze by means of the thread which Ariadne gave him. The story is told in Cat.

64 (Virgil follows his phraseology, see on 591) and in Ov.
Met. 8. 152 f. Scenes from it are portrayed on the doors of
Phoebus' temple in *Aen.* 6. 20 f. The pattern of the Labyrinth is strongly associated with dancing movements; the
dancing-floor depicted on Achilles' shield (Hom. *Il.* 18. 590 f.)
is compared with that which Daedalus built for Ariadne in
Cnossos, and Plutarch (*Thes.* 21) tells of a dance with complicated figures which was called the Labyrinth. The significance of the Labyrinth in magic and ritual is discussed by
W. F. J. Knight, *Cumaean Gates*, Blackwell, 1936; see also
the summaries and references given by Mehl (cited on 545 f.).

589. parietibus: for the consonantal *i* see note on 432.

ancipitemque: Virgil (unlike Lucretius, who has several
hundred instances; see Bailey, *Proleg.*, pp. 113–17) uses a
polysyllabic ending only with Greek words (see on 300) or
for special effect. Quintilian (9. 4. 65) says that a polysyllabic ending has about it something *praemolle*; we feel
that the long word causes the line to rush to its close without
being quite controlled. Cf. *Aen.* 10. 505 *gemitu lacrimisque*,
11. 614 f. (of the Centaurs) *perfractaque quadripedantum /
pectora pectoribus rumpunt*; see Austin on *Aen.* 4. 215 *semi-
viro comitatu* and 667 *femineo ululatu*, and Norden's *Aeneid
VI*, p. 441. Here the special effect is that the line, shorn of its
usual rhythm, conveys the strangeness of the maze and gives
a foretaste of the effect of line 591 (where see note).

590–1. qua . . . frangeret: 'so that . . . in it'. *Qua* is local, and
the subjunctive *frangeret* final.

signa sequendi frangeret . . . error: *error* here means 'maze'
(not as some have thought 'mistake'), cf. *Aen.* 6. 27 *hic
labor ille domus et inextricabilis error*. Servius glosses *frangeret* with *deciperet*, *falleret*, and it is fairly clear that the
reading *falleret* in some MSS. originates from a gloss. The
phrase *signa sequendi frangeret* is very difficult; presumably
signa means the marks or indications by which one would
follow the track on the way back; the nature of the maze
breaks the trail.

591. The line is closely modelled on Cat. 64. 114 f. *ne labyrintheis
e flexibus egredientem / tecti frustraretur inobservabilis error*.
For Virgil's debt to Catullus, particularly to the *Peleus and
Thetis*, see Heinze, *Virgils Epische Technik*, pp. 133 f., and
the references given in Pease's *Aeneid IV*, Intro., p. 14, n.
100. Virgil's adjectives are clearly both suggested by Catullus' *inobservabilis*. *Indeprensus* (equivalent to *indeprehen-
sibilis*, a word which Servius uses on 6. 27 to explain *inextricabilis*) occurs first here and very rarely afterwards. Virgil
was fond of the occasional use of this kind of word, and similar

adjectives first found in his works are *impastus, imperditus, imperterritus, implacatus, improperatus, inaccessus, inausus, inconcessus, indefessus, indebitus, inexcitus, inexpletus, infletus, insalutatus* (with tmesis), *inspoliatus, intemeratus*. The word *irremeabilis* also occurs first in Virgil (cf. *Aen.* 6. 425), and is also a type of which he was fond; similar words first occurring in Virgil are *enarrabilis, exsaturabilis* (line 781), *immedicabilis, ineluctabilis, inextricabilis* (6. 27, of the labyrinth), *inlaetabilis, irreparabilis, lacrimabilis, penetrabilis, violabilis*. See Leumann–Hofmann, p. 234, and note on 202.

Just as the diction of this line is very striking, so its rhythm (like that of the line from Catullus which Virgil is imitating) is most remarkable and effective. It has a quasi-caesura in the third foot without a strong caesura in the fourth, like 528, 781, 826 (a Greek line), and 856; but unlike the first three of these lines it is also without a strong caesura in the second foot, with the result that there is no conflict whatever in the line between the ictus and the word accent. This conveys a strange feeling of monotony and sameness, and the long words help in giving an unforgettable and magnificent representation of the feeling of being lost in an interminable maze. A similar rhythm is used in 856 (where see note) to convey the drooping drowsy effect of sleep. Norden (*Aeneid VI*, pp. 432–3) has some discussion of lines of this type. See Marouzeau, *Traité de stylistique latine*, pp. 96–103 (the effect of long words), and p. 302 (the rhythm of this line; he cites Ennius *Ann.* 43 V *corde capessere*: *semita nulla pedem stabilibat*, where also the strange rhythm gives the feeling of being lost).

592–3. vestigia . . . impediunt: 'weave a pattern of galloping movement'. On *impediunt* Servius says 'implicant, intexunt: quod est a vestibus tractum'; cf. Lucr. 1. 240, Ov. *Met.* 3. 664, and see on 585.

594. delphinum similes: *similis* with the genitive occurs only here in Virgil, no doubt to avoid the dative plural of the Greek form *delphis* (Virgil always uses *delphis* in preference to *delphinus*). For the simile cf. Ap. Rh. 4. 933 f., and compare the description of dolphins in *Aen.* 8. 673 f. (depicted on Aeneas' shield) *et circum argento clari delphines in orbem | aequora verrebant caudis aestumque secabant*; and in Ov. *Met.* 3. 683 f. *undique dant saltus multaque adspergine rorant | emerguntque iterum redeuntque sub aequora rursus | inque chori ludunt speciem . . .*

maria umida: the redundant epithet (more redundant than, for example, 859 *liquidae undae*) is perhaps due, as Servius suggests, to Homer's rather different ὑγρὰ κέλευθα.

595. Carpathium Libycumque secant: Heyne thought *-ve* preferable, but the sentence is such that either co-ordination or disjunction conveys the right sense; Wagner is surely wrong in seeing a reference to the speed of the dolphins in crossing from one sea to another. The island Carpathos is between Crete and Rhodes; cf. *Geo.* 4. 387. For the geographical localization of similes see on 448–9.

    luduntque per undas: though these words are quite unobjectionable in themselves, and indeed add to the point of the simile (cf. 593 *ludo*), they are omitted in some of the primary MSS., and must be regarded as an interpolated completion of a half-line. See note on 294. Sparrow (*Half-lines and Repetitions in Virgil*, p. 34) argues that this simile was perhaps a jotting in the margin as an alternative to 588–91, or for insertion after 582; but see note on 588 f.

596. 'the tradition of this equestrian display and these mock battles', cf. *Aen.* 3. 408. For the *lusus Troiae* at Rome see on 545 f.

597. Ascanius founded Alba Longa from Lavinium after the death of Aeneas, cf. *Aen.* 1. 271, 8. 47 f., 12. 826 f.

598. rettulit: 'revived', *innovavit* (Servius).

    priscos: some print with a capital *P*, and Servius says 'ita dicti sunt qui tenuerunt loca ubi Alba est condita'.

599. 'as he himself had done when a boy, and with him the youth of Troy'. The adjective *Troius* is a dactyl, the noun *Troia* (602) a trochee.

600–1. Compare *Aen.* 7. 602–3 for lines of very similar structure.

600. porro: 'afterwards', 'in succession', *post longum intervallum* (Servius). It is a rather archaic use of the word, cf. *Aen.* 6. 711 (applied to space not time) *quae sint ea flumina porro*. Compare the Greek πρόσω, πόρρω.

602. Troiaque nunc pueri: 'the boys are now called Troy', rather an awkward phrase meaning that the performance is called Troy. Servius quotes Suetonius as saying *lusus ipse Troia vocatur*, and we several times find in Suetonius the phrase *Troiam ludere*. It is more awkward to punctuate, as some do, after *nunc*, and to take *pueri* as the subject of *dicitur* attracted into the number of its predicate. In any case the rhythm of the line is all against such a punctuation. Nettleship proposed *cursus* or *lusus* (*J. Phil.* 1891, p. 110), or *ludi* (in his text in Postgate's *Corpus*); but we should probably accept the metonymy of the performers put for the performance.

603. hac . . . tenus: 'thus far', i.e. this was the conclusion of the games. The preposition *tenus* coalesced with its ablative

in the common words *quatenus* and *hactenus,* so that the
separation of the two component parts of the word here is an
example of tmesis; cf. *Aen.* 6. 62 *hac Troiana tenus fuerit
fortuna secuta,* and compare *quo . . . usque* (384), *quae . . .
cumque* (*Aen.* 1. 610). There is an archaic flavour in the use
of tmesis (except perhaps for the relatively common *qui . . .
cumque*), especially in the striking instances of *inque salu-
tatam* (*Aen.* 9. 288) and *inque ligatus* (*Aen.* 10. 794). Virgil uses
tmesis less often than Lucretius (see Bailey, *Proleg.*, p. 123),
and much less often than Ennius; see Marouzeau, *L'Ordre des
mots dans la phrase latine,* iii, pp. 150 f., Leumann–Hofmann,
p. 495, and Servius on *Aen.* 1. 412.

604–63. *While the games are being celebrated, Juno sends Iris
down from heaven in order to incite the Trojan women to burn
Aeneas' ships. They are gathered on the shore, weeping for
the death of Anchises and for their own unhappy fate as
wanderers over the face of the earth. Iris takes on the appearance of Beroe, and urges them to burn the ships so that their
menfolk will be forced to settle in Sicily. She herself hurls the
first torch; Pyrgo tells them that this is not Beroe, but a goddess
in disguise. As they hesitate Iris reveals her divinity, and driven
on now by the frenzy inspired by Juno they set the ships ablaze.*

604 f. The intervention of the gods in the human action is an
ever-present *motif* in the *Aeneid.* Juno's hostility to the
Trojans is described at the beginning of Book I (see note on
608), and the storm with which the narrative of Aeneas'
journey starts is caused by her. Constantly we see her at
moments of decisive importance endeavouring to alter the
course of the fates (1. 36 f., 4. 90 f., 7. 286 f., 9. 2 f., 10. 633 f.,
12. 134 f.). Venus as constantly intervenes on the side of the
fates (1. 227 f., 314 f., 657 f., 4. 90 f., 5. 779 f. (where see
note), 8. 370 f., 608 f., 12. 411 f.). Thus the fulfilment of
Aeneas' mission is set against a background of superhuman
powers. The Olympian gods in Virgil are more remote figures
than in Homer; they are partly persons and partly symbols
of forces which operate in the world of men. Thus Juno
symbolizes opposition to the process of order; she represents
individual recklessness bent on its own ends, and she inspires
furor and *violentia* in her human agents (see notes on 6 and
655). Venus is seen as the mother of the Roman race, who
upholds Aeneas as he strives to fulfil his mission and to
establish law and justice and universal peace (*Aen.* 4. 227–
31, 6. 851–3). On this theme see V. Pöschl, *Die Dichtkunst
Virgils, passim*; on the Olympian gods see Glover's *Virgil,*
chap. xi, Sellar's *Virgil,* pp. 365 f., Bailey, *Religion in Virgil,*

chaps. v–vii and ix, Warde Fowler, *The Death of Turnus*, pp. 82 f.

The episode of the burning of the ships figures early in the legend. In Dion. Hal. 1. 72 we are told that Hellanicus had such an episode in his version of the founding of Rome, and that Aristotle had an account of Greeks returning from Troy, landing in Italy, and being obliged to stay there because captive Trojan women whom they had with them burnt their ships (see Servius *auct.* on *Aen.* 10. 179). As the Aeneas legend developed, this episode figured in it with very varied localization (Plut. *Quaest. Rom.* 6), mostly in Italy; according to one version (Servius on *Aen.* 7. 1) it took place at Caieta (καίειν). The setting of the episode in Sicily may have been a current variant in Virgil's time (Dion. Hal. 1. 52. 4 refers to it), or Virgil himself may have adapted the legend to this effect. See J. Perret, *Les Origines de la légende troyenne de Rome*, Paris, 1942, pp. 396 f. By placing the burning of the ships at this stage in the poem Virgil is able to stress the association of Sicily with the early destiny of Rome (the foundation of Segesta was the direct result of the loss of part of the Trojan fleet; see on 718); and he also shows us Aeneas' fortunes and personal courage at their lowest ebb (687 f., 700 f.) at a time very shortly before the divine revelations of Book VI give him the final certainty and strength to carry out his mission. See Intro., p. xiii and pp. xvii–xviii.

604. 'At this point for the first time Fortune changed and broke faith with us.' *Primum* presumably means for the first time in Sicily; Fortune had been favourable at the landing and at the games. The phrase *fidem novavit* would by itself be ambiguous, but the presence of the word *mutata* defines the meaning. The significance of the word *Fortuna* in Virgil is discussed by Bailey, *Religion in Virgil*, pp. 234 f. He illustrates its various shades of meaning, which range from 'chance' at one extreme to 'fate' at the other; in this passage, as also in 22, 356, 710, the word has a sense intermediate between the two extremes. We might say that there is often (as here) a contrast between the inexorable march of fate and the occurrence of a set of circumstances (*Fortuna*) which may be surmounted or altered. See on 656 and 709–10.

605. **tumulo**: dative, not ablative, cf. *Aen.* 6. 380 *tumulo sollemnia mittent*.

606. This line occurs again in *Aen.* 9. 2, cf. also 4. 694. Iris, like Mercury, is a messenger of the gods; in Virgil she is particularly associated with Juno. Compare Ceres' words to Iris in *The Tempest* (4. 1. 76 f.):

Hail, many colour'd messenger, that ne'er

Dost disobey the wife of Jupiter;
Who with thy saffron wings upon my flowers
Diffusest honey-drops, refreshing showers:
And with each end of thy blue bow dost crown
My bosky acres, and my unshrubb'd down,
Rich scarf to my proud earth . . .

Saturnia Iuno: Jupiter is once called *Saturnius* (*Aen.* 4.
372), and Neptune once (line 799), but the epithet is used of
Juno again and again, especially in the later books. Servius
auct. (on *Aen.* 4. 92) says that as the planet Saturn has the
power of bringing evil, the epithet shows the evil intentions
of Juno. This astrological explanation can be dismissed;
partly the epithet emphasizes the dignity and majesty of
the greatest of the goddesses, and partly it indicates her
association with the Italy of old, before the coming of the
Trojans. Saturnus was the oldest king of Latium, according
to the myth; he took refuge there when driven from heaven
by Jupiter (*Aen.* 8. 319 f.), and he was especially associated
with the Golden Age in Italy (*Geo.* 2. 538, *Aen.* 6. 792 f.).
His image was in Latinus' palace (7. 180), and the Latins are
called *Saturni gens* (7. 203); the epithet *Saturnia* is often applied
to Italy (Ennius *Ann.* 25 V, *Geo.* 2. 173, *Aen.* 1. 569, 8. 329).

The entry here of Juno into the narrative makes explicit
the general statement in 604 about the change of fortune,
and in a moment alters the gay colours with which the games
had ended into the sombre hues of forthcoming disaster for
the Trojans.

607. ventosque aspirat eunti: 'breathes favouring winds upon
her as she goes'; compare *Aen.* 4. 223 where the winds are
to help Mercury to carry his message swiftly. *Aspirare* is
very rarely transitive, cf. *Aen.* 8. 373 (in a different sense)
dictis divinum aspirat amorem; see note on 202.

608. movens: 'plotting', cf. *Aen.* 3. 34, 10. 890.

necdum . . . dolorem: cf. *Aen.* 1. 25 f., where Juno's long-
standing anger against the Trojans because of the judgement
of Paris is given a prominent position at the very start of
the poem, and compare Hor. *Odes* 3. 3. *Saturata* is used as a
middle voice; see note on 135.

609. For the picture of Iris descending to earth by means of the
rainbow cf. Ov. *Met.* 11. 589 f. *induitur velamina mille
colorum | Iris et arcuato caelum curvamine signans | tecta petit*,
632 *remeat per quos modo venerat arcus*, 14. 838 *in terram
pictos delapsa per arcus*, Stat. *Th.* 10. 83 *in terras longo
suspenditur arcu*.

per mille coloribus arcum: the preposition is separated
from its noun by the ablative of description acting as a

compound adjective (= *multicolor*). In Macr. *Sat.* 6. 6. 4 Servius cites the phrase as an example of Virgilian variation for *per arcum mille colorum*. See Mackail, appendix A 5, and note on 663.

610. nulli visa: dative of the agent, cf. lines 305, 360 and *Aen.* 1. 440 *neque cernitur ulli*.

   virgo: the reiteration of the subject *virgo* after the demonstrative *illa* does not here give any special significance to *virgo*. Cf. *Geo.* 4. 457–8 (*illa . . . puella*), *Aen.* 12. 901–2 (*ille . . . heros*), and Wagner, *Quaest. Virg.* 21. 7. It is probably an imitation of the Homeric turn of phrase, as in *Il.* 1. 488 f. αὐτὰρ ὁ μήνιε νηυσὶ παρήμενος ὠκυπόροισι / διογενὴς Πηλῆος υἱός. See on 186 for the reiteration of the subject by *ille*, and contrast the predicative use of the noun *deus* in 841.

611. litora lustrat: 'passes along the shore', cf. 578.

612. Cf. *Aen.* 2. 28 *desertosque videre locos litusque relictum*.

613 f. The women have not been present at the games; they did not attend at *ludi funebres* in Rome, and Suetonius (*Aug.* 44) relates that Augustus excluded women from watching athletic competitions.

613–15. Observe the very slow movement of these lines; first the spondaic rhythm with alliteration of the two adjectives expressing loneliness *sola secretae*, and then the heavy spondees and elisions of 614–15, and the clash of ictus and accent. The very striking repetition of *flebant . . . flentes* in the same position in the line greatly adds to the effect. See on 136–41, and on 565–70. The scene is slightly reminiscent of Odysseus looking over the sea longing for home in Hom. *Od.* 5. 156 f., and of Ariadne in Cat. 64.

613. Trōădĕs: notice the Greek scansion; see on 265.

   acta: 'sea-shore'. The Greek word ἀκτή is not common in Latin and is found only here in Virgil and not in any other classical epic poet except once in Valerius. It occurs several times in Cicero.

615. tot vada: for the rhythm see on 274.

615–16. The construction is accusative and infinitive of exclamation; cf. *Aen.* 1. 97 f. *mene Iliacis occumbere campis / non potuisse !*, and Cic. *Ad Fam.* 14. 1 *me miserum! te . . . in tantas aerumnas propter me incidisse!* The phrase *vox omnibus una* is generally taken retrospectively in a loose apposition to the exclamatory clause; but there is much to be said for referring it forward to *urbem orant*, and punctuating heavily after *maris* and more lightly after *una* (so Mackail).

617. urbem orant: the desire for a city is one of the chief themes of the *Aeneid*; cf. Aeneas' words at Carthage (1. 437) *o fortunati quorum iam moenia surgunt*. For the structure of this line compare *Aen.* 4. 451 *mortem orat*; *taedet caeli convexa tueri.*

618. haud ignara nocendi: as Juno's messenger Iris would be required to be skilled in working evil; compare Juno's words to Allecto (*Aen.* 7. 337 f.) *tibi nomina mille, / mille nocendi artes.*

619. conicit: the word, a powerful one (cf. *Aen.* 10. 657), expresses the speed and hostile intent of Iris, and the metre reinforces the effect by the pause after the 'run-on' word; see on 480 and cf. 242, 444.

faciemque ... vestemque: for doubled *-que* ('both ... and') see on 92.

620. fit Beroe: the gods in Virgil as in Homer sometimes intervene in the action by taking on mortal form; cf. 842, *Il.* 4. 86 f., the description of how Athene in the guise of Laodocus urges the breaking of the truce, a passage imitated by Virgil in *Aen.* 12. 224 f. where Iuturna disguised as Camers urges the Rutulians to break the truce, *Il.* 3. 121 f. (Iris visits Helen in the guise of Laodice), *Aen.* 1. 314 f. (Venus assumes mortal form), *Aen.* 7. 415 f. (Allecto disguises herself as Calybe). Compare also Stat. *Th.* 10. 639 f. where in a fine passage the poet describes how the goddess Virtus assumes the mortal form of Manto.

Iris chooses the form of Beroe because the latter was away ill (650 f.), and because she was a woman of standing with the Trojans, as Virgil explains in the next line (cf. *Aen.* 12. 225–6). This Beroe is not otherwise known; a Doryclus, son of Priam, is mentioned in *Il.* 11. 489, but it is hard to see how he would be associated with Tmarus (Tomaros), a mountain in Epirus (*Ecl.* 8. 44, Claud. 26. 18, Plin. *Nat. Hist.* 4. 6). The MSS. vary over the reading *Tmarii*, but Servius attests it (as far as one can tell from the confusion in the Servian MSS. at this point), though he seems to regard it as a Thracian mountain. It is possible that Beroe went with Helenus to Epirus, married Doryclus there, and joined Aeneas' company when they came to Buthrotum (*Aen.* 3. 294 f.).

621. 'who had been of noble birth and in days gone by had had sons and a famous name'. The line describes Beroe's high status in the days when Troy still stood; *fuissent* is subjunctive because it expresses the thought in Iris' mind, the reason why she chose the form of Beroe.

622. sic: Servius says 'aut mutato habitu, aut ista dictura'. The former is right, cf. *Aen.* 7. 668.

Dardanidum: this archaic form of the genitive plural is used by Virgil instead of *Dardanidarum*, which would be very intractable metrically. Compare *Aeneadum* (*Aen.* 1.

565, etc.), *Graiugenum* (3. 550, 8. 127), and *caelicolum* (3. 21); see note on 174 for the genitive plural of second declension words.

623–35. Observe the frequency of elision in this excited and rhetorical speech. It is noticeable that as the tone changes after the proposal has been made (in 635) there are no elisions at all in the last five lines, but instead staccato sentences with mid-line stops.

623 f. 'Unhappy women', she said, 'unhappy indeed not to have been dragged off to death by some Greek band of soldiers in the war, beneath the walls of your fatherland.' For the thought cf. *Aen.* 1. 94 f. *o terque quaterque beati, | quis ante ora patrum Troiae sub moenibus altis | contigit oppetere*; *Aen.* 3. 321 f. *o felix una ante alias Priameia virgo, | hostilem ad tumulum Troiae sub moenibus altis | iussa mori*. The clause *quas . . . traxerit* is a causal relative, hence the subjunctive.

623. The rhythm of this line is unusual and jerky. The strange position of *inquit* makes sense pauses (not perhaps very strong ones, but certainly noticeable) at the end of the third foot and after the fourth trochee (for the latter see on 166–7). There is no other example of a sense pause after the third foot in this book, except once with elision (137), which is quite different. It is a very rare pause; cf. *Aen.* 2. 145, 558, and Winbolt, *Latin Hexameter Verse*, pp. 37 f.

624. The rhythm of this line too is striking. The double monosyllable in the sixth foot (see on 372) gives a heavy broken effect which is accentuated by the pause at the end of the fifth foot. This pause is common in Horace's hexameters, but is rare in Virgil, and is used mainly for excited speech (cf. 633, 670, 741, and *Aen.* 4. 593 . . . *deripientque rates alii navalibus? ite . . .*). The other instances in this book (100, 372, 646, 713) are much lighter pauses. See Winbolt, *Latin Hexameter Verse*, pp. 54 f., Marouzeau, *Traité de stylistique latine*, pp. 305–6.

625. Fortuna: see on 604; here there is some reference to the proverbial ill fortune of Troy, cf. *Aen.* 6. 62 *hac Troiana tenus fuerit fortuna secuta*. The use of *te* (with *gens*) rather than *vos* emphasizes the collective fortune of the *gens Troiana*.

626. For the chronology of Aeneas' wanderings see Intro., pp. xxviii f.

    vertitur: probably simply 'is passing', 'is running its course', rather than 'is waning'. Cf. the Ciceronian phrase (*Nat. De.* 2. 53 *et alibi*) *anno vertente* ('in the course of a year'), and Homer's περιπλομένων ἐνιαυτῶν, περιτελλομένων ἐνιαυτῶν.

627 f. cum . . . ferimur: 'while all the time we have been driven'; cf. *Aen.* 3. 645 f. *tertia iam Lunae se cornua lumine complent | cum vitam in silvis . . . | . . . traho*, and Prop. 2. 20. 21 f. The construction is an unusual one, and more often introduced by *cum interea* or *cum interim*, e.g. Cic. *Verr.* 2. 5. 162 *caedebatur virgis in medio foro Messanae civis Romanus, iudices, cum interea nullus gemitus, nulla vox alia illius miseri inter dolorem crepitumque plagarum audiebatur nisi haec, 'Civis Romanus sum'.* Cf. also *Aen.* 10. 665, and see Leumann–Hofmann, p. 750.

627–8. It is perhaps better to take all four nouns as objects of *emensae*, rather than to take *freta* and *terras* as accusative of extent after *ferimur* (for which see on 235, and cf. *Aen.* 1. 524 *maria omnia vecti*). On the meaning of *sidera* Servius says 'aut tempestates aut provincias, quae sideribus subiacent, ut *Aethiopum versemus oves sub sidere Cancri' (Ecl.* 10. 68). The second is the better explanation; compare our 'under many skies'. *Sidera* in certain contexts may mean storms, but when it is the object of *emensae* it is better to take it with a local meaning. See my note on this subject in *C.R.*, 1956, p. 104. For the tense of *emensae* see on 708.

627. inhospita: a poetic word which is first found in Horace and Virgil; cf. *infaustus* (635), *inopinus* (857), and notes on 202 and 591.

628. For the rhythm of the line ending see on 274. Observe the alliteration of *s* and *m* in this sentence.

629. Italiam . . . fugientem: 'an ever-receding Italy', cf. *Aen.* 3. 496 *arva neque Ausoniae semper cedentia retro*, 6. 61 *iam tandem Italiae fugientis prendimus oras.* For *sequi* = 'make for' cf. *Aen.* 4. 361 *Italiam non sponte sequor*, 381 *i sequere Italiam ventis.*

630. Erycis . . . fraterni: see on 24.

631. muros iacere: 'found our city-walls'. The verb *iacere* is common with words like *fundamenta*, but not normal with *muros*; cf., however, Prop. 2. 34. 64 *iactaque Lavinis moenia litoribus.*

  civibus: i.e. we shall then be citizens, not roaming exiles.

632. rapti . . . penates: cf. *Aen.* 1. 378, 2. 293, 717, 3. 148 f. Very great emphasis is laid by Virgil on the bringing of the *Penates* from Troy to Italy; see Bailey, *Religion in Virgil*, pp. 91 f. Ovid gives Aeneas the epithet *penatiger* (*Met.* 15. 450).

633. Troiae: predicative; 'shall no walls ever again be called walls of Troy?'

634. Hectoreos amnis: see on 190 for the emotional effect of the word *Hectoreus*, and cf. *Aen.* 1. 272 f. *hic iam ter centum totos*

regnabitur annos | gente sub Hectorea. Jackson Knight renders
the effect with 'rivers called Xanthus and Simois, to remind
me of Hector'. For the Trojan rivers Xanthus and Simois
cf. 261, 803, and *Aen.* 6. 88, 10. 60. For the use of the old
names in the new city cf. 756 and *Aen.* 3. 349 f., where
Helenus' town is a little Troy, with a river called Xanthus
and a Scaean Gate.

635. quin agite: *quin* with the imperative is a somewhat lively
and colloquial use which Virgil introduced into poetic
language, especially in this formula. See Austin on *Aen.* 4. 99.

infaustas: see on 627.

636. The fate of Cassandra, gifted with prophecy but never
believed (*Aen.* 2. 246 f.), is told in *Aen.* 2. 403 f.

638 f. Notice the staccato nature of these short sentences, three
in succession without the verb expressed.

638. agi res: the monosyllabic ending gives an abrupt and most
emphatic impression; see on 481.

639. nec . . . prodigiis: understand *esse potest* or *esto*. The
phrase *tantis prodigiis* is ablative of attendant circumstances,
'in the presence of', 'in the face of . . .'

640. animumque: 'will', 'intent'. The line is imitated by
Statius (*Th.* 10. 571) *ipsae tela viris, ipsae iram animosque
ministrant*; cf. *Aen.* 1. 150 *iamque faces et saxa volant, furor
arma ministrat.*

641. infensum: 'deadly', 'destructive'; cf. *Geo.* 4. 330 *inimi-
cum ignem, Aen.* 9. 793 *cum telis premit infensis*, 10. 521
infensam contenderat hastam. Many have followed Servius
in considering *infensum* to be an epithet transferred from
Iris to the weapon she uses, but it is perhaps better to regard
it as a stock epithet recalling Homer's δήϊον πῦρ.

642 f. 'and from where she stood, raising her right hand high,
with all her might she brandished it and threw'. *Procul*
emphasizes the drama of the picture; she does not approach
the ships with her firebrand, but hurls it high and far from
where she stood. Conington says for *procul* 'swung back',
presumably taking it closely with *sublata*, but *procul* will
hardly bear such a meaning. The verb *coruscare* is sometimes
transitive (as here, cf. *Aen.* 8. 661, 12. 431, 887), sometimes
intransitive, as in *Geo.* 4. 73, 98.

643. et iacit: Wagner has well drawn attention to the compelling rhythm, which is caused by the heavy pause after the
first foot where there is conflict of ictus and accent within the
foot; the effect is the more noticeable because the previous
two lines have been mainly spondaic and without pauses.
Compare *Aen.* 10. 335 f. *tum magnam corripit hastam | et
iacit; Aen.* 12. 729 f. *alte sublatum consurgit Turnus in ensem |*

et ferit. Other instances in this book of this kind of rhythm before a sense pause are 226, 368, 504, 551, 690, 742, but only the last (where see note) has such a heavy pause. See on 480 for the different effect when the pause is preceded by a single dactylic 'run-on' word.

   arrectae: 'aroused', cf. *Aen.* 1. 579, 11. 452. Mackail is wrong in saying that their minds were excited but their good sense (*corda*) stupefied. The two phrases convey a complementary picture of amazed excitement.

644. **Iliadum**: the sense pause and the conflict of ictus and accent continue the disturbed feeling caused by the rhythm of the beginning of the previous line.

645. Pyrgo is not elsewhere mentioned.

646. **vobis**: 'I tell you', ethic dative, cf. 162.

   Rhoeteia: an epithet meaning Trojan, from the promontory Rhoeteum near Troy, cf. *Aen.* 12. 456. Notice the scansion *Rhoetēǐǎ*; there is also a form *Rhōētēŭs* (*Aen.* 3. 108, 6. 505).

647. **Dorycli**: see on 620, and notice the variation in scansion, Dorȳclus here, Dorȳclus in 620. When a vowel which is short by nature precedes a mute and a liquid the syllable can either be lengthened or left short; cf. *Aen.* 2. 415 *et gemini Ātrīdae*, 2. 500 *geminōsque in limine Ātrīdas*, and *Aen.* 2. 663 *natum ante ora pătris, pātrem qui obtruncat ad aras.* See Quint. 1. 5. 28 (on *volŭcres*), and Austin on *Aen.* 4. 159.

647 f. Compare the description of Venus in mortal form in *Aen.* 1. 327 f., 402 f., and of Athene herself in Hom. *Il.* 1. 200 δεινὼ δέ οἱ ὄσσε φάανθεν.

648 f. **qui . . . eunti**: these are indirect questions parallel with *oculos* as objects of *notate*. The omission of the verb 'to be' in the subjunctive is not common, but cf. *Aen.* 2. 74, 10. 162.

648. **spiritus**: 'proud bearing', cf. Cic. *De Leg. Agr.* 2. 93 *regio spiritu,* Hor. *Sat.* 2. 3. 310 f. *Turbonis in armis / spiritum et incessum.* This is preferable to Servius' explanation 'odor: ut *divinum vertice odorem / spiravere*' (*Aen.* 1. 403–4).

649. **quis**: some MSS. have *qui*. The adjective *quis* is less common in prose, but it is frequent in verse, and much preferred by Virgil to the form *qui*, which is to be accounted for in the previous line on the grounds of euphony. See Löfstedt, *Syntactica*, ii, pp. 79 f.

   vel: *P* has *et*, and this could easily have been changed to *vel* by a scribe for the sake of the scansion; but in fact *vel* is natural enough here.

651 f. **aegram . . . munere**: 'sick and fretting because she was the only one not present at so important a ceremony'. The subjunctive represents the thought in Beroe's mind. *Tali* *munere* refers to the funeral ceremonies and the lamentation of the women for Anchises during the games (613 f.); its meaning is clarified in the next clause. Cf. *Aen.* 6. 885 f. *et fungar inani | munere*, 11. 25 f. *decorate supremis | muneribus.* Notice the heavy spondees in 651, and the unusually placed elision.

653. For the half-line see note on 294. This is one of the type which is most clearly an indication of an unfinished passage: Virgil went straight on from the speech to the narrative, and intended to write a line linking them later (cf. e.g. *Aen.* 8. 469, 9. 295).

654 f. 'But the matrons at first were uncertain, and gazed with angry eyes on the ships as they wavered between their wretched desire for the land they had reached and the kingdoms which called them with the voice of fate.' *Ancipites* (cf. *Aen.* 3. 47) anticipates *ambiguae*, a word which here only in Virgil is used of persons (see note on 326); cf. Tac. *Ann.* 1. 7. 5 *ambiguus imperandi*, 2. 40. 2 *ambiguus pudoris ac metus.*

655. spectare: 'historic' infinitive, common in Virgil; cf. 685 f., Page on *Aen.* 3. 141, Austin on 4. 422 (with references given there), Marouzeau, *Traité de stylistique latine*, pp. 212–13. Wagner (*Quaest. Virg.* 30) sets out a long list of examples. Two particular types of usage can be distinguished: (i) for vivid and exciting narrative, as in 685 f., *Aen.* 2. 685 f., 6. 489 f.; (ii) for repeated or continuous action, as here; cf. *Aen.* 2. 97 f., 4. 422, 11. 821.

miserum: Servius says 'aut magnum, ut Terentius *eam misere amat*: aut miserum, quo fiebant miseriores cum eis regna negarentur'. There is something of the truth in his second explanation; the word seems to indicate both the evil of their intention and the sadness of their folly. They become (like Dido and Turnus) victims of *furor* (659), the characteristic of those who oppose the divine plan, who for all their folly are yet to be pitied. See notes on 6 and 604 f.

miserum inter amorem: Virgil does not often elide a long syllable or a syllable ending in *-m* between the fourth and fifth foot. We find such elisions in spondaic or quasi-spondaic words at 235, 298, 821, 831; a long monosyllable is elided at 733; here only in this book is a quasi-anapaest elided before the fifth foot. There are only three instances in the whole *Aeneid* of a true anapaest elided in this position: *Aen.* 2. 658 *patrio excidit ore*, 4. 420 *miserae hoc tamen unum*, 6. 622 *pretio atque refixit.* See Norden's *Aeneid VI*, p. 455, Austin on 4. 420.

656. fatisque vocantia regna: the phrase is a condensed expression of two ideas—*regna Italiae vocant* and *fata nos vocant ad regna Italiae*. For similar free uses of the causal ablative cf. *Aen.* 10. 109, *Geo.* 1. 199. The idea of destiny calling the Trojans on to found their new city in Italy is of course one of the main themes of the poem; see Intro., pp. xix f.

657. cum . . . sustulit: for the inverted *cum* construction see on 84-85.

657-8. Cf. *Aen.* 9. 14-15, almost identical lines about Iris. Mercury (4. 276 f.) and Apollo (9. 656 f.) take their departure from the mortal scene by sudden and complete disappearance, but Iris has her own path along the rainbow (see on 609).

657. paribus . . . alis: 'on balanced wings', cf. *Aen.* 4. 252 f. *hic primum paribus nitens Cyllenius alis / constitit*.

658. 'and cut a giant rainbow beneath the clouds as she went'. *Secare* is commonly used of ships cleaving the water (218, cf. 595), or birds cutting their way through the air (*Geo.* 1. 406); we also find the phrase *secare viam* (*Aen.* 6. 899). Here the usage is extended a little, so that *secare arcum* = *secando aera facere arcum*.

660 f. The meaning is that some snatch fire from the hearths (of the Trojan encampment, cf. 668-9), while others despoil the four altars to Neptune (639-40).

661. pars spoliant: for the *constructio ad sensum* see on 108.

frondem ac virgulta: *frons* is common in Classical Latin both as a collective singular ('foliage'), and in the plural ('leaves'); cf. Varro *R.R.* 2. 5. 11 *in nemoribus ubi virgulta et frons multa*.

662. Notice the emphasis on *furit* as it begins a sentence with strong conflict of ictus and accent. It picks up the key word *furor* (659); see note on 655.

immissis . . . habenis: literally 'with the reins let loose', i.e. in full career, with unbridled frenzy. Cf. Lucr. 5. 787, *Aen.* 6. 1 (where see Fletcher), Ov. *Met.* 1. 280, and notes on 146-7, 818.

Volcanus: 'the fire-god'. In an instance like this, where the word means less than 'Vulcan in person' but more than 'fire', we see a stage leading to the full metonymy of Volcanus = *ignis*, Bacchus = *vinum*, etc. See note on 77-78.

663. transtra per: for anastrophe of prepositions see note on 370, and for *per* cf. *Geo.* 3. 276 *saxa per et scopulos*, *Aen.* 4. 671 *culmina perque hominum volvantur perque deorum* (where the genitive makes the usage easier). It is much more unusual to find monosyllabic prepositions following the word they govern than is the case with disyllabic prepositions. Except in Lucretius (who has phrases like *ignibus ex, haec loca per*; see Bailey, *Proleg.*, p. 107), such a usage is confined to instances like this one where other words governed by the preposition follow it, and to some instances with relatives.

pictas abiete puppis: 'painted ships of pine'. *Abiete* is ablative of description (or material) dependent on the noun *puppis*. This is an extended use of the ablative of which Virgil is fond; see notes on 77–78 and 609, M. E. Lees, *C.Q.*, 1921, pp. 183 f., and Mackail, appendix A, where he cites (*inter alia*) *Aen.* 2. 765 *crateresque auro solidi*. For *pictas* cf. *Aen.* 7. 431, 8. 93, and the Homeric epithets of ships μιλτο-πάρηος, κυανόπρωρος. For the scansion of *abiete* see on 432.

664–99. *The news reaches the Trojans. Ascanius immediately rides off and brings the women to a realization of their crime. But the Trojans cannot put out the flames, and Aeneas prays to Jupiter either to send help or to bring final destruction upon them. Jupiter hears his prayer; the flames are quenched by a thunderstorm, and all the ships saved except four.*

664. The rhythm of this line is unusual. Where the main caesura is in the fourth foot we generally find supporting caesurae of some kind in the second or third foot. Here there is only the hint of an 'apparent' caesura caused by the elision of *Anchisae*, and the very slight break between *ad* and *tumulum*. See note on line 1.

cuneosque theatri: these are the tiers, the wedge-shaped blocks of seats of a Roman theatre or circus; the phrase is here applied to the natural 'theatre' used for the games (288 f., 340).

665. This Eumelus is not otherwise known; the Greek Eumelus was one of the competitors in the chariot-race in Homer.

666. 'look back and see black ash eddying up in a cloud'. The word *respicere* normally has a participle with its object, but the extension here to an accusative and infinitive construction is quite natural (= *respicientes vident favillam volitare*).

667 f. 'And first of them all Ascanius, just as he was as he gaily led his galloping troop, straight away set off in hot haste towards the confusion in the camp.' For the use of *ut* cf. 388, for *sic* cf. 622. The total effect is that of the phrase *sicut erat*; he goes immediately from one activity to the other. The picture which Virgil draws of the young Ascanius is very vivid and sympathetic (see on 545 f.). He rushes straight off before anyone else reacts, and cannot be caught and dissuaded from his impetuous initiative. He speaks in simple rapid sentences, and ends with the dramatic gesture of throwing off his helmet as he stands before the women waiting for them to recognize him.

669. castra: the encampment by the ships, cf. *Aen.* 3. 519 and note on 660 f.

exanimes: the trainers are 'breathless' from pursuing him and trying to stop him; cf. *Aen.* 4. 672 *audiit exanimis trepidoque exterrita cursu . . .* Elsewhere in Virgil both *exanimis* and *exanimus* mean 'lifeless'.

670 f. Observe how the mid-line pauses in this speech give it a staccato and excited effect. For the pause after the fifth foot in 670 see note on 624. The rhythm of 672 is particularly unusual; the pause at the bucolic diaeresis after *uritis* is not common in the *Aeneid* (see on 815), and is in most cases preceded by a pyrrhic word. It is followed here by some conflict in the fifth foot (see on 274–5, and cf. 414), and preceded by a diaeresis after *spes*, the result of which is greatly to weaken the caesura between *vestras* and *spes*. In addition the conglomeration of consonants in the phrase *vestras spes* is harsh; the final *s* before the initial *s* is markedly awkward with another consonant following. See Quint. 9. 4. 37, where exception is taken to the juxtaposition of the words *ars studiorum* on this ground; for further discussion of cacophony of this kind see Marouzeau, *Traité de stylistique latine*, pp. 20 f. and 36 f., and N. I. Herescu, *Mélanges Marouzeau*, 1948, pp. 221 f.

670. novus: 'strange', suggesting something unheard of and (in this context) almost past belief; cf. *Aen.* 3. 591 *ignoti nova forma viri.*

671. cives: the word is chosen to bring the women to a realization that it is their own folk they are harming. Ascanius assumes that they must be so demented as to think that they are attacking enemy ships; hence his revelation of himself by the removal of his helmet.

673. Notice the considerable abruptness in the transition from the speech to the narrative; Ascanius stops speaking suddenly, as he waits for his dramatic gesture to take effect.

inanem: this adjective has provoked much discussion. Servius says 'concavam, sine capite', to which Servius *auct.* adds 'vacuam'. Wagner (who is followed by Lejay, Bellessort, and others) says 'tegumentum capitis in speciem galeae formatum ludo aptum, non veram galeam qua ictus telorum sustineas'. Henry is at his best as he sets about demolishing these two suggestions: '*Galeam inanem* is not *galeam vacuam*, because it had been trivial, if not absurd, to remind the reader that the helmet which Ascanius took off and threw down on the ground had not his head in it; and it is not *tegumentum in speciem galeae formatum*, because a toy or sham helmet had afforded but sorry protection to Ascanius's head in the sham battle; also because the mounted figure galloping towards them with such a helmet on its head had been less likely to frighten the women than to set them a-laughing; and especially because the context is explicit, that the battle fought by the youths was not a battle fought with sham arms, but . . . a sham battle fought with real arms.' Henry's own suggestion, which has found some support, is 'his useless helmet', useless and unnecessary now that the sham battle is over. But on the whole Servius' explanation seems the best; it is not 'absurd' unless it is forced to appear so. The phrase *galea inanis* does undeniably mean an empty helmet in *Geo.* 1. 496 *aut gravibus rastris galeas pulsabit inanes,* and in Ov. *Fast.* 4. 209 *pars clipeos rudibus, galeas pars tundit inanes.* Perhaps Virgil was thinking of Hom. *Il.* 3. 376 κεινὴ δὲ τρυφάλεια ἅμ᾽ ἕσπετο χειρὶ παχείη (where there is rather more point in the epithet); or perhaps, as the Ovid passage suggests, the word *inanis* is used to convey the clang of the helmet on the ground.

674. For the phraseology cf. 585. *Indutus* is here used with the ablative ('clad in'), cf. *Aen.* 10. 775 *indutum spoliis,* 12. 947; contrast *Aen.* 2. 275 *exuvias indutus* (see notes on 135, 264). *Exuere* shows the same variation; see note on 423.

677. sicubi: 'any they could find', literally 'if anywhere (*si, alicubi*) there were any hollow rocks, they made for them'. Cf. Stat. *Ach.* 2. 124 for a similar elliptical use of the word. For *concava saxa = antra* cf. *Geo.* 4. 49 f. *ubi concava pulsu | saxa sonant.*

678. piget . . . lucisque: 'they are ashamed of their deed and of the light of day', i.e. they want to hide in the darkness because of their shame.

    lucisque suosque: the line ending is harsh, and quite different from the doubled *-que* in 802, where see note. With *lucisque* the enclitic *-que* co-ordinates the two nouns, with *suosque* the two verbs. A trochaic pause in the fifth foot is not common; all the other instances in this book are lighter than this one (22, 50, 443, 446, 515, 665, 698, 709, 762). See Austin on *Aen.* 4. 28, Winbolt, *Latin Hexameter Verse,* pp. 50 f., Marouzeau, *Traité de stylistique latine,* pp. 305–6.

678–9. 'themselves again, they recognize their own people, and Juno is cast out from their hearts'. Cf. *Aen.* 6. 78 f. *magnum si pectore possit | excussisse deum.* The goddess is thought of as taking possession in a physical sense of those whom she inspires; cf. Hor. *Odes* 2. 19. 5 f. *Euhoe, recenti mens trepidat metu | plenoque Bacchi pectore turbidum | laetatur,* 3. 25. 1 f. *Quo me, Bacche, rapis tui | plenum ?*; and Lucan 9. 564, Val.

Fl. 1. 230, Stat. *Th.* 10. 165 f., 624, 673 (of the goddess Virtus) *seseque in corde reliquit*, 676 *iuvenis possessus numine pectus.*

680. flamma: many editors prefer *flammae*, but there is good MS. authority for the singular, and the variations in the MSS. are more easily explained if *flamma* is correct.

681. posuere: equivalent to *deposuere*, see note on 41.

681 f. 'beneath the damp timbers the caulking was still alight, belching out a slow smoke, and smouldering heat devoured the hulls, and deep in their frames penetrated the plague'.

682. tardum fumum: the pictorial effect of the words is enhanced by the comparatively unusual juxtaposition of noun and adjective with like endings; see on 845.

683. est: 'eats at', 'devours', cf. *Aen.* 4. 66 *est mollis flamma medullas, Geo.* 3. 566 *artus sacer ignis edebat*, and line 752; compare the use of the metaphor in such phrases as *ignis edax, flamma vorax.*

   corpore: the ablative of 'place where' is graphically used with a verb of motion—'went downwards till it was in . . .' See note on 88, and cf. Ernout, *R. Ph.*, 1944, pp. 193 f.

   pestis: i.e. the deadly fire, cf. *Aen.* 9. 540 (of fire) *in partem quae peste caret.* The word *prosunt* in the next line is appropriate for the metaphor of disease and cure.

684. For the elision over the caesura see note on 408.

685. pius: see on 26. Here the adjective has special reference to Aeneas' responsibility for his men and his mission, and particular force as Aeneas appeals to the *pietas* of Jupiter. To the reader it conveys something of the implication of Venus' question to Jupiter (*Aen.* 1. 253): *hic pietatis honos?*
   abscindere: 'historic' infinitive, see on 655.

686. auxilioque vocare: dative of 'purpose' or 'end in view', slightly extended from phrases like *auxilio venire, subire;* cf. *Aen.* 12. 388 *auxilioque viam quae proxima poscit.* Virgil sometimes extends this usage further, cf. Lejay on *Aen.* 1. 22 *venturum excidio*, 2. 798 *collectam exsilio pubem.* The development of this dative usage to replace a prepositional phrase is not unlike that in *it clamor caelo* (451).

687. For the form of the prayer cf. *Aen.* 2. 689 f. Aeneas' brief phrases are direct and urgent; he asks now for rescue or final destruction. This latest disaster, so soon after the short period of relaxation from the toils of men (*labores . . . humanos*) leaves him broken and weary in heart (see Intro., pp. xvii–xviii).

   exosus: active (the word is passive only in late authors), cf. *Aen.* 11. 436, 12. 517, 818, and *perosus* in *Aen.* 6. 435 (where see Norden), 9. 141. *Osus sum* occurs in early Latin for *odi*. The compound *exosus* is not found before Virgil;

see on 202. For the omission of the verb 'to be' in the second person, which is not common, see note on 192.

688. pietas antiqua: 'your loving-kindness of old'. For *pietas* applied to the gods, nearly equivalent to 'pity', cf. *Aen.* 2. 536 f., 4. 382, and see Bailey, *Religion in Virgil*, pp. 84 f.

689. da ... classi: 'grant that the fleet may escape the flames'. For the construction of *dare* see on 247–8. The transitive use of *evadere* is found in poetry and post-Augustan prose; cf. *Aen.* 3. 282 *iuvat evasisse tot urbes*, 9. 560 f. *nostrasne evadere demens / sperasti te posse manus?* See note on 437–8 (*exire*).

690. nunc: the word order gives emphasis, which is accentuated by the pause after the first syllable of the line (see on 548 f.).

et tenuis ... leto: 'and save from death the frail fortunes of the Trojans'; notice the halting movement of the second half of the line, and the assonance of long *e*.

691 f. 'If not, then in your own person do what is left to do— cast us down to destruction with your death-dealing thunder-bolt, if so I deserve, and overwhelm us here with your own right hand.' Notice the emphatic *tu, tua*: if it is Jupiter's will that they should perish, then let him act now and in person. I follow Servius in taking *quod superest* adverbially (he says 'quod congrue sequitur'); for the thought cf. *Aen.* 12. 643 *id rebus defuit unum*. Thus *me* or *nos* is to be supplied as the object of the sentence. There is much to be said for the other view which takes *quod superest* as the object, equivalent to *reliquias Troiae*, 'the remnants of Troy'; but see note on 796.

691. morti: for the dative cf. *Aen.* 2. 85 *demisere neci*, 2. 398 *demittimus Orco*, and see note on 806.

692. The pause after a trochee in the third foot is not common in Latin; it is of course very prominent in the Greek hexa-meter. Another example with a marked pause in this book is 832; there are less marked pauses at 49, 184, 800, 843. See Austin on *Aen.* 4. 164, Winbolt, *Latin Hexameter Verse*, pp. 33 f., Norden's *Aeneid VI*, pp. 431 f.

693–4. vix haec ediderat cum ... furit: for inverted *cum* see on 84–85.

693 f. 'a tempest black with torrential rain raged in wild fury, and the heights of the land and the plains shuddered at the thunder; from all heaven's expanse there came the rain pouring down in torrents, black as pitch on the misty south winds'. Compare the description of the storm in *Geo.* 1. 322 f. Day Lewis has:

Scarce were the words out when the sky grew dark and there came

A cloudburst, a storm of unparalleled violence: hill and dale

Were rocked by thunderclaps; all the firmament was one
  avalanche
Of driving rain, one blackness of cloud piled up by the South
  wind.

694–5. Notice the imitative alliteration of *t* and *r* in these two
lines; then in the phrases which follow, the *s* sounds perhaps
help to convey the hissing of the rain on the burning ships.

694. sine more: Servius says 'sine exemplo', but it is probably
better to take the phrase to mean ἀκόσμως, 'without restraint', as Henry well argues comparing *Aen.* 7. 377, 8. 635,
and Ov. *A.A.* 1. 119 (of the Sabine women) *sic illae timuere
viros sine more ruentes.*

695. ardua terrarum: 'periphrasis montium' (Servius). The
hexameter poets were fond of neuter plurals (and singulars)
of adjectives followed by a genitive (sometimes partitive,
sometimes possessive); see Bailey's Lucretius, *Proleg.*, pp.
91–92, Palmer, *The Latin Language*, p. 291, Kühner–Stegmann, ii. 1, p. 230. Livy and Tacitus followed their example;
see Anderson on Livy 9. 3. 1, Furneaux's *Annals*, Intro.,
p. 50. A phrase such as Virgil's *per opaca viarum* (*Aen.* 6. 633)
is commonly explained as a periphrasis for *per opacas vias*,
and the metrical convenience is pointed out (see Norden, ad
loc.). But it should not be thought that the phrase which the
poet has used conveys precisely the same meaning as the
phrase or word for which it is called a periphrasis. It is often
the case that more emphasis is given to the meaning of the
adjective, as in *per opaca viarum*, or Horace's *amaraque
curarum* (*Odes* 4. 12. 19 f.), or Livy's *in immensum altitudinis*
(21. 33. 7). For phrases similar to *ardua terrarum* cf. *Aen.*
8. 221 (= 11. 513) *ardua montis*, Tac. *Hist.* 4. 70 *ardua
Alpium*; compare line 180 *summa petit scopuli.*

  et campi: some MSS. read *campis*, to go with what follows,
but the picture of mountains and plains is intended to convey
the whole landscape; and the stop before *ruit* is very effective
(see on 662).

696. turbidus imber aqua: *aqua* seems at first sight to add little
to the picture, but the balance is *imber turbidus aqua et
nigerrimus densis Austris*; the storm is violent with rain and
dark with misty storm-winds. *Turbidus* is often applied to
storms, e.g. Lucr. 4. 169, *Aen.* 12. 685; it then has its primary
meaning deriving from *turba*: 'confused', 'wild'. The meaning of 'muddy', 'turbid' (as in *Geo.* 2. 137, *Aen.* 6. 296) is a
secondary one.

  densisque nigerrimus Austris: cf. *Geo.* 3. 278 *nigerrimus
Auster*, *Geo.* 3. 196 *Aquilo . . . densus*. The meaning of *densus*
is 'misty', 'rain-laden'.

697. super: there are three possible ways of taking this: (i) 'filled to overflowing', as if it were *superimplentur*; (ii) equivalent to *desuper*, 'from above'; (iii) equivalent to *insuper*, 'on top', i.e. the ships were swamped, the decks were awash with rain-water. The third seems best as giving the most natural meaning to *super*, and as providing the most striking picture.

semusta: the word is sometimes spelled *semiusta*, and in both cases is pronounced in the same way, with consonantal *i* as in *semianimis*. See on 432 and Austin on *Aen.* 4. 686.

madescunt: the ingressive form of *madere* is not found before Virgil. Other ingressive verbs which occur first in Virgil are *abolescere, crebrescere, derigescere, evalescere, inardescere, inolescere, nigrescere*. See note on 202.

698. restinctus donec: for the postposition of *donec* see on 22.

For the pause after the fifth trochee see on 678. One of the ways in which Virgil employs this pause is to repeat after it a word from earlier in the line; cf. *Ecl.* 9. 57 f. *et nunc omne tibi stratum silet aequor, et omnes | (aspice) ventosi ceciderunt murmuris aurae*; *Geo.* 2. 61 f. *scilicet omnibus est labor impendendus, et omnes | cogendae in sulcum . . .*

700–45. *Aeneas in despair wonders whether to abandon his fated mission altogether. Nautes advises him to leave behind some of his company in Sicily, and take the rest onwards to Italy. As Aeneas is pondering this advice there appears to him in the night a vision of his father Anchises, who tells him to accept Nautes' advice; but before establishing his city in Italy he is to visit the underworld to meet his father and to hear of his destiny.*

700 f. In this passage we see very clearly the tension between Aeneas' duty towards his divine mission and the human weaknesses of character with which he has to struggle. He is conscious throughout the poem of the will of the gods of which he is the chosen instrument, but again and again it seems that the task is almost too great for the frailty of a mortal man to achieve. At this stage in the poem his strength to continue is at its lowest ebb; and it is at this point that the vision of his father promises the inspiring revelations of Roman destiny which are given to Aeneas in the underworld (*Aen.* 6. 756 f.). Thereafter Aeneas' strength and determination to fulfil his mission are no longer in doubt. For a full discussion of this theme see Intro., pp. xix f.

701 f. 'kept pondering in his heart his heavy cares, turning constantly from one possibility to the other'. Virgil has a number of variations of this expression (*Aen.* 4. 285–6 = 8. 20–21, *Aen.* 4. 630); it is based on the Homeric phrases

διάνδιχα μερμήριξεν (*Il.* 1. 189) and ὡς καὶ ἐμοὶ δίχα θυμὸς
ὀρώρεται ἔνθα καὶ ἔνθα (*Od.* 19. 524). The spondaic movement
helps to portray the heaviness of his anxiety; see on 136–41,
and cf. especially 614–15.

702–3. The use of -*ne* . . . -*ne* for an indirect question (or as here
an indirect deliberative question) is rare in prose, but quite
common in poetry; cf. line 95, *Aen.* 11. 126, 12. 321.

   The jingling similarity of rhythm in the second halves
of these two lines perhaps reproduces the insistence of the
problem dinning in Aeneas' thoughts.

703. For the elision over the caesura see on 408.

   oblitus fatorum: see on 700 f.

   capesseret: cf. *Aen.* 4. 346 *Italiam Lyciae iussere capessere
sortes.*

704. Nautes: Servius tells us that Varro in his *De familiis
Troianis* said that the Nautii were priests of Pallas because
Nautes was supposed to have brought back the Palladium
(*Aen.* 2. 166) to Italy.

704 f. 'whom above all Tritonian Pallas had taught, whom she
had made renowned for great knowledge of her lore'.

704. unum: cf. *Aen.* 1. 15 *magis omnibus unam*, 2. 426 *iustissi-
mus unus*, 3. 321, 12. 143, and our expression to 'single out'.

   Tritonia: a frequent epithet of Pallas (e.g. *Aen.* 2. 171).
She is Τριτογένεια in Homer; an old legend said that she was
born (or first alighted after her birth) at Lake Triton in N.
Africa (Lucan 9. 347 f.). See H. J. Rose in *O.C.D.*, s.v.
Athena.

705. quem: for the postposition of the relative see on 22.

706–7. 'She it was who gave him replies about what the great
anger of the gods was portending or what the march of the
fates demanded.' These two lines are parenthetical, and
the subject of the main sentence (Nautes) is picked up after the
parenthesis with *isque*. *Haec* is Pallas; *quae* does not go with
responsa but introduces the indirect question. The first of
the indirect clauses refers to events caused by the anger of
individual gods (like Juno), and the second to inevitable
events (like the foundation of Rome) decreed by destiny.
Ribbeck's *hac* for *haec* (sc. *hac arte*) is attractive because it
introduces the parenthesis better, but *haec* can stand.

708. isque: the commentators compare *Aen.* 6. 684, 9. 549
where *isque* occurs with relation to the subject of a preceding
sentence. But it should be recognized firmly that here it
refers to the subject of the same sentence, or to put it another
way *senior Nautes* is left, by an anacoluthon, without a construction. If, as Sabbadini does, we follow Heyne and Wagner
and do not put the two preceding lines in parenthesis, we

avoid the anacoluthon (the construction being *senior Nautes haec responsa dabat . . . isque infit*, a sort of hendiadys). But no satisfactory sense can then be got from 706–7, because (i) Nautes' speech is not *responsa*; (ii) *dabat* is the wrong tense with *infit*; (iii) the alternative *vel . . . vel* clauses become senseless. Henry has an excellent note demolishing the views of Heyne and Wagner.

solatus: the past participle of deponent verbs is often used in this 'timeless' way, i.e. without any idea of the past tense. Cf. 86, 216, 555, 628, 766, *Geo.* 1. 293 f. *interea longum cantu solata laborem / arguto coniunx percurrit pectine telas*, *Aen.* 6. 335 with Page's note, and Palmer, *The Latin Language*, p. 327.

infit: an archaism, see on 10. The verb occurs only in this form (except for *infiunt* in Martianus Capella), and is mainly used in connexion with speaking; cf. *Aen.* 10. 101, 11. 242, Livy 1. 28. 4.

709 f. Notice the slow oracular style of Nautes' speech. There is a marked absence of mid-line pauses; the first four lines are all end-stopped and self-contained sentences which give a noticeable hortatory effect. Nautes' lack of emotion or excitement throws into clearer relief the anxiety of Aeneas, on whom rests the ultimate responsibility.

709–10. 'Wherever the fates draw us in their ebb and flow, let us follow; whatever shall betide, fortune must always be overcome by endurance.' These *sententiae* express Stoic ideas; it is by accepting destiny that a man lives *secundum Naturam*. Cf. Sen. *Ep. Mor.* 107. 11 (translating Cleanthes) *ducunt volentem fata, nolentem trahunt*; and see M. L. Clarke, *The Roman Mind*, pp. 115 f., especially 118, Heinze, *Virgils Epische Technik*, pp. 275 f., and note on 725. The attitude of Aeneas towards his destiny may in some ways (but not in all) be compared with that of the Stoic *sapiens*; see Intro., p. xx. Notice here the contrast between *fata* (destiny which we all must follow, see on 656) and *fortuna* (a set of circumstances which we may fight against, see on 604).

710. quidquid erit: Henry argues that this is a specific reference to their present situation (whatever it turns out to be), but it is better taken generally, cf. Hor. *Odes* 1. 11. 3 *ut melius quidquid erit pati*.

ferendo est: the elision (which is really a prodelision of *est*, or a coalescence of the two words) is obviously not felt to be a real elision and is quite common at the end of a hexameter (cf. 178, 224, 679, 727) as well as elsewhere in the line. It is noticeable that it occurs in Nautes' speech three times in seven lines.

711. For Acestes' divine ancestry cf. line 38.

713. The word order is *huic trade (eos) qui amissis navibus superant*; for the postposition of the relative see on 22. *Superant* means 'are left over'; see on 519.

et quos: for the double monosyllable in the sixth foot see on 372.

714. pertaesum: cf. *Aen.* 4. 18 *si non pertaesum thalami taedaeque fuisset.*

716. 'and any you have who are frail and fearful of danger'. For the use of the neuter *quidquid* applied to people cf. *Aen.* 1. 601 f. *quidquid ubique est | gentis Dardaniae,* Hor. *Epod.* 5. 1 *at o deorum quidquid in caelo regit,* Cat. 37. 4 *quidquid est puellarum.* It is doubtful whether we are justified in seeing, as many commentators do, something contemptuous in the use of the neuter here.

metuensque: the word is used as a pure adjective, with an objective genitive; cf. Hor. *Sat.* 2. 2. 110 *metuensque futuri,* Livy 22. 3. 4 *ne deorum quidem satis metuens.* Other present participles used in this way include *timens* (Lucr. 6. 1240, where see Munro), *cupiens, neglegens, amans, fugiens, patiens.* See Kühner–Stegmann, ii. 1, pp. 450–1.

717. Here again the word order is complicated (cf. 713); the normal order would be *et sine (ut) fessi moenia his terris habeant.* Notice the rather awkward repetition of *fessi* after *fessas* (715); see on 254. For the jussive subjunctive in parataxis with *sine* see on 163, and cf. 548 f.

718. permisso nomine: the participle has conditional force, 'if the name be allowed'. Servius takes the meaning to be 'if Acestes allows the use of his name', but it could equally well be 'if you (Aeneas) allow the name'. Nautes' phrase is deliberately unspecific.

Acestam: the town was called Egesta by the Greeks, Segesta by the Romans. For etymological connexions of this kind (Acestes > Acesta > Egesta) see notes on 2 and 117. The belief that the Trojans came to this part of Sicily had been firmly founded for a very long time; cf. Thuc. 6. 2. 3. Ἰλίου δὲ ἁλισκομένου τῶν Τρώων τινὲς διαφυγόντες Ἀχαιοὺς πλοίοις ἀφικνοῦνται πρὸς τὴν Σικελίαν, καὶ ὅμοροι τοῖς Σικανοῖς οἰκήσαντες ξύμπαντες μὲν Ἔλυμοι ἐκλήθησαν, πόλεις δ' αὐτῶν Ἔρυξ τε καὶ Ἔγεστα.

The association of these Trojans with Aeneas would very easily follow in Roman times; cf. Cic. *Verr.* 2. 4. 72 *Segesta est oppidum pervetus in Sicilia quod ab Aenea fugiente a Troia atque in haec loca veniente conditum esse demonstrant.* By altering the legend so that Aeneas visits Sicily twice, and thus setting the whole of this book in Sicily, Virgil has given special prominence to Italy's nearest neighbour; see Intro., p. xiii.

For early Sicilian peoples and places see notes on 24, 38, 73–74, 523–4, 604 f., 759 f., and T. J. Dunbabin, *The Western Greeks*, pp. 335–7, T. R. Glover, *Virgil*, pp. 95 f., with references.

719 f. While the ships were ablaze Aeneas was in despair (685 f.); when Jupiter answered his prayer and saved them, he was still worried and uncertain what to do (700 f.); now after Nautes' proposal the fires of anxiety burn him. The task which the gods had laid upon him was almost too great for human endurance. But he is at this point given new strength by the vision of his father, to whom he had owed so much in the past, and from whom now he receives Jupiter's assurance.

720. 'then indeed is he racked in mind with every kind of torment'.

    tum vero: for *tum vero* following a subordinate clause cf. *Aen.* 7. 376, 11. 633, and Livy 2. 29. 3 *quo repulso tum vero . . . devolant*, Sall. *Cat.* 61. 1 *confecto proelio tum vero cerneres*; cf. also *Aen.* 12. 6, and line 382. Compare the use of *sic* in *Aen.* 1. 225, 7. 668, 8. 488, and see note on line 14 (position of *deinde*).

    animo: this is the reading of the main MSS.; Servius reads *animum* and explains it as a Greek accusative.

721. et: the nature of the connexion here is extremely difficult to see. Servius says 'quasi maior causa cogitationis', presumably linking the line very closely with the preceding line; but this is inappropriate both because of the sense and because of the different tenses. Commentators quote *Aen.* 10. 256 f. *tantum effatus. et interea revoluta ruebat / matura iam luce dies* (where *interea* makes all the difference); *Aen.* 2. 780 f. *longa tibi exsilia et vastum maris aequor arandum: / et terram Hesperiam venies*; *Aen.* 2. 760 f. *procedo et Priami sedes arcemque reviso: / et iam porticibus vacuis Iunonis asylo / custodes lecti Phoenix et dirus Ulixes / praedam adservabant*. But all of these are much easier, and we can only conclude that Virgil has left this passage in an unrevised state, without having finally completed the links in the transition of the narrative.

    bigis: Night (like Phoebus, line 739) drives across the sky in her chariot, and the stars follow in her train; cf. Eur. *Ion* 1150 f., Theoc. 2. 166, Enn. *Scen.* 112–13 V (*sacra Nox*) *quae cava caeli / signitenentibus conficis bigis*, Tib. 2. 1. 87 f. *iam Nox iungit equos, currumque sequuntur / matris lascivo sidera fulva choro*, Val. Fl. 3. 211 *lentis haeret Nox conscia bigis*, Milton, *Comus*, 553–4 'The drowsy frighted steeds / That draw the litter of close-curtain'd sleep'.

722. dehinc: the word is scanned here as an iambus (cf. *Geo.* 3. 167, *Aen.* 3. 464), but as a single syllable in *Aen.* 1. 131, 256, 6. 678. It sometimes refers to the future ('henceforth'), but more often, as here, looks from the past to the present ('after this', 'then'). It does not afford a good connexion with the previous line; see note on 721 (*et*).

facies: the actual shade of Anchises is in Elysium (735). This is an apparition or vision (*imago*, cf. *Aen.* 4. 353, 6. 695) sent by Jupiter; compare the apparition of Hector in *Aen.* 2. 270 f. Dreams and visions play a considerable part in the development of the story of the *Aeneid*. It is only rarely that they are psychological revelations of a state of mind (like Dido's dream in 4. 465 f.; cf. the dream simile in 12. 908 f.). Most of them are waking visions or dreams of gods or dead heroes, like this appearance of Anchises to Aeneas. They serve to emphasize the connexion of the gods with the human action, and to show how the future greatness of Rome is part of the divine plan. Notable examples are the appearances to Aeneas of Hector (2. 270 f.), of the Penates (3. 147 f.), of Mercury (4. 556 f.), of Tiberinus (8. 31 f.). On this theme see H. R. Steiner, *Der Traum in der Aeneis*, Bern, 1952.

724 f. Notice the entirely different movement of Anchises' speech from that of Nautes (see on 709 f.); here there are many heavy mid-line pauses (see Marouzeau, *Traité de stylistique latine*, pp. 308 f.). The speech begins gently, and Aeneas' anxiety is set at rest with the simple phrases *imperio Iovis huc venio, consiliis pare*. Anchises gives his instructions in precise and direct terms, and ends with two lines of rich poetic beauty.

724–5. Cf. Cat. 64. 215–16 *nate, mihi longa iucundior unice vita, / nate, ego quem . . ., Aen.* 1. 664 f. *nate, meae vires, mea magna potentia, solus, / nate, patris summi qui tela Typhoea temnis . . .*

725. Iliacis exercite fatis: 'hard-pressed by Trojan destiny'; there is the same phrase in *Aen.* 3. 182, used by Anchises in life to Aeneas. For the idea of the ill fate of Troy see on 625. The word *exercite* suggests the phraseology of Stoicism; cf. Sen. *Dial.* 1. 4. 7 *hos itaque deus quos probat, quos amat, indurat, recognoscit, exercet.* Compare the Stoic ring of Aeneas' words in *Aen.* 6. 103–5 (where see Norden) and in 8. 131 f. *sed mea me virtus et sancta oracula divum / . . . fatis egere volentem.* See also note on 709–10.

726. imperio Iovis: notice the emphasis on the divine motivation; cf. 747, 784, and see Intro., pp. xix f.

classibus: dative, see on 845. The plural *classes* is used of Aeneas' fleet a number of times (*Aen.* 3. 157, 4. 313, 582, 6.

697), and sometimes the singular is used to mean one ship (see Norden on *Aen.* 6. 334, Servius on *Aen.* 1. 39, *Aen.* 6. 1). The usage then seems to be metonymy of *classis* = *navis* rather than poetic plural.

728. For the placing of *pulcherrima* in the relative clause, a common Latin usage, cf. *Aen.* 3. 546 *praeceptisque Heleni dederat quae maxima* . . .

729. fortissima corda: 'bravest hearts'; cf. *Aen.* 2. 348 f. *iuvenes, fortissima frustra | pectora.*

730. aspera cultu: 'rough in its way of life'; cf. *Aen.* 1. 263 f. (Jupiter's prophecy) *bellum ingens geret Italia populosque feroces | contundet,* and the fine speech of the Rutulian Numanus in *Aen.* 9. 603 f. *durum a stirpe genus natos ad flumina primum | deferimus* . . .

731. debellanda: Servius says 'bene victoriam, non bella sola, praedicit'. Compare *Aen.* 6. 853 *parcere subiectis et debellare superbos.* The word does not occur before the Augustan Age; it is a great favourite with Livy, who has it more than fifty times.

731 f. In *Aen.* 3. 441 f. Helenus prophesied that on arrival at Cumae Aeneas would receive instructions about his future destiny; in that passage, however, it was to be the Sibyl and not the shade of Anchises who would reveal the future. This is one of several inconsistencies between prophecies made in Book III and their fulfilment elsewhere in the poem, supporting the generally held view that Book III was written early and was in need of some revision to bring it into line with the rest of the poem. Compare the prophecy of eating the tables, given in III by Celaeno but attributed in VII to Anchises; and the sign of the white sow, referring in III to the foundation of Lavinium but in VIII to that of Alba Longa. See M. M. Crump, *The Growth of the Aeneid*, Blackwell, 1920, pp. 20 f., and Intro., pp. xxiii f.

731. Ditis: Virgil generally calls the king of the underworld Dis, but never uses the nominative; the sole occurrence of the name Pluton is where the nominative is needed (*Aen.* 7. 327).

For lines ending in two disyllables see on 274–5. This instance, however, is of a particularly striking type; in most instances a monosyllable precedes so that the ictus and accent coincide at the beginning of the fifth foot, though there is a clash on the next syllable. Here there is no coincidence in the fifth foot at all. This is the only case of this rhythm in the first six books (except for the slightly different instance in *Aen.* 3. 695 *subter mare qui nunc*); there is one in *Aen.* 8. 382 *sanctum mihi nomen*, and nine in Books X and XI. There is no instance at all in Ovid. For a strikingly effective use of this rhythm cf. *Geo.* 2. 153 f. *nec rapit immensos orbis per humum neque tanto | squameus in spiram tractu se colligit anguis.* See Winbolt, *Latin Hexameter Verse*, pp. 137 f., and Norden's *Aeneid VI*, p. 447.

732. Averna: Virgil sometimes uses the neuter plural form *Averna* and sometimes the masculine *Avernus* (813); cf. *Tartara* (734) and *Tartarus* (*Aen.* 6. 577). The word is used both of the lake with its fabled entrance to the underworld (*Aen.* 3. 442) and of the underworld itself (*Aen.* 7. 91); here it probably has the latter meaning. *Avernus* was connected with ἄορνος because the fumes from the lake, situated in an old volcanic crater, kept birds away. Cf. *Aen.* 6. 239 f.; although 6. 242 *unde locum Grai dixerunt nomine Aornon* is generally regarded as spurious, the previous lines clearly indicate that Virgil accepts the derivation (see note on 2).

733. congressus . . . meos: 'seek a meeting with me'. Except in its military sense (e.g. *Aen.* 12. 514) the word *congressus* is very rare indeed in poetry, and is found only once elsewhere in Classical times (Ov. *Met.* 7. 501 *postquam congressus primi sua verba tulerunt*). It is common enough in prose, and perhaps had tended to acquire a somewhat formal sense;—this may be the reason why Virgil has used it in a 'poetic' plural, for there is little force in Mackail's suggestion that the plural conveys 'occasions of meeting'. For poetic plurals see on 98.

non me impia namque: the connexion of thought is that Aeneas would not be allowed to visit Tartarus, cf. *Aen.* 6. 563 *nulli fas casto sceleratum insistere limen*. For the postposition of the word *namque* cf. *Ecl.* 1. 14, *Aen.* 7. 122, 10. 614, and note on 5. Virgil does not often end a line with a colourless word of this kind. As a general rule the key position at the end of the line is occupied by a noun or a verb; adjectives are less common in this position (sometimes they may be given emphasis in this way, e.g. 100); adverbs and particles are rarer still (cf. 415). See Norden's *Aeneid VI*, pp. 400 f. for some statistics and a comparison with Lucretian usage.

734. tristes umbrae: some inferior MSS. have *tristesve umbrae*, and commentators have suggested a reference to the tripartite division of the underworld into Tartarus, Elysium, and the neutral region (of the untimely dead). But it is more effective to take *tristes umbrae* in apposition to *Tartarus*, *umbrae* being used in its local sense (region of darkness). Cf. *Aen.* 6. 534 *tristes sine sole domos*, 6. 404 *imas Erebi descendit ad umbras*. Tartarus with its legendary sinners is described in *Aen.* 6. 548 f.

734 f. Elysium, the abode of the blessed, is described in *Aen.* 6. 637 f., a passage of memorable and haunting beauty.

735. There is hiatus between *colo* and *huc*; for Virgil's use of hiatus see Austin's full treatment (with references) on *Aen.* 4. 235. Many of the instances are in imitation of Greek rhythm; some are of the type *o ubi*, where hiatus is regular; in nearly all other cases the hiatus occurs before a pause, and the unelided vowel is at the ictus of the foot. There is a very similar instance to the present one at *Aen.* 1. 16 *posthabita coluisse Samo: hic illius arma* . . . For the much rarer device of shortening in hiatus see on 261.

  casta Sibylla: the Sibyl of Cumae (*Aen.* 3. 441 f., 6. 10 f.) was the prophetess of Apollo; originally perhaps Sibylla was a personal name, but it came to be the type name of succeeding priestesses (this Sibyl is called Deiphobe, *Aen.* 6. 36). The Sibylline oracle played a most important part in Roman religion, and in 18 B.C. Augustus had the Sibylline books recopied and transferred to his new temple dedicated to Apollo on the Palatine. See Pease in *O.C.D.*, s.v. Sibylla.

736. 'when you have duly paid rich sacrifice of black cattle'; *multo sanguine* is ablative of price. The sacrifices are described in *Aen.* 6. 243 f.

737. This promise is fulfilled when Anchises describes the long and splendid pageant of Roman heroes yet to be born, waiting at the stream of Lethe, *Aen.* 6. 756 f.

738. 'dewy Night is sweeping round past the mid-point of her course', i.e. in her chariot has passed the mid-point of her orbit through the sky; cf. 721, 835.

739. saevus: because the day banishes ghosts. Cf. the Ghost in *Hamlet* (1. 5. 58 f.). 'But soft! Methinks I scent the morning air; / Brief let me be.' Virgil has a very similar line at *Geo.* 1. 250 *nosque ubi primus equis Oriens adflavit anhelis* . . . For *adflare* used transitively cf. *Aen* 2. 648 f. *ex quo me divum pater atque hominum rex / fulminis adflavit ventis*, Ov. *Tr.* 1. 9. 22 *ignibus adflari*, Livy 30. 6. 7 *adflati incendio.*

740. tenuis . . . in auras: cf. *Geo.* 4. 499 f. (*Eurydice*) *ceu fumus in auras / commixtus tenuis fugit diversa, Aen.* 2. 791 (*Creusa*) *tenuisque recessit in auras*, Lucr. 3. 456, Hom. *Il.* 23. 100.

741. Compare Hom. *Od.* 11. 210, where Odysseus begs the phantom of his mother to stay. Notice the broken urgency of this line and the next, accentuated by the omission of the reflexive with *proripis* (cf. *Aen.* 10. 796 *proripuit iuvenis seseque immiscuit armis*, though there the reflexive can be supplied from the following clause). The effect is assisted by the large proportion of monosyllables, and by the internal pauses, especially *quem fugis?* with its marked conflict; see on 643, and cf. *Aen.* 6. 466, the same phrase with similar effect.

deinde: Servius says 'ordo est: Aeneas deinde "quo ruis?" ', but this is hardly possible. The meaning seems to be equivalent to *posthac*, in the context implying 'so soon'; some take it to have the force of *tandem*, adding emphasis to the interrogative word, but there is no real authority for this. There is a very similar phrase in *Aen.* 9. 781 *et Mnestheus 'quo deinde fugam quo tenditis?' inquit*, where from the next line (*quos alios muros, quae iam ultra moenia habetis?*) it appears that the meaning is *posthac*. Cf. also Pers. 5. 143.

743 f. Sacrifices are made after supernatural appearances at *Aen.* 3. 176 f., 8. 542 f. The phrase *cinerem . . . ignis* occurs again in *Aen.* 8. 410. Notice how the agitated excitement of Aeneas is calmed by the ritual performance of these religious ceremonies, described in the appropriate sonorous and formulary diction.

744. Compare *Aen.* 8. 542 f. *et primum Herculeis sopitas ignibus aras | excitat hesternumque Larem parvosque Penates | laetus adit*: and for the phraseology *Aen.* 9. 258 f. *per magnos Nise Penates | Assaracique Larem et canae penetralia Vestae | obtestor*. For the Trojan Penates and the undying fire of Vesta brought by Aeneas from Troy cf. *Aen.* 2. 293 f., and note on 632. Vesta was closely associated with the Lar and the Penates, and like them of great importance in the State worship at Rome (*Geo.* 1. 498); see Bailey, *Religion in Virgil*, pp. 91 f., 95 f. For her epithet *cana* cf. *Aen.* 1. 292 *cana Fides et Vesta*; Servius says 'aut antiquae aut propter ignis favillas', of which the former is preferable.

745. farre pio: cf. Hor. *Odes* 3. 23. 20. This is the *mola salsa* used in sacrifices, cf. *Aen.* 2. 133, 4. 517, 12. 173. For *pius* cf. also *Aen.* 4. 637 *pia tege tempora vitta*; in these contexts it means 'required by religion'.

plena . . . acerra: cf. Hor. *Odes* 3. 8. 2 f. *acerra turis | plena.*

746–78. *Aeneas follows out the new plan, and a city is founded under Acestes' rule for those staying behind; a temple is dedicated to Venus at Eryx and Anchises' tomb has a priest and a sanctuary appointed for it. After nine days of celebration in honour of the new city the Trojans say their farewells to those staying behind; sacrifices are made, and they sail for Italy.*

746. accersit: some MSS. have *arcessit*, the alternative spelling; see *Thes. L.L.*, s.v. *arcesso, init.* The form *accersit* is perhaps preferable here on grounds of euphony, but in either case the line ending has a harsh sound; see note on 670 f. (*fin.*).

748. 'the plan which now was firmly settled in his mind'; cf,

Cic. *Ad Att.* 8. 11. 1 *constitit consilium*, and the use of *stat* in *Aen.* 2. 750 *stat casus renovare omnis*, and compare *mens eadem perstat* in line 812.

750. transcribunt urbi: 'they enrol for the city'. According to Servius this is a technical term: 'Romani moris verbum est: transcripti enim in colonias deducebantur'. The much commoner term is *adscribere*; *transcribere* would presumably imply the transfer from one register to another, cf. *Aen.* 7. 422.

751. deponunt: Servius rightly says 'quasi de navibus'.

animos... egentis: 'hearts with no craving for great glory'. The word *magnae* is intended to convey that Acestes' settlers are not spiritless, but lack the final qualities of the indomitable spirit. The fourth foot rarely consists of a single spondee, so that emphasis is thrown on *magnae* (as on *bello* in 754); see on 116.

752. ambesa: literally 'eaten round', hence here 'charred'. It is a very rare word, occurring also in *Aen.* 3. 257 *ambesas . . . absumere mensas*, otherwise only once in Plautus and once in Tacitus in Classical Latin. See note on 202. For the metaphor cf. 683.

753. remosque rudentisque: for the doubled *-que* ('both . . . and') see on 92; for the hypermetric *-que* see on 422.

754. 'few they are in number, but their valour in war never sleeps'. The phrase *vivida virtus* is a powerful one; the adjective *vividus* is mostly poetic and has emotional overtones, and the marked alliteration enhances the effect. Compare Lucr. 1. 72 (of Epicurus) *ergo vivida vis animi pervicit*, *Aen.* 11. 386 f. *possit quid vivida virtus / experiare licet*, *Aen.* 10. 609 f. *vivida bello / dextra viris*. For a similar shift from a personal to an impersonal subject cf. *Aen.* 11. 338 f. *largus opum et lingua melior, sed frigida bello / dextera*.

755 f. Compare the building of Carthage (*Aen.* 1. 423 f.), and o Pergamum in Crete (*Aen.* 3. 137 *iura domosque dabam*).

755. urbem designat aratro: for the custom of marking out the site for the walls of a new town see Servius, ad loc., and *Aen.* 7. 157 *ipse humili designat moenia fossa*.

756. 'this he bids be their Ilium, these lands their Troy'; see on 634. As the town is to be called Acesta, these are presumably names of the different quarters. Others take the meaning to be that Acesta is to be their Ilium (though not called Ilium) and its surrounds their Troy (though not called Troy). This seems less likely in view of 633 f.

Ilium et: for the elision of the final syllable of a quasi-cretic see Austin on *Aen.* 4. 684, Norden's *Aeneid VI*, pp. 455 f. It is rare in Virgil and occurs mainly with the word

Ilium (eight times, seven times followed by *et* and once by
in). Without such an elision the word could not of course
have been used. Austin points out that all eight occurrences
are in the first six books, and *Ilia tellus* is used instead in
9. 285, 11. 245. Other notable instances of this kind of
elision are *Aen.* 4. 387 *audiam et*, 4. 684 *abluam et*, 12. 569
eruam et; 1. 599 *omnium egenos*, 2. 667 *alterum in alterius*,
10. 514 *ardens limitem agit*.

For the double disyllable at the end of the line see on 274.

758. indicitque forum: 'proclaims an assembly', arranges for
the assembly to meet, cf. *forum agere* (Cicero), *comitia indicere*
(Livy). Servius says 'tempus et locum designat agendorum
negotiorum, qui conventus vocatur'. Notice the very Roman
terminology here (as in 750, 755), associating the foundation
of Acesta with the later greatness of Rome.

patribus dat iura vocatis: 'summons the senate and
administers justice', i.e. sets up laws, begins the process of
government. For *dare iura* cf. *Aen.* 1. 293, 507, 3. 137, 7. 246,
8. 670.

759 f. This temple of Venus on Mt. Eryx (see on 24) was a very
famous one in Greek and Roman times; cf. Thuc. 6. 46. 3,
Theoc. 15. 100 f. (quoted below), Tac. *Ann.* 4. 43. 5. There
was a temple of Venus Erycina at Rome near the Colline
Gate (Livy 23. 30. 13, Ov. *Fast.* 4. 871 f., Hor. *Odes* 1. 2. 33).

760. Idaliae: Idalium in Cyprus was one of Venus' most
favoured abodes; cf. *Aen.* 1. 681, 10. 52, 86, Cat. 64. 96,
Theoc. 15. 100 f. δέσποιν᾽, ἃ Γολγώς τε καὶ Ἰδάλιον ἐφίλησας /
αἰπεινάν τ᾽ Ἔρυκα, χρυσῷ παίζοισ᾽ Ἀφροδίτα. Gow (ad loc.)
suggests that Theocritus perhaps coupled Eryx with Idalium
as the opposite extremes of the goddess's domain; Virgil
may have chosen the epithet *Idalia* simply as one of the
most famous of the places associated with Venus (in Cat.
36. 12 f. Idalium comes first in a list of her seats of worship),
or he may be recalling the passage from Theocritus.

760 f. Compare Andromache's sacrifices at Hector's cenotaph,
Aen. 3. 300 f. For the significance of this worship see on 42 f.;
the deification of Anchises is implied rather than stated.
There is perhaps some thought of the deification of Julius
Caesar in Virgil's mind, but it is going too far to relate the
sacerdos here with Antony as *flamen* of Caesar (Cic. *Phil.*
2. 110 f., Suet. *Iul.* 76, Dio 44. 6. 4). We may concede this
much to allegorical interpretation (see, for example, D. L.
Drew, *The Allegory of the Aeneid*, chap. ii, N. W. DeWitt,
A.J.Ph., 1920, pp. 369 f.), that contemporary events and
current attitudes obviously helped to form Virgil's whole
approach to his theme; but the general poetic intention of the

Aeneid is such that we should resist any suggestion of hidden meanings, or enigmatic references to historical facts.

761. **Anchiseo**: the adjective is formed in the Greek way, the ending *-ēus* representing *-εῖος*. Compare *stirpis Achillēae* (*Aen.* 3. 326), *moenia Pallantēa* (9. 196, a line ending of the same rhythm as this one), *Cytherēa* (line 800), and words like *Phoebēus*, *Grynēus*. For the rhythm of the line ending see on 300 and 320.

762. Aeneas had decreed for Anchises a religious ceremony of nine days with games on the ninth (see on 64–65). This further period of nine days is to celebrate the foundation of the city.

764. 'and the south wind blowing steadily calls them out to sea again'. For the postposition of *et* see on 5; for *creber* cf. *Aen.* 3. 530 *crebrescunt optatae aurae*. The adjective is used adverbially with the present participle; see on 278, and cf. *Aen.* 3. 70 *lenis crepitans vocat Auster in altum*.

765. **procurva**: the word is not found before Virgil; cf. *Geo.* 2. 421. *Recurvus* (*Aen.* 7. 513) also occurs first in Virgil. Of the two words *procurvus* is not found again in Classical Latin, but *recurvus* became quite common. See on 202.

766. **noctemque diemque morantur**: probably 'they delay a night and a day' rather than 'they prolong night and day' by trying to make them last longer. For the doubled *-que* ('both . . . and') see on 92.

768. **numen**: 'its power'. I should, however, prefer to accept *nomen*, the original reading of *M*, in the sense 'the very mention of it'. This gives more force to the sentence, and a better balance with *facies*. Confusion in MSS. between *nomen* and *numen* is very common; cf. *Aen.* 4. 94.

770 f. Aeneas is now completely in control of the situation again, consoling rather than consoled (708), calmly making all the necessary arrangements.

772. Eryx was the guardian deity of the place, see on 24.

    Tempestatibus agnam: cf. *Aen.* 3. 120 *nigram Hiemi pecudem, Zephyris felicibus albam*, Hor. *Epod.* 10. 23 f. *libidinosus immolabitur caper / et agna Tempestatibus*. There was a temple to the *Tempestates* near the Porta Camena, cf. Cic. *Nat. De.* 3. 51, Ov. *Fast.* 6. 193.

773. For the variation of voice after *iubere* (*iubet eos caedere . . . et funem solvi*) cf. *Aen.* 11. 83 f. *indutosque iubet truncos hostilibus armis / ipsos ferre duces inimicaque nomina figi*; compare also *Aen.* 3. 60 f.

    ex ordine: 'duly'. Servius says 'rite peragi sacrificium, et sic solvi funem', and cites *Aen.* 7. 139 f. *Phrygiamque ex ordine matrem / invocat*; compare note on 102. It is also possible that the meaning is that the ships are to cast off in turn.

774–8. Almost the whole of this passage is made up of lines which occur elsewhere; see note on 8–11.

774. For the construction of *caput* see on 135; for *tonsae* see on 556. Cf. *Geo.* 3. 21 *ipse caput tonsae foliis ornatus olivae*.

775. procul: 'apart', high up, away from the rest.

775–6. extaque . . . fundit: this is almost an exact repetition of 237–8, where see notes. Here, as there, I would prefer to read the form *porricit*.

777. prosequitur: 'attends', 'escorts' them. This line occurs at *Aen.* 3. 130, and the following line at *Aen.* 3. 290. The familiar phrases give a calm ending to this section of the poem.

779–826. *Meanwhile Venus complains to Neptune of Juno's hostility to the Trojans, and asks for his promise that the Trojans will safely cross his domain to Italy. Neptune gives his promise, and recalls how he has helped Aeneas in the past; but he says that one life must be lost so that the others shall be safe. The seas are calmed as Neptune rides over them, attended by his retinue.*

779 f. At this critical moment of the narrative of the human events, as Aeneas sets out on the last stage of his long journey, the scene moves on to the divine plane so that the events which follow are seen to be part of a larger context. This is typical of Virgil's intention throughout the whole poem to link the human action with the divine purpose; see note on 604 f.

781 f. The speech of Venus is vivid and emotional; her angry resentment against Juno runs through it and is emphasized by the insistent theme of Juno's disregard of the Fates, of Jupiter, and of Neptune himself (792).

781. Notice the emphatic position of *Iunonis* as the first word of the speech, the word which comes immediately to Venus' lips. We might translate: 'Juno, with her fierce anger and implacable heart, forces me . . .' Juno's hostility to Troy is discussed in the notes on 604 f. and 608. This line is without a strong caesura in third or fourth foot; see note on 591. Observe, however, the very marked difference of rhythm in the first half of 591 compared with this line. 591 is entirely without any conflict of word-accent and metrical ictus, but here there is conflict in both the first and the second foot, with the word accent on *gravis* (an emphatic word) in particularly marked conflict with the ictus. The rhythmic effect helps to portray the unrestrained indignation of Venus. Exactly similar in rhythmic structure, and with something of the same effect, is the magnificent and memorable description of the sound of the city's grief at the suicide of Amata, borne to Turnus on the breezes, *Aen.* 12. 619 *confusae sonus urbis et inlaetabile murmur*; compare too *Aen.* 2. 483 (the breaching of Priam's palace) *apparet domus intus et atria longa patescunt*.

neque exsaturabile: = *et inexsaturabile*; cf. Prop. 2. 28. 52 *vobiscum Europe nec proba* (= *et improba*) *Pasiphae*, Ov. *Met.* 1. 109 f. *mox etiam fruges tellus inarata ferebat, | nec renovatus* (= *et non renovatus*) *ager gravidis canebat aristis.* The word *exsaturabilis* does not occur elsewhere except for one instance in Stat. *Th.* 1. 214; in *Aen.* 7. 298 the participle *exsaturata* is used (of Juno). See note on 591 for adjectives in *-bilis*, and on 202 for words not found before Virgil.

782. preces descendere in omnis: 'have recourse to every kind of prayer', i.e. the humblest prayers. Cf. Caes. *B.C.* 1. 9. 5 *ad omnia descendere paratum*, Hor. *Odes* 3. 29. 58 f. *ad miseras preces | decurrere*.

783–4. It has been pointed out that the grammatical arrangement of these lines is somewhat clumsy, with *quam* separated from its antecedent *Iunonis* and the change of subject in 784. But the abruptness, which in any case is only slight, is suitable for the excited feelings of Venus.

783. longa dies: cf. *Aen.* 6. 745 *donec longa dies . . .*; for the gender of *dies* see on 42–43.

pietas nec: for the postposition of *nec* see on 5. *Pietas* means *Aeneae pietas*, both in general (*Aen.* 1. 10 *insignem pietate virum*) and towards Juno (*Aen.* 3. 547 *Iunoni Argivae iussos adolemus honores*). Cf. Venus' cry (*Aen.* 1. 253) *hic pietatis honos?*, and see note on 26. Others less well relate the word to Juno and take the meaning to be 'pity', cf. 688.

784. The commands of Jupiter and the fates are virtually identical; cf. *Aen.* 4. 614 *fata Iovis*, 8. 398, and Bailey, *Religion in Virgil*, pp. 229 f. See also Intro., p. xix.

infracta: 'valde fracta', Servius; cf. *Aen.* 7. 332, 9. 499, 10. 731, 12. 1. The adjective *infractus* = 'unbroken' occurs only in late Latin.

quiescit: cf. the ironic words of Juno in *Aen.* 7. 297 f. *at credo mea numina tandem | fessa iacent, odiis aut exsaturata quievi.*

785 f. 'It is not enough that in her accursed hatred she has devoured their city from the heart of Phrygia's people.' The language is very harsh, partly probably in imitation of Hom. *Il.* 4. 34 f. (where Zeus supposes that Hera will not be satisfied until she has eaten Priam and his children raw) and of similar passages in Homer, but it is also appropriate to Venus' anger against Juno. Some of the most powerful language of the *Aeneid* issues from the mutual hatred of these two goddesses; cf. *Aen.* 10. 16–95.

785. The rhythm of this line too is unusual (cf. 781 and note there). The third foot has a quasi-caesura, and in the fourth foot the caesura is 'apparent' only, after an elided syllable.

786. odiis: the plural means 'acts of hatred', cf. *Aen.* 4. 623, and note on 98.

786 f. 'nor that she has dragged the remnants of Troy through the utmost retribution'. This seems the best punctuation; others punctuate after *omnem* or after *reliquias*. The image is perhaps that of dragging captives off in chains, or even dragging a dead body (like Hector's) behind a chariot in order to satisfy the desire for vengeance. For *traxe* (by syncope for *traxisse*, a mark of archaizing style) cf. Lucr. 3. 650 *abstraxe*, 5. 1159 *protraxe*, *Aen.* 4. 606 *exstinxem* (where see Austin and Page), 4. 682 *exstinxti*, 6. 57 *derexti*, 11. 118 *vixet*. Compare also *Aen.* 1. 201 *accestis*. The contraction of perfect forms in -*v*- is of course much commoner (e.g. line 42 *fugarat*, 107 *complerant*, etc.). See Leumann–Hofmann, pp. 335–6.

787. reliquias: for the scansion see on 47, for the phrase cf. *Aen.* 1. 30 *Troas, reliquias Danaum*, 1. 598, 3. 87.
   For the comparison of a city with a human body cf. Cic. *Ad Fam.* 4. 5. 4 *oppidum cadavera*. Henry well points out that the suggestion of savagery against a dead body conveys the height of barbarism.

788. sciat illa: 'be it hers to know' (Fairclough); i.e. it is completely inexplicable to all right-minded persons. The words which Venus uses here recall Virgil's question (*Aen.* 1. 11) *tantaene animis caelestibus irae?*

789 f. Venus refers to the storm, aroused by Aeolus at Juno's instigation, with which the adventures of the Trojans begin in the *Aeneid*, 1. 84 f. Compare *molem* (790) with 1. 134; *maria omnia caelo miscuit* with 1. 133 f.; *Aeoliis procellis* with 1. 65 f.; *in regnis hoc ausa tuis* with 1. 138–9.

791. nequiquam: in vain because Neptune's intervention saved the Trojans.

792. For the half-line see on 294.

793. per scelus: notice the very emphatic position of this phrase, placed as it is in front of the words *ecce etiam* which would naturally begin a sentence; see note on 5. Henry explains it as adverbial with *exussit*, equivalent to *scelerate*, cf. Cic. *De Dom.* 147 *domo per scelus erepta*; but it is better to take it in a local sense with *agere* ('started our Trojan mothers on a path of crime', Jackson Knight). Compare 786 and Hor. *Odes* 1. 3. 26 *gens humana ruit per vetitum nefas*.

794–5. The object to be supplied for *subegit* is *Aenean*. Some MSS. have *ignota terra*, but the dative is preferable as *lectio difficilior*; it is the indirect object of *linquere* with a slight personification of *terra*—'to the mercies of an unknown land'. Notice the rhetorical exaggeration in *classe amissa* and *ignotae terrae*. On *ignotae* Servius says 'ignobili . . . et dixit ignotam Italiae comparatione: nam ignota non erat ad quam bis Troiani venerant'; but Venus' exaggeration is deliberate, and should not be explained away.

796. quod superest: adverbial, 'for the rest', 'henceforward' (τὸ λοιπόν); cf. 691. The phrase occurs twice in the *Georgics* (2. 346, 4. 51) in the Lucretian way, to introduce a new topic, and we find it in a slightly different adverbial construction (similar to the present one) in *Aen.* 9. 156 f. *nunc adeo, melior quoniam pars acta diei,* / *quod superest, laeti bene gestis corpora rebus* / *procurate*; and *Aen.* 11. 14 f. *maxima res effecta, viri; timor omnis abesto,* / *quod superest*; cf. Stat. *Th.* 10. 47, *Ach.* 1. 49. It is very tempting to take the phrase here and in 691 to mean 'all that remains of them'; in that case it would act in this passage as the object of *liceat*, and would pick up the word *reliquias* (787); for this meaning of the verb cf. *Aen.* 1. 383 (*naves*) *vix septem convulsae undis Euroque supersunt.* But the formulary nature of the phrase and the other Virgilian instances cited above make the adverbial construction more likely.

796 f. dare tuta per undas vela tibi: most commentators take the phrase to mean 'commit their sails in safety to you', and this is probably best; cf. *Aen.* 3. 9 *dare fatis vela, Geo.* 2. 41 *pelagoque volans da vela patenti, Aen.* 12. 263 f. *penitusque profundo* / *vela dabit.* Others, arguing that *dare vela* means 'to sail' (cf. *Aen.* 3. 191 *vela damus*) take *tibi* as ethic dative (= *per te*, 'through your help'), but this is not the kind of relationship which an ethic dative bears to the sentence.

797. Laurentem: the *ager Laurens* evidently extended from the Tiber to Ardea (*Aen.* 7. 650). The noun Laurentum was the name either of this region or of an ancient town within it, perhaps identical with Lavinium; on this see Fairclough's Appendix to *Aen.* 8. 1 (Loeb, p. 514), and B. Tilly, *Vergil's Latium*, Blackwell, 1947, pp. 83 f.

798. As Servius says, *si* here has no real conditional force but is equivalent to *siquidem*, 'as surely as'; compare the extension of this use in 64, and *Aen.* 6. 529 f. *di, talia Grais* / *instaurate, pio si poenas ore reposco.*

    ea moenia: 'a city there'.

    Parcae: the three Fates (Lachesis, Clotho, and Atropos), cf. *Aen.* 1. 22, *Ecl.* 4. 47 *et saep.* See R. B. Onians, *Origins of European Thought*, pp. 416 f.

799. The epithet *Saturnius* is normally used of Juno (606); in applying it to Neptune (who was of course also a child of Saturnus) Virgil is perhaps remembering the line with similar rhythm in *Aen.* 4. 372 (of Jupiter) *nec Saturnius haec oculis pater aspicit aequis.* A diaeresis after the second foot when there is no caesura in the second foot is not uncommon in Lucretius, but is very rare in Virgil, and mostly reserved for special effect. There are three instances in *Aen.* 4 besides the one already quoted: 316 *per conubia nostra*, 385 *et cum frigida mors*, 486 *spargens umida mella* (see Austin's notes on these). Other examples are *Geo.* 2. 61 *scilicet omnibus est labor impendendus*, *Geo.* 3. 344 *armentarius Afer agit*, *Geo.* 4. 448 *sed tu desine velle*; see Winbolt, *Latin Hexameter Verse*, pp. 100 f. The reason for the rarity of this rhythm in Virgil is that there is coincidence of word accent with the ictus in each of the first three feet; this gives an insistence to the beat of the rhythm which would tend to be monotonous if frequently used in normal narrative, but when it is very rarely employed it can give an effect like the tolling of a bell (*et cum frigida mors . . .*) or the beat of a hammer (*scilicet omnibus est labor impendendus . . .*). When there is a caesura in the second foot, a diaeresis after it is not uncommon, because the rhythmic effect is entirely different (cf. 127, 260, 418, 639, 675).

800 f. The tone and movement of Neptune's speech contrasts most markedly with the emotional excitement of Venus. It is calm and slow and reassuring; and the sentence beginning at 804 is unusually long and complex (almost rambling) compared with Virgil's normal style (see note on 101–3). It is the speech of a revered old counsellor.

800. fas omne est: 'it is altogether right', cf. *Aen.* 3. 55.

    Cytherea: a frequent epithet of Venus, born from the sea near Cythera in S. Greece (here it is used with special reference to *unde genus ducis*). Hence her name Aphrodite (ἀφρός = foam), and her epithet Anadyomene (ἀναδυομένη = rising up). For the story see Servius, ad loc., Hesiod, *Theog.* 188 f., and cf. Ov. *Met.* 4. 531 f. For the scansion Cytherēa see on 761.

801–2. The storm aroused by Aeolus at the instigation of Juno (note on 789 f.) was calmed by Neptune; and although he is not specifically mentioned, we may assume that he was also responsible for the calming of the storms in 3. 192 f., 5. 10 f.

802. caelique marisque: this use of doubled *-que* ('both . . and ') provides a convenient metrical close to a hexameter, and it is frequently employed by the poets (some fifty examples in the *Aeneid*, more than a hundred in Statius' *Thebaid*). See note on 92.

803. Xanthum Simoentaque: see on 634.

805. exanimata: 'breathless', 'panic-stricken', quite a common word, but this is the only place where Virgil uses it. Cf. *exanimes* (669).

　　impingeret: Statius imitates this in *Th.* 10. 765 f. *captaeque impingite Lernae | reliquias turpes*; cf. also *Th.* 7. 28. For the dative *muris* see on 34.

806. daret: supply *et cum*.

　　daret leto: this phrase is common in Latin from very early times (cf. the archaic formula in Cic. *De Leg.* 2. 22 *suos leto datos divos habento*); compare *demittere morti* in 691, where the dative of the indirect object is natural with a noun capable of personification. See also notes on 233, 451.

806–8. This is a close imitation of the words of the River Scamander (Xanthus) to Achilles (Hom. *Il.* 21. 218 f. πλήθει γὰρ δή μοι νεκύων ἐρατεινὰ ῥέεθρα, | οὐδέ τί πη δύναμαι προχέειν ῥόον εἰς ἅλα δῖαν | στεινόμενος νεκύεσσι). Cf. also Cat. 64. 357 f.

807. amnes: the unusual effect of a spondaic first foot followed by a pause perhaps here helps to give an idea of heaviness and absence of movement; see on 80.

808 f. The meeting of Aeneas and Achilles, son of Peleus, is described in *Il.* 20. 158 f., and the rescue of Aeneas by Poseidon (who sheds a mist over Achilles' eyes) in *Il.* 20. 318 f.

808. Pelidae: the dative after verbs of 'striving', 'fighting with' (where the common construction is *cum*), occurs in early Latin but becomes much more frequent in Augustan poetry and post-Augustan prose, chiefly through Greek influence (μάχεσθαί τινι); cf. *Aen.* 1. 475 (*Troilus*) *impar congressus Achilli*, 1. 493 *viris concurrere*, and Pease on *Aen.* 4. 38.

　　For the double disyllable at the end of the line see on 274, and cf. especially 414, 672.

809. nec dis nec viribus aequis: for the thought cf. line 466; there is perhaps a reminiscence of Poseidon's words to Aeneas in *Il.* 20. 334 (Πηλείων) ὃς σεῦ ἅμα κρείσσων καὶ φίλτερος ἀθανάτοισιν.

810. nube cava: 'enfolding cloud'; cf. *Aen.* 1. 516 *nube cava speculantur amicti*, 2. 360 *nox atra cava circumvolat umbra*, *Il.* 20. 444 ἐκάλυψε δ' ἄρ' ἠέρι πολλῇ.

　　cuperem cum: 'although I desired'; for the postposition of the conjunction see on 22.

　　vertere ab imo: Servius cites *Aen.* 2. 610 f. *Neptunus muros*

magnoque emota tridenti | fundamenta quatit and refers to
Poseidon's epithet ἐνοσίχθων (Earth-shaker); cf. also 2. 625
ex imo verti Neptunia Troia.

811. Neptune and Apollo helped to build the walls of Troy
(hence *Neptunia Troia*), but were cheated of the agreed reward
by Laomedon (Hom. *Il.* 21. 441–55); cf. Hor. *Odes* 3. 3. 21 f.
ex quo destituit deos | mercede pacta Laomedon, and *Aen.* 4. 542
Laomedonteae . . . periuria gentis, Geo. 1. 502.

813. Notice the slow spondaic line to give due impressiveness to
his promise; cf. 484, and see note on 136–41. For the emphasis falling on the single spondaic word *tutus* which fills
the first foot see on 80, and cf. line 815. The line as a whole
well illustrates Cicero's remark on the spondee (*Orat.* 216)
habet . . . stabilem quemdam et non expertem dignitatis gradum.

813 f. Servius punctuates after *accedet* in order to make *Averni*
depend on *gurgite*, not on *portus*, because Venus' request had
been that the Trojans should reach the Tiber, not Avernus.
This is an interesting indication of how far Servius was ready
to go in order to explain some alleged contradiction in Virgil,
perhaps one of the many brought forward by Virgil's *obtrectatores.* See on 404 and 521. Servius also maintains that
unus in 814 refers to Misenus and *unum* in 815 to Palinurus
—again a violence to the language, arising from his punctuation in 813 and perhaps also connected with the difficulty
about the Misenus–Palinurus 'doublet'; see Intro., p. xxvii.

813. portus . . . Averni: i.e. Cumae, see on 732, and cf. *Aen.*
6. 2 *et tandem Euboicis Cumarum adlabitur oris.* The construction by Agrippa of the sea-works which made Avernus
a part of the *Portus Iulius* is mentioned in *Geo.* 2. 161 f.
For the poetic plural *portus* see on 57. The accusative after
accedere is common in the poets, cf. Lucr. 1. 927, *Aen.* 1. 201.

814. The fulfilment of Neptune's prophecy is described in the
last part of this book.

    quaeres: so the best MSS.; some editors following inferior
MSS. read *quaeret,* but the second person is used because here
Venus is identified with the fortunes of Aeneas. *Quaerere*
here shades into the meaning of *requirere, desiderare,* 'look
for in vain', 'miss'; cf. Prop. 1. 17. 18 *optatos quaerere
Tyndaridas,* Tib. 2. 3. 26, Ov. *Met.* 2. 239, Stat. *Th.* 4. 704,
and *Aen.* 1. 217 *amissos longo socios sermone requirunt.* See
note on 41 (simple verbs for compounds).

815. For the incomplete line see on 294.

    The repetition of the word *unus* from the previous line is
given special emphasis by the comparatively unusual rhythm
caused when the first foot is composed of a single spondaic
word; see on 80. The incomplete line ends at a bucolic

diaeresis (the term given to a pause after the fourth dactyl),
as do four other incomplete lines: *Aen.* 2. 468, 787, 6. 835,
9. 721. A pause after the fourth dactyl occurs quite frequently in Greek hexameters from Homer onwards, but it
came to be called 'bucolic' diaeresis because it was especially
favoured in pastoral poetry (there are sixteen instances of
a heavy stop at this point in the line in Theocritus' first
idyll—152 lines, and very many more lighter stops). It is
markedly rarer in Latin than in Greek, and particularly so
in the high style. The *Eclogues* have about four heavy stops
in this position per hundred lines, but the *Georgics* about
one per hundred, and the *Aeneid* less than one. Again,
Horace has about seven per hundred in his *Satires*, and
Juvenal four, but none of the Silver Age epic poets has it as
often as twice in a hundred lines. In this book the only heavy
stops at a bucolic diaeresis are in this speech (801, 812) and
in 672 (see note on 670 f.). Examples of much lighter stops
occur at 83, 111, 130, 139, 176, 237, 274, 382, 414, 415, 755.
See Winbolt, *Latin Hexameter Verse*, pp. 45 f., Marouzeau,
Traité de stylistique latine, p. 306, and for a detailed discussion
J. Perret, *R.E.L.*, 1956, pp. 146 f.

816. **laeta . . . permulsit**: 'soothed and gladdened', a particularly clear example of the proleptic use of an adjective. Servius says 'permulsit et laeta fecit, ut *animumque labantem
impulit* (*Aen.* 4. 22–23): aut certe perpetuum est epitheton
Veneris'. Of these explanations the first is correct and the
second absurd.

    pectora: for the poetic plural, an extremely common one,
see on 98.

817 f. The picture of Neptune driving over the waves in his
chariot, attended by his retinue of creatures and deities of
the sea, is painted in the most brilliant colours. It is based on
Homer's memorable description of Poseidon's journey in *Il.*
13. 23 f., and it has points of similarity with Virgil's earlier
description of Neptune in *Aen.* 1. 142 f.; but it has a more
sustained pictorial imagery than either of these passages,
culminating as it does in the long and sonorous pageant of
the gods and nymphs of the deep.

817–18. 'Father Neptune yoked his horses in their golden
harness, then put the bit in their foaming mouths as they
chafed to be away, and let all the reins run out free through
his hands.' Poseidon's horses in *Il.* 13. 23 f. have golden
manes, and Poseidon himself wears gold and holds a golden
whip; the horses which Latinus gives to the Trojans (*Aen.*
7. 278 f.) have golden trappings and harness. The word
feris conveys the high-spiritedness of the horses, cf. *Aen.*

LINES 815–22 195

4. 135 *frena ferox spumantia mandit.* Servius, followed by many, says that *feris* is simply equivalent to *equis*, comparing *Aen.* 2. 51, but it certainly conveys more than that in this context.

818. manibusque . . . habenas: cf. *Aen.* 12. 499 *irarumque omnis effundit habenas*, and see note on 662.

819 f. Compare the description of Neptune calming the storm in *Aen.* 1. 142 f., especially 147, 154–6.

820–1. tumidumque . . . aquis: 'the swelling surface of the waters is stilled beneath his thundering chariot'; cf. *Aen.* 8. 89 *sterneret aequor aquis.* *Aequor* has its meaning of the surface, the expanse, of the sea; *aquis* is perhaps possessive dative, perhaps local ablative. *Axis* is normally taken to mean the 'axle' of Neptune's chariot (*Geo.* 3. 107, 172, *Aen.* 12. 379). But the epithet *tonans* is not wholly appropriate to the placid context described by the previous line, with the picture of Neptune's chariot skimming lightly over the waves, and it is possible that the phrase means that the ocean was 'swelling beneath the thundering sky', as Lewis and Short appear to suggest s.v. *tono.* In this case cf. *Aen.* 2. 512, 8. 28 *sub aetheris axe*, 8. 239 *intonat aether*, Lucan 5. 632–3 *arduus axis / intonuit.* On the whole, however, the traditional rendering is perhaps preferable.

821. vasto: this is a rather unexpected use of the word, which normally implies dread, and means 'wild', 'savage', rather than simply 'vast'; see Conway on *Aen.* 1. 146. On this account Wagner (ad loc.) objected strongly to its use here. But we may compare Lucretius' use of the word applied to space, 1. 957 *an immensum pateat vasteque profundum* (see Bailey, ad loc.). There is then no question of a violent usage of the kind which the Silver Age poets often employ to benumb the senses of the reader; but we may still ask why Virgil has chosen this particular epithet here. His normal adjectives with *aethere* are *alto, summo, magno, toto*; he is certainly not forced by metrical or other necessities to use *vasto* here. The intention surely is to contrast the good weather which Neptune now brings with the threatening storm-clouds which he drives away. The aspect of a sky beset with storm-clouds could well be described by sailors setting out as *vastus.*

822 f. It has been suggested that Virgil's description of Neptune's retinue was based on a piece of sculpture by Scopas in the circus of Flaminius, described thus by Pliny (*Nat. Hist.* 36. 26): *Neptunus ipse et Thetis atque Achilles, Nereides supra delphinos et cete aut hippocampos sedentes, item Tritones chorusque Phorci et pistrices ac multa alia marina . . .* Whether this is so or not, the passage has a most marked visual impact. Virgil was brilliant at using the sonorous effect and descriptive imagery of lines consisting largely of proper names; see Page, ad loc., Marouzeau, *Traité de stylistique latine*, pp. 91 f. Compare the long list of nymphs in *Geo.* 4. 334 f., and lines like 240 in this book or *Geo.* 1. 437 *Glauco et Panopeae et Inoo Melicertae*; and (with a rather different effect) *Aen.* 6. 482 f. *Dardanidae, quos ille omnis longo ordine cernens | ingemuit, Glaucumque Medontaque Thersilochumque, | tris Antenoridas Cererique sacrum Polyboeten, | Idaeumque etiam currus, etiam arma tenentem.*

822. 'Then there come the manifold figures of his company'; for the absence of a main verb in a descriptive passage cf. *Aen.* 1. 639 f., 3. 618 f., 4. 131; see also note on 32.

    cete: 'sea-monsters'; the Greek neuter word κῆτος is here used in the Greek form of its plural, as always in Classical Latin (cf. Stat. *Ach.* 1. 55, Sil. 7. 476). Lucretius uses Greek neuters like *mele* and *pelage*; compare the common use of *Tempe* (e.g. *Geo.* 2. 469). For the imagery of the line cf. Hom. *Il.* 13. 27 (describing Poseidon's retinue) ἄταλλε δέ κήτε᾽ ὑπ᾽ αὐτοῦ, and *Geo.* 4. 430 f. (Proteus and his escort of seals).

823 f. For these deities of the sea cf. lines 239–42. Compare the great pageant of river-gods and sea-deities at the marriage of Medway and Thames (Spenser, *The Faerie Queene*, 4. 11. 11 f.), and Milton, *Comus*, 867 f.

> Listen and appear to us
> In name of great Oceanus,
> By the earth-shaking Neptune's mace,
> And Tethys' grave majestic pace,
> By hoary Nereus' wrinkled look,
> And the Carpathian wizard's hook,
> By scaly Triton's winding shell,
> And old sooth-saying Glaucus' spell,
> By Leucothea's lovely hands,
> And her son that rules the strands,
> By Thetis' tinsel-slipper'd feet,
> And the songs of Sirens sweet . . .

Glaucus was a fisherman who became a sea-god; cf. Plato, *Rep.* 10. 611 d, Servius, ad loc., Ov. *Met.* 13. 896 f., and *Geo.* 1. 437. Palaemon, also called Melicertes, son of Ino (Leucothea), is identified by Servius with Portunus (line 241). The story was that Ino, pursued by her maddened husband Athamas, threw herself with her son into the sea, and they both became sea-deities (cf. Ov. *Met.* 4. 416 f.). Triton

(*Aen.* 1. 144, Ov. *Met.* 1. 331 f., cf. *Aen.* 10. 209 f.) was a son of Neptune, whose skill at trumpeting with a sea-shell Misenus vainly tried to emulate (*Aen.* 6. 171 f.). Cf. the final lines of Wordsworth's 'The world is too much with us . . .'

> So might I, standing on this pleasant lea,
> Have glimpses that would make me less forlorn:
> Have sight of Proteus rising from the sea,
> Or hear old Triton blow his wreathéd horn.

Triton became 'pluralized' in works of art; see Daremberg–Saglio, s.v. *Triton*, and cf. Stat. *Ach.* 1. 55 *armigeri Tritones eunt scopulosaque cete*. Phorcys, an old man of the sea, is mentioned in Hom. *Od.* 13. 96, Hes. *Theog.* 237; cf. Val. Fl. 3. 726 f., where his retinue of seals is described. Thetis, the mother of Achilles, was the most famous of the Nereids (Cat. 64 *passim*); she led them as they guided the Argo through the Planctae (Ap. Rh. 4. 930 f.). Melite and Panopea (*Geo.* 1. 437, line 240) were Nereids; cf. Milton, *Lycidas*, 98–99

> The air was calm, and on the level brine,
> Sleek Panope with all her sisters play'd.

The nymphs in the next line are from Hom. *Il.* 18. 39 f. Θάλειά τε Κυμοδόκη τε / Νησαίη Σπείω τε. This line occurs also at *Geo.* 4. 338, but its MS. authority there is poor, and it is generally regarded as interpolated from here. A very long list of Nereids is given in Hes. *Theog.* 240 f.

825. laeva tenent: by this it is implied that the male sea-deities already described are on the right. For the use of the neuter plural *laeva* see on 168.

826. For the Greek rhythm of this line see on 300 (line-ending) and 591 (caesura). In a number of places (e.g. *Geo.* 1. 437, 4. 336) Virgil has lines consisting entirely or almost entirely of Greek words where the metrical pattern also is Greek; see on 822 f.

827–71. *The Trojans proceed on their voyage, Palinurus leading. During the night the god Sleep comes to Palinurus, disguised as Phorbas, and urges him to rest from his vigil. Palinurus refuses, and Sleep sheds the dew of Lethe over him and, as he loses consciousness, casts him into the sea. His cries for help are not heard, and the fleet sails on; not until it reaches the rocks of the Sirens is the loss of Palinurus discovered. Aeneas takes over the control of the ship, and in deep sorrow speaks his farewell to his helmsman.*

827 f. The story of Palinurus with which the book ends leads into the atmosphere of Book VI; the liquid notes of sorrow

which are so marked a feature of the *Aeneid* are here heard
at their clearest. It is very typical of Virgil's poetic method
that when the Trojans come at last in sight of the 'ever-
receding shores' of Italy there should be sorrow to be endured
at the moment of joy and triumph. These two contrasting
sides of human experience are in the *Aeneid* never far apart;
and at the end of the whole poem, when the final victory is
won, Virgil mutes the joyful notes of triumph with the sorrow
of Turnus' death.

There are some differences in the account which Virgil
gives here of Palinurus' death compared with the sequel in
Aen. 6. 337 f. It seems likely that this passage was written
later than Book VI, and that Virgil's death prevented him
from harmonizing the two parts of the story. For a full
discussion of the discrepancies see Intro., Sect. V.

The origin of the legend of Palinurus, the helmsman who
gave his name to Cape Palinurus near Sicily, is a typical
aetiological story to account for the foundation of a town.
The Sibyl says to the shade of Palinurus in *Aen.* 6. 378 f. that
the inhabitants of the place where he was killed will be led by
prodigies from heaven to pay honour to his dead body and
set up a tomb and call the place after his name. Servius
(on *Aen.* 6. 378) comments: 'de historia hoc traxit. Lucanis
enim pestilentia laborantibus respondit oraculum manes
Palinuri esse placandos; ob quam rem non longe a Velia
ei et lucum et cenotaphium dederunt'. Norden in his full
discussion (on *Aen.* 6. 337–83) cites the story of the Phoceans
and the plague in Herod. 1. 167. It seems likely that the
Palinurus legend can be traced back to Timaeus in the third
century, and it probably came to Virgil through Varro (like
the similar episode about Misenus, and much more of the
legendary material). Certainly by Varro's time, if not before,
Palinurus had become associated with Aeneas and the Trojans.
The outlines of the story are given in Dion. Hal. 1. 53. 2.

This then was the factual material, probably in brief and
prosaic outline, which was available to Virgil. For its trans-
figuration into poetry a number of Homeric passages set
Virgil's imagination working. The appearance of the shade
of Palinurus to Aeneas in the underworld is modelled on the
appearance of Elpenor to Odysseus in the Νέκυια of *Odyssey*
XI. Elpenor had died from a fall when he was suddenly
awakened after feasting in Circe's palace, and his corpse
had been left unburied. The points of similarity are marked;
both Elpenor and Palinurus died following a fall, both ask
for burial, both are the first of the apparitions in the underworld. But the differences are very marked too, both in

detail and in tone. Elpenor was not a helmsman, and the manner of his death was not appropriate for Virgil's purpose. Again, the account in Homer is simple and direct; that of Virgil is more intense emotionally, more pathetic (see Heinze, *Virgils Epische Technik*, p. 465).

The part of the Palinurus story which occurs in Book V is suggested perhaps by the brief account in *Od.* 3. 278 f. of the death of Phrontis, the helmsman of Menelaus who was slain by the gentle darts of Apollo. Virgil has greatly enlarged and developed this theme in his own picture of the helmsman who struggles against the divine power of Sleep and cannot be persuaded to abandon his duty but only compelled by irresistible force. The intervention of the god Sleep recalls *Il.* 14. 231 f., and the circumstance of his appearance in the guise of Phorbas may be suggested by *Il.* 2. 5 f., where Zeus sends the Dream-god to Agamemnon in the guise of Nestor. On these sources see H. R. Steiner, cited on 840.

Thus in the story of Palinurus we can see how passages from Homer's poems, deeply assimilated in Virgil's mind, formed a large part of the rich store of poetic imagery with which he could transform a prosaic legend into an episode of typically Virgilian tenderness and beauty.

The construction of this final episode in the book is a masterpiece of verbal economy, and excellently illustrates Virgil's ability to describe a scene in the most telling way, combining sensitivity and pathos with restraint. There is no unnecessary elaboration, no apparent effort to compel the reader's attention. The passage begins with a general description of Aeneas' fleet, followed by a specific mention of Palinurus in his normal position of responsibility. Then the scene changes to night-time; the picture of midnight peace upon the waters is drawn with the haunting beauty so characteristic of Virgil, and this leads to the description of the god parting the darkness on his silent journey from heaven, with its climax at line 840, a line of unforgettable power and pathos.

The speech of Somnus—four lines of soft persuasive words—is balanced by the four lines of Palinurus' indignant and vehement reply, and in the next two lines (852–3), lines with very marked rhyming assonance, the encounter is concluded as far as Palinurus is concerned; the mortal Phorbas cannot prevail upon him. But it is not the mortal with whom he contends, and the completeness of divine power is revealed with the phrase *ecce deus* and the sonorous inevitability of his victory (854–6). The sequel follows just

as inevitably; even in sleep Palinurus clings to the helm,
but the god leans over him and casts him easily into the sea.
He is deprived of all human assistance, for sleep has overcome his friends who might have saved him. Then Somnus
departs, and is gone as lightly as he came (861).

As the scene was introduced by a passage describing the
movement of the fleet, all in due order, led by Palinurus, so
now it ends with the movement of the fleet, still in order as
long as Neptune guides it, but as soon as he leaves it,
pilotless and drifting. And the final two lines convey a note
of profound pathos and poetic irony as Aeneas attributes
Palinurus' death to that very over-confidence which he had
so resolutely refused to entertain.

827–32. Day Lewis has:

> Aeneas had been in suspense; but his mood changed now,
>   and a calm joy
> Thrilled through his heart. He gave orders that all the masts
>   should at once
> Be stepped and the sails broken out from the yards. The
>   crews all set
> Their mainsheets and all together slanted the lofty yard-arms
> This way or that, to keep the sails filled, as the breeze shifted
> To port or starboard quarter. A fair wind bore them on.

827. suspensam: 'anxious', cf. *Aen.* 4. 9 *Anna soror, quae me
suspensam insomnia terrent!*

828. pertemptant: 'came over', 'pervaded'; this is a poetic use
of the word, cf. *Aen.* 1. 502 *Latonae tacitum pertemptant
gaudia pectus*, and *Geo.* 3. 250, *Aen.* 7. 355.

828 f. Aeneas had taken his fleet out of harbour by means of
oars (778); now they go over to sails, which is the normal
way of proceeding in the *Aeneid* except in serious emergencies
(cf. line 15). See S. L. Mohler, 'Sails and Oars in the *Aeneid*',
T.A.Ph.A., 1948, pp. 46 f. for a full discussion of seamanship
in the *Aeneid*. He shows that Virgil's ships were essentially
contemporary Roman ships, very different from those in
Homer, and that Virgil had a good knowledge of their
abilities and performance. See also E. de Saint-Denis, *Le
Rôle de la mer dans la poésie latine*, Paris, 1935, pp. 183 f.;
he argues that the relative absence of technical nautical
terms in the *Aeneid* indicates that Virgil writes of the sea
from a landsman's point of view.

829. attolli malos: the masts could be taken down when the
ships were not being sailed. The mast of Serestus' ship had
been removed and set up on land for the archery contest
(487).

intendi bracchia velis: 'the yard-arms to be hung with their sails'. For the phrase cf. line 403 with note. *Bracchia* in the sense of *antennae* seems not to occur before Virgil, and is not common; cf. Val. Fl. 1. 126. Two of the main MSS., followed by Janell, read *remis* for *velis*; but the point of the whole context here is that all is well, and the fleet goes over from oars to sails. The corruption probably arose from recollection of 136.

830 f. Notice the emphasis on the regularity and precision of the manœuvre given by the repetition of *una, pariter, una*. The serene description here of ordered progress heightens the pathos of the night's disaster.

830. fecere pedem: 'set the sheets', i.e. fastened their tacks. The square sail was unrolled from the yard-arm which ran across the top of the mast, and the operation described as *facere pedem* was to secure the ropes at the bottom of the sail so that it made the desired angle with the wind. Homer uses the word πόδες in this sense (*Od.* 5. 260); cf. Cat. 4. 20 f. *sive utrumque Iuppiter / simul secundus incidisset in pedem*, Ov. *Fast.* 3. 565 *nancta ratem comitesque fugae pede labitur aequo*.

830–1. pariterque . . . sinus: 'and together they let out their sails now to the left, now to the right', i.e. as they tacked. Supply *nunc* to the first clause.

831 f. 'in unison they turn their lofty yard-arms now this way, now that'. *Cornua* is the technical term for the ends of the yard-arms, cf. *Aen.* 3. 549. This phrase amplifies and explains the previous phrase as a description of tacking. Mohler (loc. cit. on 828 f., p. 58) gives a suggested diagrammatical representation of this tacking manœuvre, and says that the ships perhaps 'started abreast aligned in the direction of their second tack, so that when they came about they were in a file "following the leader", "in line ahead"'.

832. For the sense pause after the third trochee see on 692.
ferunt . . . classem: 'its own breezes bear the fleet onwards', i.e. fair breezes. For this use of *suus* see on 54.

833 f. Observe how the attention is concentrated on Palinurus before the fresh start in the narrative at 835. See note on 827 f.

834. ad hunc . . . contendere: 'direct their course towards him', 'set their course by him'. *Contendere* in this sense is much more commonly used absolutely, but for the accusative with it cf. Plaut. *Cist.* 534, Sil. 5. 125.

835 f. The new scene is set in peaceful descriptive verses, with alliteration of *m* and assonance of long vowel sounds. See on 721 for Night's chariot; *meta* is here the half-way mark of her course through the sky, see on 129.

838 f. Homer tells in *Il.* 14. 231 f. how the god Sleep charmed
the eyes of Zeus at Hera's request. There are fine descriptions
of Somnus and his home in Ov. *Met.* 11. 592 f., Stat. *Th.* 10.
84 f.; cf. also Sil. 10. 340 f. and the well-known invocation
in Stat. *Silv.* 5. 4. A discussion of ancient concepts of the
god, and of representations of him in art, is to be found
in Frère's introductory note to Stat. *Silv.* 5. 4 in his Budé
edition; see especially P. Friedländer, *Die Antike*, 1932, pp.
215 f.

    cum . . . dimovit: for inverted *cum* see on 84–85.

838. levis . . . delapsus: for the adverbial use of the adjective
see on 278; for the tense of the participle see on 708.

839. 'sundered the dusky air and parted the darkness', i.e. in
his flight. *Dispulit* does not mean 'dispelled', 'drove away',
for such an action would be no proper function of the god
Sleep. The diction of this line conveys a strange other-
worldly effect of midnight powers at work.

    tenebrosum: the word is not found before Virgil (cf. *Aen.*
6. 107), but probably already existed (*tenebricosus* is Ciceronian). Ernout (cited on 352, where see note) compares
latebrosus in Plautus to show that the word is not likely to
have been a Virgilian innovation.

840 f. Here Virgil's art in giving emphasis by rhythmical and
other means to an emotional part of the narrative can be very
clearly seen. Line 840 is balanced with an effective simplicity
by means of the repetition of *te . . . tibi* and the similar endings of *petens* and *portans*; there is very marked alliteration
of *p* and *t*, and the insistent beat of the rhythm on the two
dactylic words *somnia tristia* which fill the fourth and fifth
feet is made the more marked because they have similar
grammatical endings. Finally *insonti* (the key word for the
pathos of the whole passage) is given great emphasis by its
position in the sentence (last word), by its position in the
line (first word before a heavy pause), and by its spondaic
slowness after the dactylic movement of the previous line.
For other examples of these various points see notes on 5 f.,
81, 136–41, 198, and 480.

840. te Palinure: the use of the vocative in apostrophe is not
uncommon in Virgil, and it may at times be no more than
a metrical convenience, or a device to secure variety. The
other examples in this book (122, 495, 564) do not aim at any
very marked effect. But when it is used in a context where
an idea of sorrow is already present, or when it is linked with
other effects (see previous note), it can bring a personal
element into the portrayal of pathos. Compare *Aen.* 4. 408 f.
quis tibi tum, Dido, cernenti talia sensus, | quosve dabas

gemitus! The Silver Age poets seized on apostrophe as one of the many rhetorical figures with which style could be 'adorned', and Lucan especially used it to such an extent that it was necessarily shorn of the expressive power which it might otherwise have possessed (see the preface to J. D. Duff's Loeb edition of Lucan). E. Hampel (*De Apostrophae apud Romanorum poetas usu*, Diss., Jena, 1908) shows by statistics that apostrophe is used by Ovid, Statius, Silius, and Valerius about twice as often as by Virgil, and by Lucan more than three times as often. For some observations on the use of apostrophe see Quint. 9. 2. 38–39, 9. 3. 23; see also Austin on *Aen.* 4. 27.

somnia tristia: a vague phrase of foreboding. *Somnia* here does not mean specifically 'dreams', but rather more generally refers to what the god has the power to bring, here 'the sleep that spells doom', cf. 854 f. Servius saw this when he glossed the word with *soporem*, though the remainder of his note cannot be upheld—'bene autem discernit ista Vergilius, ut *Somnum* ipsum deum dicat, *somnium* quod dormimus, *insomnium* quod videmus in somnis'. The passage with its sources is discussed at length by H. R. Steiner, *Der Traum in der Aeneis*, Bern, 1952, pp. 78 f. He extends the implication of *somnia tristia* beyond the meaning of 'a fatal sleep' to include all the disasters which befell Palinurus, quoting the scholiast on Hom. *Il.* 10. 496 ὅταν γάρ τις νυκτὸς κακῷ τινι περιπέσῃ, φαμὲν ὅτι κακὸν ὄναρ εἶδεν ὁ δεῖνα, and arguing that in the Homer passage also it is not a question of a real dream but of disaster in the night.

841. deus consedit: 'alighted in his divine power'. The word *deus* has some predicative force, the subject still being *Somnus*; cf. *Aen.* 1. 411 f. *at Venus obscuro gradientes aëre saepsit,* | *et multo nebulae circum dea fudit amictu,* and *Aen.* 1. 691 f. See also note on 521.

842. Phorbanti similis: 'in the likeness of Phorbas'. This is probably the Phorbas mentioned in Hom. *Il.* 14. 490, the father of Ilioneus. The appearance of gods in the likeness of men is discussed in the note on 620; for this passage compare especially *Aen.* 7. 406 f., where Allecto appears in disguise to Turnus and, like Somnus, first tries persuasion and then uses her divine power; and Hom. *Il.* 2. 6 f., where Zeus sends Oneiros (the dream-god) disguised as Nestor to urge Agamemnon to give battle.

loquelas: this is not a common word, and is employed here, as Page well says, to suggest the 'soft insinuating words he uses'. Cf. Lucr. 1. 39 f. *suavis ex ore loquelas* | *funde,* 5. 231 *nutricis blanda loquela,* and see note on 163 (diminutives).

843. Iaside: Iasius, son of Jupiter, a founder of the Trojan race, is mentioned in *Aen.* 3. 168. Palinurus was one of his descendants, Iapyx (*Aen.* 12. 392) another. For the Greek vocative ending in long *-e*, normally used with Greek patronymics, cf. *Aen.* 6. 126 *Tros Anchisiade*; compare also *Menoete* (166), *Polite* (564).

844. aequatae: probably 'steadily', 'evenly', as opposed to gusty or veering winds (so Henry). Others take it to mean 'filling the sails evenly', i.e. blowing from straight behind, comparing *Aen.* 4. 587 *aequatis velis*; but this would be rather a strange transference of the epithet from the sails to the breezes.

845. fessosque . . . labori: 'steal your weary eyes from their vigil'. The metaphor is a vivid one; Statius imitates the phrase in *Silv.* 4. 4. 28 f. *exue curis | pectus et adsiduo temet furare labori*. The dative is normal in Latin with words of 'taking away' (*demere, eripere, subtrahere*, etc.), and is essentially the same usage as with words of 'giving'. Compare 260, 726, *Aen.* 6. 524 *fidum capiti subduxerat ensem*, 10. 615 *pugnae subducere Turnum*; and for the dative with *furari* cf. *Aen.* 7. 282 f. *patri quos daedala Circe | supposita de matre nothos furata creavit*.

fessosque oculos: the juxtaposition of words with similar case endings is generally avoided by Virgil; see on 81. Because it is comparatively rare, a certain emphasis can be given when it is employed; see Wagner, *Quaest. Virg.* 33. 8 'singularis captatur ex ea re gravitas'. This is especially so when an adjective and noun are of the same metrical length and the similar syllables are in the arsis of successive feet. In this book cf. particularly 376 *umeros latos*, 682 *tardum fumum*; and for notable examples cf. *Aen.* 2. 251 *involvens umbra magna terramque polumque*, 6. 469 *illa solo fixos oculos aversa tenebat*, 6. 269 f. *perque domos Ditis vacuas et inania regna, | quale per incertam lunam sub luce maligna* . . ., and especially 6. 638 f. (with Norden's note) *devenere locos laetos et amoena virecta | fortunatorum nemorum sedesque beatas*. See Marouzeau, *Traité de stylistique latine*, pp. 51 f., especially p. 57.

847. vix attollens . . . lumina: 'hardly lifting his eyes' (so intent on steering that he barely glances at Somnus) or 'barely able to lift his eyes' (because of the power of the god). Servius gives both explanations, and prefers the second, which certainly gives a natural meaning; but the other is much more appropriate to the context. Palinurus' indignant reply, with its vigorous diction and vehement rhetorical questions, its wakeful-sounding movement, gives a most marked contrast to the persuasive and sleepy tones which Somnus had used to him; and the two lines which follow Palinurus' answer do not at all suggest that he is yet under the spell of sleep. It is not until Palinurus shows that he cannot be persuaded that Somnus uses his divine power: *ecce deus ramum . . .* (854).

848. mene: very emphatic—'do you ask me of all men?' (Jackson Knight). Others may be tricked by the smiling face of the sea, but not so the helmsman of long experience. Compare the fine descriptions of the treachery of the sea (*placidi pellacia ponti*) in Lucr. 2. 557 f., 5. 1002 f.

849. ignorare: 'forget what I know of', 'act as if I did not know'.

monstro: the word in this usage conveys the idea of a vast and supernatural agent of evil. It is used of the wooden horse (*Aen.* 2. 245), of the Harpies (3. 214), of Polyphemus (3. 658), of Fama (4.181), of Cacus (8. 198).

850. Aenean credam: the pathos of this episode is greatly enhanced by the stress laid on Palinurus' loyalty as a helmsman, his sense of duty to the trust placed in him; see note on 870–1. In the underworld (*Aen.* 6. 351 f.) his shade says to Aeneas: *maria aspera iuro | non ullum pro me tantum cepisse timorem, | quam tua ne spoliata armis, excussa magistro, | deficeret tantis navis surgentibus undis.*

quid enim?: it is perhaps best to take these words as parenthetical—'for what then?'; cf. Hor. *Sat.* 1. 1. 7, 2. 3. 132, Cic. *De Fin.* 2. 72, 93. Others prefer to regard them as postponed from the beginning of the sentence; for this see note on 5.

851. et caelo: sc. *fallaci*, 'to the uncertainties of wind and weather'. Most MSS. have *caeli* (a noun for *sereni*), but the original reading of *P* was *caelo*, and Servius read *caelo*, as is evident from his note on *sereni*: 'serenitatis, ut *servantissimus aequi* (*Aen.* 2. 427)'. Servius *auct.* added 'alii legunt *deceptus fraude caeli sereni*'. For *serenum* as a noun cf. *Geo.* 1. 393 *aperta serena*, Lucan 1. 530 *fulgura fallaci micuerunt crebra sereno*, Livy 31. 12. 5, Val. Fl. 1. 332, 2. 403, and notes on 127 (*tranquillum*), 508 (*alta*), 695 (*ardua*). The fatal objection to the reading *caeli* is that *et* is senseless. Forbiger, ad loc., gives a long list of all kinds of suggestions for explaining it, the best of which is to regard it as equivalent to καὶ τοῦτο, *cum praesertim* (Wagner, *Quaest. Virg.* 34. 2). It is difficult, however, to see how this makes a possible sentence, much less an elegant one. Conington suggests that Virgil has confused two constructions, and Mackail says that the sentence is deliberately left incomplete, implying that we must imagine a verb for *et*. There seems no reason to resort to such desperate measures when the other reading is well attested and makes good sense.

totiens . . . sereni: 'when I have been so often cheated by the false promise of bright weather'. *Deceptus* does not imply that Palinurus was deceived or tricked into a sense of security, but only that his hopes were played false.

853. amittebat: for the lengthened final syllable see note on 284; here Virgil is perhaps using the archaic long vowel of the imperfect ending *-bat*. Notice the assonance of *dabat, amittebat, tenebat*, which here has the effect of emphasizing the steady monotonous determination of Palinurus; see on 181–2 and 385–6. The disyllabic internal rhyme of 853 is called 'leonine'; see Austin on *Aen.* 4. 260.

854 f. 'Then behold, the god shook over both his temples a branch dripping with the dew of Lethe, made sleepy with the power of Styx, and as he gradually yielded closed his swimming eyes.' These lovely lines were remembered and imitated by Valerius Flaccus (8. 84) *cunctaque Lethaei quassare silentia rami*, and by Silius (10. 354 f.) *quatit inde soporas / devexo capiti pennas oculisque quietem / inrorat, tangens Lethaea tempora virga*. For Lethe, the river of forgetfulness, cf. *Aen.* 6. 749 f., *Geo.* 1. 78 *Lethaeo perfusa papavera somno*, and Milton, *P.L.* 2. 582 f.

> Far off from these a slow and silent stream,
> Lethe the River of Oblivion rolls
> Her wat'ry Labyrinth, whereof who drinks,
> Forthwith his former state and being forgets,
> Forgets both joy and grief, pleasure and pain.

Styx is the river of death, here mentioned partly because Sleep is the brother of Death (*Aen.* 6. 278), but mainly to show, as Servius saw, that this sleep is a fatal one.

855. soporatum: this verb, like the adjectives *soporus* and *soporifer*, is not found before Virgil; cf. *Aen.* 6. 420 *melle soporatam et medicatis frugibus offam*. See notes on 16 and 202.

856. Cf. *Geo.* 4. 496 *conditque natantia lumina somnus*. There is no strong caesura at all in this line (see notes on 528 and 591); the ictus and accent coincide in each foot, and the effect is one of lilting drowsiness. Cf. *Aen.* 4. 486 *spargens umida mella soporiferumque papaver* (with Austin's note). The word *cunctanti* is generally taken to mean 'though he struggled'. Joseph Trapp in his translation (1718) rendered it 'as he nods'; in the later edition with notes (1731) he changed to agree with the majority, but expressed the view in a footnote that he thought he was perhaps right the first time. There is a good deal to be said for his view (for the idea of faltering in *cunctari* cf. *Aen.* 7. 449, 12. 916, 919); the word does not contain the notion of positive resistance so much as of slowness of action. Cf. *Aen*. 6. 210–11 (Aeneas plucking the golden bough) *avidusque refringit / cunctantem* (where see Fletcher's note). For the phrase *lumina solvit* cf. *Aen*. 10. 418 *ut senior leto canentia lumina solvit . . .*

857–60. Day Lewis has:

As soon as, taken off guard, he was relaxed in unconsciousness,
The god, leaning down over him, hurled him into the sea
Still gripping the tiller; a part of the taffrail was torn away:
As he fell, he kept calling out to his friends, but they did not hear him.

857. primos: the word conveys a picture of the onset of sleep upon the body as a gradual process of penetration until the innermost being is finally conquered; here the god acts as soon as Palinurus is lightly asleep. Many commentators say that *primos* is used for the adverb (= *vix primum*), but it must have some application to its noun; see on 375.

inopina: the word is first found in Virgil as a more manageable form of the prose word *inopinatus*. See on 202 and 627.

858. et: the word *et* here links two clauses in the sense of inverted *cum* (see note on 84–85). This is fairly frequent in poetry especially after *vix*; see Page on *Aen*. 2. 172, Wagner, *Quaest. Virg.* 35. 6, Leumann–Hofmann, p. 660.

superincumbens: 'leaning over him' or even 'looming over him'; the word *incumbere* often conveys a threatening notion, with the idea of 'swooping' or 'looming', cf. 325, *Geo*. 2. 377, *Aen*. 1. 84, Stat. *Th*. 10. 148 f. (of Sleep) *cum vero umentibus alis / incubuit . . .* For the compound verb *superincumbens* see on 202, and cf. *supereminere* (*Aen*. 1. 501), *superimponere* (4. 497), *supervolare* (10. 522). It is, however, very possible that it should be printed as two separate words.

858–9. Palinurus even in sleep does not relax his hold, so that the helm and a part of the ship are torn away with him; cf. his words in *Aen*. 6. 349 f. *namque gubernaclum multa vi forte revulsum, / cui datus haerebam custos cursusque regebam, / praecipitans traxi mecum.*

861. ales: Sleep is often depicted in literature and art as winged; see on 838, and cf. Prop. 1. 3. 45 *iucundis lapsam Sopor impulit alis* (with Enk's note), Stat. *Th*. 10. 137–8 and 148 (quoted above on 858). In Hom. *Il*. 14. 290 f. the god Sleep assumes the shape of a bird.

862. iter: for the use of the accusative, which well illustrates how 'extent of space' developed from 'cognate', see on 235.

863. interrita: 'without alarm', a slight personification of the fleet.

864. iamque adeo: see on 268.

864-7. 'And now the fleet voyaging on was approaching the
cliffs of the Sirens, in former days perilous and white with the
bones of many men—at this time the rocks were re-echoing
with roaring afar in the ceaseless surf—, when father Aeneas
saw . . .' Editors punctuate these lines in various ways, but
it seems clear that the construction must be *iamque subibat
cum pater sensit* (for inverted *cum* see on 84–85), and that
Mackail is wrong in putting a full stop after *albos*. Servius
rightly insists on the antithesis between *quondam* and *tum*
when he says: 'ac si diceret, antehac delectabili voce resona-
bant, tunc fluctibus solis'. Many commentators have denied
this antithesis, and argued that because Aeneas is a contemporary of Odysseus it follows that *quondam* must be used
from Virgil's point of view, not from that of Aeneas; but
Virgil is surely referring (as Servius saw) to the part of the
legend which said that the Sirens killed themselves when
Odysseus had successfully got past them. Cf. Lycophron
712 f., 1463 f., Servius on 864 *has Ulixes contemnendo
deduxit ad mortem*, Hyginus *Fab.* 141 *his responsum erat tam
diu eas victuras quam diu cantantes eas audiens nemo esset
praetervectus. quibus fatalis fuit Ulixes; astutia enim sua
cum praeternavigasset scopulos in quibus morabantur, prae-
cipitarunt se in mare.* See also the vase painting reproduced
in Roscher's *Lexicon*, s.v. *Seirenen*, p. 605. Thus the point
of this passage is that before the time when Aeneas reached
the rocks of the Sirens Odysseus had already caused them
to kill themselves, so that no enchanting voices were to be
heard, only the harsh booming of the sea against the lonely
rocks.

864-5. Cf. Hom. *Od.* 12. 39 f., especially 45 f. πολὺς δ' ἀμφ' ὀστε-
όφιν θὶς / ἀνδρῶν πυθομένων. Some of the famous sea stories
from the *Odyssey* find their echo in *Aen.* 3 (the Cyclops, Scylla
and Charybdis), but this passing reference is Virgil's only
mention of the Sirens, whose song had by now been silenced
for ever (see previous note). The Alexandrians had established geographical locations for Homer's stories, and the
Sirens were placed in the islands called Sirenusae (now Galli)
near Capreae; see E. de Saint-Denis, *Les Études Classiques*,
1938, pp. 472 f.

866. rauca: perhaps adverbial with *sonabant* rather than agreeing with *saxa*; cf. *Aen.* 9. 124 f. *amnis / rauca sonans*, and
see note on line 19.

Note the alliteration of *s*, imitative (as Servius points out)
of the hissing of the surf; cf. *Aen.* 2. 209 *fit sonitus spumante
salo*, and compare note on 84 (the hissing of a snake). For

the triple initial alliteration at the line ending see on 444–5;
Servius quotes this line in his comment on *Aen.* 3. 183 *casus
Cassandra canebat*, where he says 'haec compositio iam
vitiosa est, quae maioribus placuit, ut *Anchisen agnovit
amicum* (3. 82) et *sale saxa sonabant*'. See Marouzeau, *Traité
de stylistique latine*, pp. 17 f., especially p. 28, for a discussion
of the effect given by various letters in alliteration, and pp.
33–34 for a well-put warning about the danger of seeing
imitative effect in all alliteration: 'L'effet des procédés
phoniques est latent et pour ainsi dire facultatif; il n'est
exploité que si les circonstances s'y prêtent.' Compare also
his words on p. 339: 'Les procédés de style ont une valeur
latente, facultative, qui n'apparaît que si les circonstances la
font apparaître, s'il y a intérêt à la dégager; ils sont expres-
sifs en puissance, et non nécessairement.' For instances of
alliteration in this book see Index s.v., and especially notes
on 75–76, 287 f., 444–5, 451–2.

867. fluitantem: 'drifting', cf. Lucr. 3. 1052 *atque animi incerto
fluitans errore vagaris*. Supply *ratem* from the following
clause; see on 26–27.

868. Two difficulties have been raised here: the first is why
nobody had previously noticed the absence of Palinurus and
a part of the ship, and the second is how Aeneas was now able
to steer it without its rudder. To these points it may be
answered firstly that the movement of the whole fleet is
under the divine guidance of Neptune (813, 863) and sub-
jected to the intervention of the god Somnus, and the
moment at which the human actors become responsible again
(in this case as they approach the Sirens) is a matter for the
poet to decide; and secondly that there are a number of
possible ways in which a sailing boat with oars may be kept
under control without a rudder (*rexit* is perhaps 'took control
of' rather than 'steered'), and Virgil does not feel it necessary
or appropriate to go into details.

nocturnis: the adjective is used with adverbial force in a
way which is rather an extension of normal prose usage. Cf.
Aen. 4. 303 *nocturnusque vocat clamore Cithaeron*, 4. 490
nocturnosque movet manis, 4. 118 f. *crastinus . . . Titan*, Hor.
A.P. 268 f. *vos exemplaria Graeca | nocturna versate manu*,
versate diurna; and (rather more striking instances) *Geo.* 3.
538 *nocturnus obambulat*, *Aen.* 8. 465 *Aeneas se matutinus
agebat*. See Löfstedt, *Syntactica*, ii. 368 f.

869. multa gemens: for the adverbial accusative cf. *Aen.* 4. 395
(the same phrase), and note on 19; compare 866 above.

animum: for the construction see on 135.

870–1. It is a most effective piece of poetic irony that Aeneas in his last farewell to Palinurus attributes his death to the very thing which he had so resolutely refused to do (848 f., see note on 850). Observe how in these closing lines Virgil has two effects which he rarely uses: the assonance of case endings in *-o* (see on 81), and in the last line a trochaic break in both the fourth foot and the fifth (see on 52). Notice too how the last line is made sonorous by the assonance of *nu-* and *no-*.

871. nudus: 'unburied', because Aeneas will not be able to recover his body.

   ignota: cf. *Aen.* 11. 866 (*illum*) *obliti ignoto camporum in pulvere linquunt*, Prop. 3. 16. 29 *aut humer ignotae cumulis vallatus harenae*.

   According to Servius Virgil had the first two lines of Book VI at the end of Book V, but Varius and Tucca marked the end of Book V here. See Intro., pp. xxv f. The sequel to the story of Palinurus' death is told in *Aen.* 6. 337 f.

INDEX RERUM ET VERBORUM

The numbers refer to the line references of the notes. There are sub-headings for 'metre' and 'prosody'.

PRINTED IN GREAT BRITAIN
AT THE UNIVERSITY PRESS, OXFORD
BY VIVIAN RIDLER
PRINTER TO THE UNIVERSITY